The History and Politics of Latin American Theology

Volume 2:
Theology and Civil Society

Mario I. Aguilar

scm press

© Mario I. Aguilar 2008

The Author has asserted his right under the Copyright, Designs and
Patents Act, 1988, to be identified as the Author of this Work

British Library Cataloguing in Publication data

A catalogue record for this book is available
from the British Library

978 0 334 04160 3

First published in 2008 by SCM Press
13–17 Long Lane,
London EC1A 9PN

www.scm-canterburypress.co.uk

SCM Press is a division of
SCM-Canterbury Press Ltd

Typeset by Regent Typesetting, London
Printed and bound in Great Britain by
William Clowes, Beccles, Suffolk

Contents

To the memory of
Dom Bernard Orchard OSB (1910–2006)

A man who listened to my stories from Chile and
I listened to his stories about God

Omnia mutantur nos et mutamur in illis

Acknowledgements

Every book is like a blank canvas, a tapestry on which choices of subject, colour, style and aesthetic narrative are made by the artist. However, during the time in which the artist works and creates the canvas or the page, he is influenced by people, beauty, suffering: the life that surrounds him. Thus, my acknowledgements are to those who have made the process of filling this particular canvas fruitful, painful, controversial and personal.

This work has been inspired by the great Mexican artists who dreamt many years ago of changing the world through their art, and I think particularly of Frida Kahlo (1907–54) and Diego Rivera (1886–1957); their love and their anger have remained an inspiration for my ongoing commitment to intensity in my own recreation of social and personal realities through writing.

I am thankful to Professors Marcella Althaus-Reid and Alistair Kee in Edinburgh for their encouragement, support and ongoing friendship; to Dr Iván Petrella goes my gratitude for allowing me to read his forthcoming work – I hope that my comments encourage his future work on the context of liberation theology – and to Fr Gero McLoughlin sj for his detailed comments on developments within the 34th General Congregation of the Jesuits (1995), and for guiding my personal journey with gentleness and wisdom.

I am grateful to Professors Philip Esler and Ron Piper and to Drs Ian Bradley and Esther Reed for encouraging this kind of research, and for their friendship. I have discussed parts of this book with my doctoral students: Dr Cheryl Wissmann, Dr David Wilhite, Dr David Brannan, Jennifer Kilps, Jeff Tippner, Rob Whiteman, Jonathan Rowe, Yumi Murayama, Casey

Nicholson, George Hargreaves, Gordon Barclay, Alissa Jones Nelson and her husband Matt, and Joanne Wood. I thank all of them for their ideas and challenges. My family in St Andrews and Edinburgh has been always supportive, and I thank Laurel and Sara for allowing writing to become a way of life rather than a part-time occupation.

This book is dedicated to Dom Bernard Orchard OSB, a Benedictine monk of Ealing Abbey in London, who, starting in 1982 and for several years, listened to my personal search for God and told me about his own journey. At that time I didn't realize that Dom Bernard was such an important person; to me he was an older friend who trusted that a Chilean on the move could find a home in books and in God. Monthly, he provided me with wonderful tea and toast, and he tenderly fashioned my own memories of brokenness. Sadly, Dom Bernard died in 2006; but he is still very much alive in my research.

Finally, a word of thanks to Barbara Laing, SCM Senior Commissioning Editor, for believing once again that an idea shared over an extended lunch could become an academic work.

Mario I. Aguilar   *St Andrews, April 2007*

Introduction

Globalization and Civil Society in Latin American Theology

In Volume 1 of this work I highlighted the complexity of Latin American theology, a liberating reflection coming out of praxis that has evolved into a large body of works.[1] Within that complexity the 'problem of generations' as outlined by Karl Mannheim has allowed us to depart from a single unified tradition of praxis and theology in order to outline generational patterns, generational metaphors, and ways of doing theology that have shown that the so-called liberation theology has become a diversified subject; that within its theological umbrella are contained many diverse theologies using the social metaphor of liberation in order to stand with the marginalized in the name of God, a person who through the writings of those Latin American theologians sustains a defence of human rights and the rights of those on the fringes of society. Their tools include cultural theory, anthropology, history, literary criticism, and mostly a simple way of life that challenges the centrality of profit and consumption within a contemporary capitalistic society and the globalized hedonistic phenomenon of consumerism. In the words of Marcella Althaus-Reid 'liberationists are responsible for the multitude of theologies that surround us, including feminist theologies, Black American, African, Asian, Aboriginal, queer, lesbian and gay'.[2]

The 'problem of generations' within any group and certainly within a group of theologians relates to the external perception that there is an entity out there called 'liberation theology' while in reality there is a group of older and younger theologians with different perspectives on the same subject owing to the fact that the context, which in the case of Latin American theology changes, produces theology as 'a second step' which also changes. Members of a group agree on some ideas but in general they continue being shaped by the Christian tradition or community they have experienced and by the ongoing socio-political contexts, forever changing from one political utopia to another. Within that theological context, Gustavo Gutiérrez is not the teacher or master of the other theologians but the brilliant pastor who catalysed a larger Christian concern for the oppressed and the poor by providing a common metaphor: liberation. Thus, different generations of Latin American theologians responded to changes within the socio-political environment in Latin America so that, using the words of Mannheim, 'the teacher–pupil relationship is not as between one representative of "consciousness in general" and another, but as between one possible subjective centre of vital orientation and another subsequent one'.[3]

Within Latin American theology I have outlined three generations, not as a fixed taxonomy but as a tool for thinking on the victims and their context. For it is to the victims of social and economic processes within Latin America that we must return once and again and always. The poor and the marginalized are those who suffer because of others, not because of themselves. The victims are most of the time economically poor, mixed-race, indigenous peoples, landless peasants, women, gay and lesbians, separated and divorce parents, victims of genocides and military offensives, HIV/AIDS sufferers, alcoholics, substance dependants and drug addicts, those without a future and those without a history that do not matter for the forces of neo-liberalism, profit and greed.

The first generation includes pioneers such as Gustavo Gutiérrez, Jon Sobrino and José Míguez Bonino, while a second generation is marked by the critique of the first male generation of theologians by Elsa Tamez or the continuity of anti-colonial discourse by Pablo Richard. A third generation has taken those previous concerns and has moved parameters of theological action and reflection on behalf of the victims to social realms outside the Roman Catholic Church and outside the churches through cultural and gender critiques about theological methodologies – they include Iván Petrella and Marcella Althaus-Reid. If 'the problem of generations' remains a positive problem and not an empirical system of classification it is because theologians, as feeling and sometimes loving human beings, explore changing responses to the social realities of Latin American victims and can be perceived as having theological rebirths that allow them to be located within different generations. If Gutiérrez, as the totemic father of the first generation, remains firmly located there, Jon Sobrino retains a theological mobility that allows him to pursue practical actions and reflections on behalf of the victims that locate him within all generations. Sobrino could have been a victim himself in November 1989, as his Jesuit companions of San Salvador were all assassinated and he escaped because he was in Thailand at that time. Other theologians, such as Ignacio Ellacuría, assassinated in San Salvador, remain ever present within the world of Latin American theology because others published their works after their death and the works continue being part of an ever growing corpus of Latin American theology previously silent.

In assessing theological generations one must remain alert so as not to create systematic theological systems, because that is not the task of a liberating theology. Those attempts at systematizing liberation theology during the early 1990s have since been forgotten. The danger in creating a systematic liberation theology by Jon Sobrino and others was that they tried to comply with European parameters of theological classification.[4] The project of a Latin American *Summa Theologica* was never completed but it almost brought an abrupt end to a theology from the side of the victims and the oppressed.[5] It is to the victims of oppression, those preferred by God, that we turn in order to follow God's work in the world in general and within Latin America in particular. For a new theological paradigm from the side of the poor and the oppressed continues arising today, providing a theological shift by a new generation but also allowing a continuity of purpose with the first generation of Latin American theologians. After all, and in the words of Sobrino, 'giving new life to the victims is fullness, and overcoming selfishness and the risks and fear it involves is triumph'.[6]

However, if the first generation of theologians grew up under the courageous challenge of the churches to the Latin American military regimes in the context of the Cold War, a second generation challenged the given paradigms of faith interpretation within the churches and provided an ongoing feminist critique of traditional patriarchy following the American and European critiques.[7] Those critiques pointed less to a challenge to church structures, for example, the possibility or impossibility of women's ordination to the priesthood, than to a critique of the involvement of the Church within society and within a post-Cold War situation. Within that situation of the 1990s the challenge to the churches was to remain central to Latin American societies within an ever increasing secularism, a ruthless imposition of globalized neo-liberal economic models and the social unrest created by indigenous populations, the direct victims of 500 years of oppression and genocide. Thus, Franz Hinkelammert has characterized 'globalization as a strategy for capital accumulation' with insight and, in the case of Latin America, as experienced through imposed 'structural adjustments'.[8] Against that ongoing economic view of society vis-à-vis globalization Jon Sobrino responded with an interesting and challenging theological trope, 'the civilization of poverty' as a contrast to the failed 'civilization of wealth'.[9]

The response by the Latin American theologians was not an intellectual response to what was happening, that would presuppose that theology is 'a first step', but an ever increasing involvement with civil society, with a large number of organizations formed by groups that belonged neither within the state apparatus nor within the churches. There is within the second theological generation a movement towards the periphery, not from the churches point of view of centrality in society but from the fact that the churches themselves became part of civil society. One of the reasons for that particular shift was the fact that the Latin American nation-states with their ever hopeful new democracies found themselves controlled by international monetary systems, international corporations and economic groups.[10] That movement towards a landscape that was not familiar to the churches created the impression that the churches were not involved in society any longer; however, in the case of those involved with the victims of state oppression and international neo-liberal genocidal processes, liberation remained as central to theological concerns as it was before. It is within that ongoing changing context that some theologians remained within the structures of the churches while others, such as Leonardo Boff, opted for a location of theological praxis outside the churches' structures, in his case the movement of landless people in Brazil and the ecological movement.[11]

Within the following pages I explore some of the changing socio-political and religious contexts that affected the ongoing pastoral commitment by Latin American theologians during the 1990s and that triggered a different Christian liberating praxis in preparation for the arrival of the twenty-first century.

The Human Rights Generation

The first and second generation of Latin American theologians had to deal with the changes in pastoral and theological approaches that took place within Latin America after the Second Vatican Council (1962–65), and the conferences of Latin American bishops in Medellín (Colombia, 1968) and Puebla de Los Angeles (Mexico, 1979). Most of those theological concerns related to an active support for the Christian communities that were under close scrutiny by a number of military regimes because of their defence of the persecuted, many of them members of Christian communities. There was no concerted effort to theorize the relation between church structures and human rights but a pragmatic response to gospel values and the immediacy of providing a hearing ear, a lawyer, or a public voice for the persecuted and their bewildered families. For example, in Chile, Cardinal Silva Henríquez supported the formation of an ecumenical group (Pro Paz – COPACHI) after the 1973 military coup, and when in 1975 Pinochet's government threatened the Church with full-scale persecution and the forced closure of that group the Chilean Cardinal founded a pastoral-Episcopal vicariate within the archdiocese of Santiago, with the name Vicariate of Solidarity. The same phenomenon took place in the archdiocese of San Salvador while Oscar Romero was archbishop. Within the model of engagement with civil society and the state the Church was at the centre of society and used her public voice and political power to influence the political spheres, requesting a quick return to democratic institutions.

With the return to democratic systems there was a new social utopia quickly filled by the neo-liberal system, hedonism and capitalism. The Vatican did not help matters with the appointment of conservative/traditional bishops, a notorious trend since 1979 and during the pontificate of John Paul II.[12] However, a whole generation of Christians and pastoral agents had grown under the wings of the Church and her ongoing concerns with human rights. As democracies started their own legal and historical investigations into human rights violations and many criminal cases were opened, the Church facilitated Truth and Reconciliation Commissions but slowly left the arena of human rights to the state and to civil society and returned to some pressing pastoral and educational matters in order to prepare for the advent of the twenty-first century. Throughout this process many of those who had already worked with civil society for human rights continued their work not within church structures but within civil society.

During the 1992 Meeting of Latin American Bishops in Santo Domingo (Dominican Republic) new pastoral concerns and realities that needed liberation were pointed to: indigenous peoples, culture and the youth. There were problems for the theologians of liberation during that meeting in that under the guidance of Pope John Paul II most of them were not allowed to accompany the bishops to the meeting and part of the documents had already been prepared in advance of the meeting.[13] Indeed, there was a theological climate change and, according to Sobrino's assessment, 'in theology, there has been a retreat. Fundamentally, theology has retreated in its procedure, its method. The events of history are no longer seen as a sign of the times in a strictly theological sense, that is, as the place where God can speak his word and in which he himself can be present, as God.'[14] In practice, the presidency of the bishops' meeting provided the discussions with a theological framework that was European and traditional, the judge–see–act axis, that provided the start of a theological reflection in doing theology first and taking action later.[15] In its Christology the documents of Santo Domingo provide a starting point from the Christ of faith rather than from the God of history and therefore not via the historical Jesus, present and active in the contemporary history of Latin America.[16] Despite the fact that communities can live with different theologies the shocking reality of the Santo Domingo meeting was that it did not include the martyrs within the document because they could not be central to a high theology of faith. Romero and others were remembered in prayer but the social realities of martyrdom and genocide did not make it to the final document, which after all was produced in order for Christian communities to reflect upon their own faith and involvement in the world.[17] Gutiérrez had a more positive view of the meeting and certainly argued that the preferential option for the poor and other themes outlined by Medellín and Puebla had been continued within new contexts such as ecology, the indigenous peoples and the general new evangelization of incoming cultures.[18] Nevertheless, it was after this meeting and following new questioning by the Vatican that Leonardo Boff decided to resign his priesthood and became a lay theologian teaching outside pontifical universities.

If in the short term this moment within the development of a Latin American theology could have been considered bleak and uneventful it had its own dynamics and those dynamics were to create the possibility of a critique of the previous project of liberation and to ask questions about involvement with other groups within civil society in a search for an ecological theology, a theology that could include gays and lesbians, a queer theology and a full critique of globalization as a dehumanizing project.

In my analysis this socio-political and theological moment provided a natural progression within Latin American theology, a fruitful moment of inclusion in diversity, a close return to the social experience of the first Christians and the possibility of a political Christianity for the twenty-first century. The Second Vatican Council had already had an impact on Latin American theology because of the experience of religious and pastoral agents who chose to live outside large convents, cathedrals and well-to-do Christian educational institutions. The movement of the Spirit after 1992 was similar. Instead of being able to assume the glories of martyrdom and pastoral service within the new democratic regimes, pastoral agents felt challenged by the new models of democratic states that were once again running the lives of the poor and the marginalized with their economic policies and by the fact that in reality they did not have and they still do not have the full willingness of the international community to eradicate poverty and suffering.

Theologies of liberation towards the late twentieth century arose out of a liberating praxis within a different Latin American context in which new socialist-oriented governments tried once again to challenge globalization and the power of the North American empire. The political lives of Hugo Chávez of Venezuela, Lula of Brazil and Michele Bachelet of Chile provided Latin American governments with members of that previous human rights generation who suddenly embraced the social discontent with globalization and looked forward to diverse, multi-cultural and all-inclusive societies within a climate of youth unrest, indigenous protests, increasing economic poverty and a general apathy towards contemporary democratic systems.

Within the socio-political climate of Latin America during the late 1990s it became clear that the 'reproductive battles', political battles over contraception and individual rights over life and death, between the Church and the State alienated those who were closer to the poor and drove them deeper into NGOs and groups that independently of Church and State policies worked through a liberating praxis for the liberation of those at the margins of society.[19] Within those new challenges Christian activists remained part of a localized theological model in that they were able to mediate the tensions between the Church and the State through their firm engagement and participation within a larger civil society. Thus, because of an ever increasing involvement of Christians within civil society during the 1990s it is crucial to reflect on what the social entity known as 'civil society' actually is and on its various manifestations, including the idea and role of a globalized civil society, a concept that by itself is not always conducive to a liberating praxis of inclusion and rouses theological suspicion.

Models of Civil Society

The political idea of civil society has a long history, many meanings and an enormous amount of literature attached to it.[20] However, it can be described as an 'ideal type', and when applied as a global concept of encounter and cooperation it can also be described as a utopia coming out of a comparative analysis of formal or informal cooperation between partners smaller than the State and larger than the family. John Keane, for example, has suggested that global civil society 'refers to a dynamic non-governmental system of interconnected socio-economic institutions that straddle the whole earth, and that have complex effects that are felt in its four corners'.[21] However, Keane forgets the possibility that life is not just regulated by economics and that the full dichotomy between religion and politics does not operate as a successful normative dichotomy for all areas of the world. A universalistic approach to civil society becomes as contested as a universal approach to rules and norms, however much it lies behind all necessary attempts to politicize diversity and to theologize society.

Mary Kaldor has argued that the concept needs to be under-

stood in relation to five particular historical contexts that provide five possible models to any futuristic development of its
possibilities.[22] Those five models are:

1 *Societas civilis* as a peaceful order based on the rule of law
  and the consent of individuals.
2 *Bourgeois society* or *Bürgerliche Gesellschaft*, proposed by
  Hegel and Marx, and drawn from the Scottish enlightenment
  (Adam Ferguson and Adam Smith) in which civil society is
  the ethical life that exists between the State and the family,
  for example, markets, social classes, civil law and welfare
  organizations.
3 *The activist version* that proposes a post-Marxian and
  utopian concept based on a rule of law by the State but with
  a redistribution of power.
4 *The neo-liberal version* as a market in politics resembling the
  general politics of the West and particularly as it operates
  within the United States.
5 *The post-modern version* in which the universal principle of
  tolerance is required but civil society provides an arena for
  civility and 'incivility', for example, Islamic society composed of religion, the bazaar and the ruler.

Thus, Kaldor proposes, the initial idea of a single civil society
has become larger because of the changes experienced after the
1990s and the rising idea of globalization as a world phenomenon of both integration and diversity. Following from her
schema it is possible to argue that the framework proposed by
the theologians of liberation and their ideas about religion and
society fit within a redistribution of power and therefore within
model 3 and *the activist version*. I am aware that Latin America
does not seem to occupy a central place in the literature on
global civil society and that within a non-Western context
writers seem to find an important parallel within Asia and the
Middle East, and particularly in the rising economic power of
China and the rising of political Islam within the Middle East.[23]
However, despite the omission of Latin America from Euro-

pean discussions on civil society it is possible to argue that theologians of liberation assumed the same challenges posed by the fall of the Berlin Wall and found new agendas within globalization and the rising of popular movements of protests within late twentieth-century Latin America, that is, civil society.

The development of the ideas of liberation theology and those of a global civil society can be chronologically connected because liberation theology used the social sciences, and Marxism, in order to analyse the localized context in the same way as ideas of civil society were analysed, at a level smaller than the political State but at a level larger than the family or the local parish. As a result and by the time that the socialist societies of Eastern Europe were collapsing, theologians of liberation were facing the end of the military regimes that had dominated the social and political life of Latin Americans. They also lived the short utopian dream of a newly unified world symbolized by the collapse of the Berlin Wall in Europe and the end of the authoritarian regimes in Chile, El Salvador and Guatemala.

By the 1990s Latin American elites had started enjoying the possibilities of globalization and freedom without realizing that the network connections that united Latin American civil societies into a globalized system of communication were only available to a few, all linked to the neo-liberal economic models embraced happily by the military and those who enriched themselves by global cooperation, free trade and universal policies. Thus, by the start of the twenty-first century the ideal of a global civil society had become a shattered dream because the new Latin American democracies were not able to foster a continuous economic flow between private industries without a dependency on the big corporations, most of them owned and directed from within the United States. With the advent of a war on terror and the security measures that followed 9/11 Latin America ceased to have the same freedom to negotiate free exchanges and the theologians of liberation took up a fresh agenda related to three important areas: indigenous rights and eco-theology, gender issues and a theology of liberation from empire. That new agenda continued using the same tools of action–reflection–action but developed networks of interaction and cooperation that, while resembling participation in a global civil society, contested the possibility of making local changes by means of that association. In many ways the newly found agenda of liberation theology questioned the structures of a Church that previously had replaced civil society, but that within globalization could represent yet another form of global corporatism rather than a place where civil society could develop.

Within those socio-historical changes theologians of liberation found themselves connected not by a localized system of oppression that needed to be challenged but by a global phenomenon of social incorporation that amounted to empire, with only one major actor, the United States. The exclusion/social injustice became clear through economic systems of globalization/oppression and the local responses to those social processes required a more globalized approach, not always liked by many Latin American theologians but certainly at the forefront of Asian and African theologies and their inter-religious dialogue.

The founding of an international association of Third World theologians, the Ecumenical Association of Third World Theologians (EATWOT), created the possibility of coordinating a global theological response to global events and a clear coordination of efforts for a just civil society within globalization.[24] That association rejected globalization as neo-colonialism and mobilized theologians using the concept of a political global civil society. While during the 1990s Europeans were focusing on the possibility of rebuilding democracies within former Yugoslavia and the former Soviet Union, Latin Americans and their theologians analysed the five-hundredth anniversary of the encounter between Christopher Columbus and the indigenous populations (1492) with the challenge of liberating those same populations from the ills of free trade, economic control, lack of land, and economic profit arising out of globalization and greed.

Introduction

The Indigenous Protests

Once again, and as was the case with the Latin American bishops' meetings at Medellín and Puebla, the pastoral discussions undertaken by the bishops at Santo Domingo did not dictate a new socio-theological agenda for Latin America but dwelt on changes and new phenomena within the pastoral realities of the continent. Within the context of 500 years of Christian evangelization in the Americas the history of injustice, genocide, slavery and poverty was acknowledged as a negative factor while the increase in numbers of Christians within Latin America was seen as a positive sign and as a sign of God's presence within the Americas. Attempts to shadow those promises of a bright Christian future disappeared as soon as Pope John Paul II arrived in Santo Domingo and a continent that loved the papacy became enchanted by his visit and the global attention given to a continent that after the end of the Cold War had disappeared from international strategies.

The bishops highlighted the indigenous question and indigenous rights as one of the major topics of the conference.[25] Within that pastoral stance Latin American theologians connected directly with the ongoing realities of the indigenous peoples, and the pastoral commitment to them became central to the development of a strategy of pastoral witness to indigenous rights. The case of Bishop Ruiz in Chiapas is a clear example of that pastoral commitment to justice, equality and social inclusion as discussed in Chapter 6; he did not condemn the uprising by the indigenous peoples of Chiapas (Mexico) in 1994, instead he collaborated with a process of ongoing mediation between the rebels and the Mexican Government. Within that commitment to the social realities of the indigenous movements the Church was not the only voice. Indigenous groups in North America and Australia were already using international indigenous rights for the repatriation of human remains and for an improvement in health and education. The violent protests by indigenous groups against the State in the 1990s suggested that the indigenous groups did not want the Church and the theologians as mediators any longer but preferred, and some said 'rightly so', to run their own affairs. The socio-political reflections of 1992 brought disengagement between the indigenous peoples and the churches and a return to a more essentialist challenge to the State as well as to the churches.

The Case of Chile

The indigenous crisis was more drastic within Latin American nations where the indigenous populations were a minority. For example, the Araucanía Region of southern Chile witnessed significant organized violence against landowners, and massive arrests and repression of the indigenous population by the police. Despite those protests the Chilean legislators negated the possibility of a multi-cultural society within the Chilean constitution as the Chilean Congress declared once again that all Chileans were part of one nation, one history and one language rather than a multi-cultural society; they voted against a constitutional change by which the indigenous populations (*Mapuche*) of Chile could have had their own language, their traditions and history upheld and maybe a federal region with some kind of autonomous or devolved powers. Throughout these years the bishop of the Araucanía Region, Manuel Camilo Vial, has been a good mediator between the indigenous populations and the State but the level of violence and social unrest has increased with the arrival of international supporters of indigenous movements and the lack of inclusive political measures by the recent administrations of Presidents Ricardo Lagos and Michele Bachelet.

The possibility of giving more rights and a separate identity to the Mapuche within Chilean Law was supported by the Catholic bishops of southern Chile who in January 2003 prepared a document alerting Christian communities to the deep crisis of the indigenous populations within Chile, and indeed within Latin America, and requested a period of communal reflection by all Christian communities.[26] Within the document the bishops called for reforms in order to alleviate that unjust poverty in which the indigenous populations live and for all citizens to recognize that the nation-state is multi-ethnic and multi-cultural. However, the liberation of the indigenous population, according to the bishops, has to coincide with the recognition of their dignity and the injustices they faced during colonial times and during the period of the military regime in Chile (1973–90). Historically, the Mapuche were able to start recovering their land through the indigenous law of 1972 that coincided with a national process of agrarian reform by the government of Salvador Allende (1970–73). However, the military government reformed that law in 1979 and allowed the private ownership and division of communal lands so that those who had it could rent it for up to 99 years. The indigenous lands ceased to be part of the so-called ancestral lands and became owned by individuals with the disappearance of communal rights and the social strength of communal decisions and demands under Chilean Law. At that time the bishops protested against that legal reform but their protests were ignored. With the return to democracy, a large Mapuche gathering (*congreso mapuche*) took place in Temuco in 1991 in order to push for indigenous demands, for their recognition as a people and for a general demand to the Chilean State for their right to have their own ancestral lands back. A new indigenous law was approved by the Chilean Congress in 1993 and the creation of a development body within the Chilean Government, Corporación Nacional de Desarrollo Indígena (CONADI), opened the possibilities for educational and agrarian opportunities within the Chilean State. Despite those efforts the economic neo-liberal model did not allow for quick progress in areas of indigenous development, and the indigenous peoples' lands for the most part were not classified as productive because their owners were growing traditional agricultural products. Consequently, the farms were opened to development by forestry companies. That situation put enormous pressure on the indigenous peoples by companies that for the most part wanted to use the land in order to plant trees to satisfy an international demand for timber and expensive woods for furniture. Thus, and according to the declaration by the Catholic bishops in 1993, Chilean law had neither protected the lands of the indigenous peoples nor managed to mediate between their need for land and water and the economic pressure put on the Chilean State by multinational corporations.

Several groups within the indigenous populations have opposed with violence the taking over of their lands, supported by a narrative of ecological concerns that has granted them the backing of some international activists who lobby for the preservation of the global climate and for solutions against global warming. The police have used brutal force to evict indigenous communities, and many Mapuche activists have been imprisoned. Some of them have publicly renounced their Chilean nationality and the whole situation has created a new context for the Christian communities within an ailing nation-state that is not able to cope any longer with international pressures and with the changing rules of neo-liberalism and a globalized economy. The problem, arising from centuries of social injustice, will not go away. It is within that conflict that the nation-state is in danger of collapsing altogether by not being able to integrate all citizens within the same set of rights and obligations, and it is within that situation of conflict, violence and social injustice that the theologians are called once again to challenge the State, to walk with the poor, the oppressed and the marginalized and to reflect on the presence of the God of Life among all, but with a divine preference for the poor.

It is within the so-called 'death of the nation-state' that more liberating praxis and theological reflections are needed. Globalization and the global markets have increased the possibilities of those who have some economic means but have helped to decrease the national sense of community together with the need to solve political problems: injustice, social exclusion and equal rights remain, in practice, unsolved social problems within Latin America. Thus, the indigenous question is one of those that has to be debated within a climate of solidarity and social justice rather than within old parameters of nationalism or the history of a country, realities that can always change and indeed must change in order to allow social justice and the ongoing liberation of the poor and the marginalized of Latin America. Within those social processes the God of Life is present and Christians taking part must search for the signs of God's presence outside the communities and within the realm of a civil society that has become more meaningful and more open to a constant cooperation between the NGOs and the Basic Christian Communities.

New Questions, New Contexts

It was within that changing Latin American context (remember that the only certainty in life is change) that, in 1995, Jon Sobrino asked poignant reflective questions about an all-inclusive and by then already recognized as complex and diverse liberation theology:

1 He challenged the fact that questions about the context of a theology of liberation have been dominated by the socio-economic sphere and wondered if more questions should be asked about other types of oppression within the areas of culture, ethnicity, religion, women, children and nature.
2 He proposed to explore not only the needs of the poor but also their faith – after all, the basis for a Latin American theology.
3 He questioned the fact that theologians seemed to be present at times of revolution and made the point that they should also be there during the most ordinary times of peoples' lives.
4 He argued that theologians must recognize that world changes bring other concerns and move on.
5 He suggested that a theology of liberation still has 'deficiencies and limitations' related to exegetical, systematic and historical understandings.[27]

Thus, Sobrino summarized the new and different areas within an ongoing work of theologizing in Latin America at the end of the twentieth century and, without realizing, reminded us of the possibility of diversity within a single theological umbrella and many different socio-political realities. The theological works by Leonardo Boff and Diego Irarrázaval have already responded to those concerns and their work has reflected their own experience of involvement with popular religiosity and with the world of civil society and the 'popular church'. Certainly they have moved on with the changing world, and Boff's work on ecological issues and the death of our planet seems to be directly connected with the concerns of civil society and the pressure on the international community and the G-8 nations to respond to public demands on climate change.

Where I am not too sure that there is enough theological engagement is with Sobrino's more systematic concerns. One of the challenges of Latin American theology has been to remain as a 'second step' vis-à-vis communities and civil society while several Latin American theologians have established the discipline within academic posts in Latin America, Europe and the United States.[28] Within communal reflections of EATWOT the establishment of Third World theologies within academic institutions has been perceived as problematic in so far as such recognition has taken away some of the communal theological reflection that arose out of a theological movement rather than out of an academic organization.[29]

A point of clarification, which I made in the previous volume, is in order here. There are those who understand feminist critiques and other critiques towards the first generation of liberation theologians as new theologies with different names. I perceive and understand Latin American theology as an umbrella for many kinds of theologies and thus for *all* of those theologians using the metaphor 'liberation' for their reflection on Christian praxis and the actions of the God of history within the Latin American context – hence my reluctance to identify liberation theology solely with a phenomenon of socio-economic engagement, exemplified by the lives and works of the first generation of Latin American theologians. For theology remains a 'second act', the first act being praxis, so that the plural expression as in 'theologies of liberation' fits better the purpose of plurality, diversity, variety, and ongoing suspicion that allows Christians and Christian theologies to open new areas of pastoral activity and theological writing from within many changing contexts.

Theological Choices

In the first section of this book I explore the theologies of Jon Sobrino SJ, Ignacio Ellacuría SJ and Juan Luis Segundo SJ, all of them Jesuit priests. Despite my own suspicion about systematic tools for the Latin American theologies of liberation, Jon Sobrino remains important to all three theological generations and therefore his theology is assessed at the start of the first section of this book. The choice of Juan Luis Segundo and Ignacio Ellacuría is twofold: they brought an engagement with two main areas of Latin American life and apostolate: the parish and the university. The three of them were also Jesuits and it is possible to argue that within the theological literature there is a reluctance to acknowledge the fact that the Jesuits triggered some of the concern for the poor among religious congregations by opting themselves as an ecclesiastical institution and as a religious community to serve the cause of the poor, the refugees and those without voice after the Second Vatican Council.

Thus, within the second section of this book I explore the history and charisma of the Jesuits, the theology of human rights vis-à-vis the phenomenon of forced disappearance, and the theological praxis of Bishop Ruiz during the Chiapas uprising of 1994. The role of the Jesuits in supporting those without a voice, through education, parish work and their own testimony of social involvement and martyrdom, has been crucial to the contemporary history of Latin America. The Jesuits articulated before anybody else had done so the importance of an ongoing dialogue between the Church and the State and between the Christian communities and civil society. They were part of an institutional effort to support those who faced human rights violations and were present in Chile and El Salvador within diocesan structures that challenged such violations as well as the growing phenomenon of kidnappings, arrests and forced disappearances.

Within the third section of this book I examine the theology of Pedro Casaldáliga, Marcella Althaus-Reid and Iván Petrella. Pedro Casaldáliga, Catholic bishop in the Amazonia region of Brazil, remained physically within the periphery of the indigenous populations, showing solidarity with the poor by fostering poetry and a spirituality of liberation. Sometimes, and within discussions on the praxis of liberation, the central issue of spirituality (and contemplation) has been forgotten; spirituality opens commonality within human concerns for other worlds and other experiences, human and divine. In the same way the work of Marcella Althaus-Reid opens new avenues within theological explorations about a god with different names, and the social experience of women and the queer realities of God's creation and human society in Latin America. Finally, the work of Iván Petrella brings us full-circle to the questions posed by the first generation: how do we describe God's actions alongside his people and how do we continue exploring liberation and the theology of liberation within ongoing theoretical models, which evolve after action, after love and after grace have been given.

Petrella's manifesto connects Latin American theologies with the language and the metaphors of the North and this in itself is a challenge of hermeneutical mediation for all those involved in liberation and all those writing about Latin American theology. The manifesto brings glimpses of hope for the future, a future of commitment and liberation to be lived not within the centre but at the periphery, because it is from the periphery that God liberates and accompanies the whole diversity of humanity and it is within the periphery that the Kingdom of God is realized, 'now and not yet'.

One of the many unresolved issues within Latin American theologies remains the enactment, actualization and ongoing understanding of social memory. A concept so important within in a whole range of symbolic and ritual activities, memory remains crucial to any understanding of the contrarieties/contradictions of a social experience.[30] For the oppression of the poor takes place when a particular or ethnocentric memory by a single social group or agreed by a State mechanism takes precedence over other memories. If a social memory is not absolutely inclusive it could never generate liberation because it is through the re-enactment of history that the soul is freed from prejudice and from social oppression. The history and politics of Latin American theology remain an active proposition of sociability but at the same time a social text of contradiction whereby actors of this history challenge the possible centrality of other narratives and of other social actions. In the case of the churches the centrality of a single authoritarian narrative cannot effect liberation; liberation is effected by an inclusive, all-embracing proposition of sociability where social divisions in the name of money, class, ethnicity and gender are challenged and where human experience is seen as the realm of divine companionship for the poor and the marginalized. Maybe the self-reflections by Sheila Cassidy give us a glimpse of a theology of the periphery and the ordinary, as requested by Sobrino, when she confides in her memoirs:

> He or she [God] has led me a merry dance into the torture chamber and out, into the convent and out, and then through twenty years of the most satisfying work a woman could wish for. Now I have emerged into a sunlit meadow and I feel God's love like the sun on my back. I have no idea what joy or suffering the future may bring but I am ready for either.[31]

Shall I dare to add: I am also ready for joy or suffering but within the periphery!

Part 1

Ecclesial Theology

I

Jon Sobrino SJ

The theological contribution of Jon Sobrino over a 30-year period has been marked by his own life within El Salvador, a small country in Central America, where he has taught at the Jesuit university and where Sobrino experienced periods of intense public violence, intimidation, insecurity, the assassination of the Jesuit Rutilio Grande in 1977, of Archbishop Oscar Romero in 1980 and the torture and assassination of his six Jesuit companions at the Jesuit house in El Salvador in November 1989.[32] Sobrino was abroad at that time, the reason why he escaped assassination and why a new theological paradigm arose out of his bereavement and pain.

Among those killed by the soldiers was Ignacio Ellacuría, rector of the Jesuit community and a great intellectual and religious inspiration for Sobrino. As Sobrino received the news in Thailand where he was giving a course on Christology he went into psychological shock for a few days and went through bereavement for a long period. As in many cases where a survivor faces the question 'Why me?' he confronted his personal demons by digging deep into the experience of martyrdom of thousands of Salvadorians and of the pain of their relatives and friends. It was at that moment that a new theological project started locating Sobrino within a third generation of theologians, those who had seen long periods of suffering under military regimes and took those lessons into other conflicts and others experiences of oppression and liberation around the world.

Through the experience of losing his Jesuit companions (for a celibate they were his family and loved ones), Sobrino became a victim rather than a companion because his family had been killed. He returned to El Salvador to rebuild a Jesuit community with the help of many other Jesuits who immediately volunteered to replace those killed in San Salvador and was subsequently sustained by the visit of the Jesuit Superior General who decided to spend Christmas of 1989 in El Salvador.[33]

Sobrino's initial contribution to Latin American theology and his ongoing theological field of study was Christology and the person of Christ within the Latin American context and the role of the Church.[34] The assassination of Oscar Romero moved him towards an ongoing examination of Romero's writings and spiritual life but after the assassination of his community he started developing the concept of martyrs that he associated with the people of El Salvador and with the Jesuits as companions of Jesus through their journey with the people of El Salvador. He has called those weeks and months after the assassination of the Jesuits 'the most decisive weeks and months of my life'.[35] Lately, Sobrino has called for a third Vatican Council in order to reshape the Catholic Church as to fit God's demands for the twenty-first century but forgetting her fear of geography and hosting a council outside Europe, for example, Bombay I rather than Vatican III.

Life in El Salvador

As was the case with other Latin American countries El Salvador as a nation arose out of the colonial conquest by the Spanish empire and over the centuries consolidated a national identity based on a group of elite families that owned the land and the economic means of production. El Salvador is a small country in Central America, bordering with the North Pacific Ocean, Guatemala and Honduras. The whole of El Salvador covers 20,720 sq km, an area smaller than the state of Massachusetts. The estimated population of El Salvador is 6 million with 75 per cent of its people considering themselves Catholics, and a growing number of Protestant Evangelicals reaching 20 per cent of the total population. The country is divided into 14 counties (*departamentos*) and the majority of the population lives in the rural areas.[36]

In a small country such as El Salvador the Church has enormous influence and the archbishop of El Salvador before Romero had worked very closely with the elite families and the government. El Salvador became independent from Spain on 15 September 1821 and remained within a close network of Central American States that were heavily influenced in their economic activities by the United States. After the 1929 Great Depression there were protests and economic uncertainty in El Salvador and in 1932 thousands of peasants were shot on orders from General Maximiliano Hernández Martínez, following a direct confrontation with the trade unions inspired by the Communist Party.[37] Hernández consolidated his power and established a dictatorship that lasted from 1931 to 1944. Successive military takeovers followed massive demonstrations in 1944 and the military consolidated a strong political position within the country.

Particular benefits and privileges were given to the economic elites during the governments of Major Oscar Osorio (1949–56) and President José María Lemus (1956–60). In 1960 young army officers deposed President Lemus and started a new line of army officers that ruled El Salvador.[38] It was only in 1976 during the military government of Arturo Molina that the first proposals for an agrarian reform were prepared.[39] Before that reform there was a close alliance between 'an agro-exporting (coffee) oligarchy and a praetorian guard'.[40] Public protests and a generalized armed conflict between the Salvadorian Army and the guerrillas followed the agrarian reform until a peace accord signed in Mexico in January 1992 ended years of violence.[41] The violations of human rights during the 1980s were widespread and the Catholic Church and her Christian communities were the main recipient of death threats, occupation of churches and general harassment for defending the rights to life of thousands of Salvadorians.[42] Sobrino lived in El Salvador throughout this violent period and his own personal changes in outlook were influenced by the social context and the work by staff and university students at the Jesuit University.

Sobrino, a Basque, was born on 27 December 1938 in Bilbao, Spain.[43] He joined the Jesuits when he was 18 and was sent the following year to El Salvador. His studies as a Jesuit included engineering at St. Louis University in the United States and then theology in Frankfurt.[44] After his theological studies he returned to El Salvador where he has lived most of his life, working at the University of Central America (UCA). Sobrino recently confessed that his own life's journey has seen several major changes over the years. He started his life in El Salvador as a young priest who wanted to be holy and then changed into an existential philosopher who wanted to be authentic. Later, he became a liberation theologian who wanted to be a revolutionary and finally he has developed a desire to be real, living a fully incarnational life.[45] In his formative years in El Salvador Sobrino 'did not see anything'; however, after his return from studies in 1972 he perceived a change in the local church and became slowly involved in the lives of the Salvadorian people.[46] The change had taken place in 1968 when the Latin American bishops meeting in Medellín (Colombia) decided to look more closely at the social and pastoral realities of Latin America and involved all pastoral agents within society and particularly the poor and the oppressed, that is, the majority of Latin Americans.

The 1968 call by the Latin American Jesuit provincials to immerse themselves in the realities of Latin America after the Second Vatican Council included Jesuit schools and universities.[47] Thus, if Gutiérrez worked and lived all his life in a slum in Lima, Sobrino worked all his life as a teacher, and following the foundation of the Jesuit-run José Simeón Cañas University (UCA) in San Salvador he worked there as one of its professors.[48]

The university was founded in September 1965 by the Jesuits in order to bring education to those who didn't have access to it and as a project of liberation where the values of the gospel as understood by Vatican II and Medellín would be promoted through the leadership of the Jesuit community. At the time of its foundation the state-run Universidad de El Salvador was the focus for students' protests and social awareness, perceived by the government of Colonel Julio Adalberto Rivera as promoting Marxist ideas and of threatening the social order. Thus, when the Jesuits requested permission to start a university, the new foundation fitted nicely into the law that regulated private universities, assuming that students from the best private schools of El Salvador would attend the UCA and that they would study with the best Jesuit members of staff. At the beginning the UCA offered courses in economics, industrial engineering and business administration. Later, in 1969, the new courses in philosophy, psychology and the humanities were created.

The UCA campus started to be built in 1970 through financial loans from the Inter-American Development Bank (Banco Interamericano del Desarrollo – BID). The UCA under Román Mayorga Quirós as rector moved quickly into a progressive line following changes within the Jesuits, and in 1976 Professor Ignacio Ellacuría attracted the animosity of El Salvador's President Arturo Armando Molina after he wrote an editorial in the university's magazine criticizing the halting of the Salvadorian agrarian reform. The government withdrew educational subsidies to the UCA and the attacks on the Jesuits started after the assassination of the Jesuit Rutilio Grande in March 1977 and after the UCA supported all pastoral plans by Archbishop Romero through its department of theology, headed by Jon Sobrino. In 1979 Ellacuría became Rector of the UCA and moved the university into research programmes related to the national realities of El Salvador while immersing students, staff and the university community in the social realities of the poor of El Salvador. As the Civil War continued Ellacuría became very prominent within the movement to mediate peace accords and he spoke strongly against injustice and human rights abuses through the television, the UCA radio and the UCA publications.

Ignacio Ellacuría SJ, at the time of his assassination Rector of the university, articulated this particular ministry in the following words: 'the university should be present intellectually where it is needed: to provide science for those who have no science; to provide skills for the unskilled; to be a voice for those who have no voice; to give intellectual support for those who do not possess the academic qualifications to promote and legitimate their rights'.[49] Sobrino was less romantic about the possibilities of a university because of past experiences where Jesuit universities became top educational institutions but in doing so compromised their opportunities for challenging unjust and sinful structures within society.

Sobrino advocated the option for the poor within a Christian university by arguing that while it was unrealistic to suggest that a university should be located among the poor, all activities and in particular the central activities of a Christian university should look towards the poor. For him, one of the central activities within this kind of university is the dialogue between faith and science and therefore the importance of the teaching and research of theology as a discipline and as a reflection on the life of the poor and the marginalized from a Christian perspective. Sobrino's statement about theology within a university becomes central to understand the challenges that the Jesuits posed to the powerful in El Salvador and the inspiration they provided to many of the communities linked to their extra-mural courses and training of leaders of Christian communities within El Salvador. Sobrino argues very strongly that

> theology must be turned, then, towards the people of God; it should be inserted effectively among them, draw its agenda from them and accompany them. In this sense, university theology should be a moment of theo-praxis for the whole people of God and should be considered as a theo-culture, a Christo-culture, an ecclesio-culture – that is, an instrument that cultivates and nurtures faith, hope, and love of God's people.[50]

It is difficult to understand Sobrino and the other Jesuits without understanding their life in community and their university venture, as it is difficult to disentangle the educational context of Sobrino from the ongoing presence and challenging university life of Ellacuría. From 6 January to November 1989 15 bombs were planted at the Jesuit university campus, with the destruction of the printing press and other university installations. The campus was blocked; the buildings raided; attempts were made to end government financial aid; teachers, students and staff had to flee the country because of political persecution. Sobrino and Ellacuría, however, remained there. Even before his assassination Ellacuría didn't know if he was going to be allowed back into the country. In 1990 the UCA was awarded the Príncipe de Asturias Prize in Spain for communications and humanities because of the UCA's defence of human rights and freedom of expression.

A Latin American Christology

The Christology of Jon Sobrino of the 1990s advances without a theological apology the social context of Latin America in which there is a need to return to the historical Jesus as well as a need to understand that the social context of the Jesus of history needs liberation today as it was at the historical time portrayed by the Gospels.[51] For Sobrino, it is not sufficient to confess that Jesus is Lord in order to become a Christian because Christological creeds and assumptions without a context have already created so much violence and contradictions within the world.[52] Instead, Sobrino argues that the Jesus of history preaches a kingdom that is eschatological, already here and not yet, a kingdom and a God of the Kingdom that interacts with contemporary history in which salvation is proclaimed here and now and not yet fully. The Christological 'rapture' of Sobrino comes out of his link between Christology and soteriology, so that salvation for humanity became a reality during Christ's life on earth. Thus it has been present throughout history, with the proviso that Christological understandings have been manipulated and used for many reasons.

Those who received Good News at the time of the historical

Jesus were the poor, the dispossessed, the sick, those rejected by society, the prostitutes and all those that Sobrino identifies with the poor within society. Therefore Sobrino searches for the poor and the marginalized within Latin American society because salvation has been shown to them in history, even though their tribulations and sufferings under the oppression of the military regimes and other structural developments impede the preaching of the Kingdom and the realization of the good news of the Kingdom here and now. The *locus theologicum* (*lugar teologal*) for Sobrino are the poor because it is clear within the Gospels that Jesus made a clear connection between the poor, the Kingdom of God and an ongoing process of salvation.[53] The poor acquire a certain authority because it is with the poor and the marginalized that Jesus teaches the values of the Kingdom of God. Thus the place of the poor becomes a significant and privileged stand-point for the development of a Christology related to the preaching of salvation by the historical Jesus.

Sobrino is clear that the first stand-point of a study of Christological issues within Latin America locates itself within the Church, because the study of the historical Jesus follows from faith in Christ. Without faith in Christ there are no possibilities of examining the historical Jesus and his history, and without faith in Christ there is no correlation between contemporary history, the values of the Kingdom and the world of the poor and the marginalized. Thus, Sobrino remains as a theologian within the Church and within the locations where the Church is living the values of the Kingdom through the poor and those who suffer. Although 20 years earlier and within the models of economic development within Latin America questions about the poor had an enormous economic weight, Sobrino reiterates the value of the world of the poor for theological action and thought by introducing the term 'victims', equated with the world of the poor. Jesus of Nazareth was a victim of the Roman Empire and was crucified because he preached the Kingdom of God and mixed with the poor; the Christ of faith through the Church intends to do the same in

Latin America; and he finds a central place for action and theology within the contemporary victims of political violence, economic policies and other types of crucifixion that remind us of a crucified Christ who is always crucified when the poor, as victims, are crucified within a particular socio-political context.

For Sobrino, the leap between the study of Christology and the realities of the contemporary Christ in Latin America is breached by a single epistemological principle: the following of Christ. Study and research leads to a commitment towards those who are following Christ, the victims, and generates a hermeneutical circle centred upon a social following of those who symbolize the values of the Kingdom and therefore are privileged in their knowledge of Christ through their life of following in very difficult circumstances.

Sobrino had already attempted these contextual approaches to Christ in Latin America in his earlier work and he had introduced apologetic polemics vis-à-vis other approaches to Christology, particularly those immersed in biblical criticism and hermeneutics where a preoccupation for the intention of the Christ vis-à-vis the Logos seems to dominate discussions on theological issues.[54] Within that initial confrontation of more traditional and universalistic approaches to the Christ of faith Sobrino recognizes the centrality of the early work of Ignacio Ellacuría where a historical framework to the historical developments of Christology is introduced and where Ellacuría advocates a movement towards a historical Logos in order to avoid mere speculation.[55] Within that theological progression there is a need to understand the historical process by which the early Christians arrived at the conceptions of the high logos so that belief does not forget any experience and doctrine does not disentangle itself from a historical and human experience of divine revelation within an empirical and incarnated world. Sobrino and Ellacuría influenced each other within the context of a theological thinking that is already, years after Vatican II, challenging the centrality of a rationalistic and speculative theology of reason, a predominant phenomenon within European theology since the European scientific revolution.[56]

Further, for Sobrino the relation of the Logos within the Trinity is also in need of a historical hermeneutics because the God of the Kingdom does not remain above as a God of creation and rests thereafter but throughout the biblical text shows an enormous energy and an enormous compassion, an empathy towards those who are oppressed in Israel, in exile and those who have followed Jesus of Nazareth throughout his ministry. God raises Jesus from the dead in order to allow a human contact between the Logos and the early Christians who immediately recognized him in a human activity, a meal, and bring their own joy to others (the disciples on the road to Emmaus). The high Christological treatments of the Christ of faith should complement the initial and very important experience of humanity, men and women who in their own realms of life and social activities encounter the God of history who is on their side and who through the Church walks, eats and works with them.

Sobrino questions the status quo faced by the poor in Latin America and wonders if the Christ preached to them by the institutional Church as Christ-love, Christ-power and Christ-reconciler has not invaded and negated the biblical paradigm of the prophetic Jesus who instead of complying with the socio-historical and religious experience of his time questioned Jewish society because it paid lip service to the covenant and was not looking after the poor and the marginalized.[57] Indeed, the councils seem to highlight, following the writings by the Fathers of the Church, the existence of the true man, the *homo verus*, the exalted Son of God who walks the earth as an incarnational Logos, forgetting the fact that the human Jesus cannot be essentialized through the Logos because he was a true man with all the attitudes, feelings and emotions of a man not of an exalted Logos of the later councils of the Church. These theological lacunae suggest not a contradiction between Jesus of Nazareth and the Christ of Faith but a theological simplification by European theology that points to an over exultation of humanity rather than to a critical assessment of what is said of the historical Jesus within the Synoptic Gospels.

If Sobrino associates salvation with Christology within a historical context it is because faith in Christ has not managed to alleviate poverty and oppression within Latin America. The prophetic attitudes of Jesus of Nazareth have not been widely followed by those who believe, in Latin America, and the majority of Latin Americans remain surrounded by and under the effects of poverty and oppression. The reason for that, according to Sobrino, is the separation between the Christ of faith and the historical Jesus, a reality that united by the incarnation was historically separated by the Church on the one hand and by those oppressed on the other.[58] The contribution by Medellín and Puebla to mediate this dichotomy has been enormous and the admonition of Jesus the liberator has created a sense of hope and resurrection in the victims of oppression in Latin America. For it is the resurrection of Jesus by the Father that inaugurates the eschatological time of salvation and gives hope to the poor and the marginalized. However, unless the resurrection is understood as a moment in which a man, Jesus, is vindicated by the justice of God, the resurrection could remain an event at a spiritual level that only looks to the future. The just man, Jesus, is resurrected because as victim he is loved by the Father who is with him. Thus, the God of justice and the God of the resurrection remains with all victims, gives them hope and justice and proclaims a resurrection of the oppressed in their human life here and now and for the future. As was the case with Israel, faith in the resurrection of the dead arises at a time of persecution in which theologically the sacred authors recognize that the God of history must save by resurrecting bodies and by resurrecting peoples.

For Sobrino God the liberator is God the crucified.[59] Therefore the message of the resurrection is that there is no redemption without embracing sin and there is no liberation without embracing suffering and oppression. This is a liberating embracing in which suffering is not to be praised but lived with a purpose as Jesus of Nazareth did. The resurrection is not only the triumph of life over death and grace over sin but also the triumph of Jesus over his oppressors.[60] Sobrino concludes that the historical salvation of Jesus comes out of a central core of values associated with the Kingdom of God that push him into confrontation with different groups within society. Those confrontations are not related to a resurrection but to a set of values that prepare people to be raised again after death. In the case of Latin America that confrontation is between the followers of Jesus and the idols because for Sobrino idolatry is the central paradigm that antagonizes the values of the Kingdom of God within a Latin American context. Idolatry remains contextually a thirst for riches and for economic gain whereby all divisions that create injustice and oppression come out of an idolatrous behaviour in which the values of money rather than the values of the Kingdom are at the centre of people's lives and particularly of those who oppress the poor by wanting more and more.

The Christology of Sobrino is structured in relation to the Kingdom of God rather than in relation to the resurrection, and brings the person of Christ closer to human life, human need and human suffering. The concrete implications of that Christology point to the need for a just life for the poor because if they have a just and dignified life society would have acquired the values of the Kingdom and the social injustices would have been alleviated. The utopian touch of this Christology becomes the utopian touch of the Kingdom of God, realized in the poor and authenticated by the exaltation of those who are considered less important within society. The task and the challenge posed by Sobrino is for all Christians: to prepare for the resurrection and therefore eternal salvation by a constant life that complies with the values of the Kingdom of God. Christ is present in the crucified peoples who complete the sufferings of Christ in their lives so that the crucified peoples are the cause and beginning of God's salvation. In Sobrino's words: 'To call the peoples of the Third World "crucified people", "Yahweh's Suffering Servant", "the presence of the crucified Christ in history", is the most important theological statement we can make about them. Nevertheless, I also want to call them a "martyred people", not because this adds anything new, but for immediate pastoral reasons and broader theological reasons.'[61]

This is a scandalous proposition for the world, as it was a scandalous proposition that God would save through his son's crucifixion and that the symbol of hope and resurrection would be the Roman symbol of criminality and shame. However, if this social proposition is a scandal at least Christians can recognize that it is not possible to ascertain a resurrection through suffering and that it is necessary to bring the crucified down from their crosses so that the liberating power of God is recognized among those who have been liberated. The following of this Christ requires a way of life in which the values of the Kingdom are at the centre and in which justice and solidarity are the values that identify the followers of Christ who walk together with those whom God loves: the poor, the oppressed, the lonely, the sick, and those rejected by society.

Sobrino takes a methodological option within his Christology, that of emphasizing the Kingdom of God rather than the councils or the Church and therefore clashes with other aspects of Christological preference. Thus, Costadoat has criticized him for not allowing a more fluent relation between the historical Jesus and the faith of Christians and the Christ of faith vis-à-vis the involvement of the Logos within human history.[62] One can only argue without going into a whole section on Christological polemics that Sobrino's Christological centrality of victims and of the centrality of the Kingdom of God grounds itself completely in the reading of the Synoptic Gospels and allows the Christian communities of Latin America to regain a sense of biblical perspective within a contextual social suffering which in the past has always been linked to a future eschatological time rather than to the divine chronology of the Kingdom, 'here and now' but 'not yet'.

A Theology of the Victims

Sobrino's understanding of the relation between the crucified Jesus and the Christ of the resurrection connects with his understanding of the socially deprived, the oppressed and the victims of violence in Latin America in general and in El Salvador in particular. For it is of interest theologically that there is both theological continuity and contextual rupture between the social situation of Latin America and the theology of Jon Sobrino. By 1992 the civil war in El Salvador had ended and most of the military regimes throughout Latin America ceased to exist. By that time Sobrino's loss of his community had been theologically channelled into larger questions about globalization and the future that coincided with the post-Santo Domingo state of affairs and Sobrino's own engagement with a globalized community through lectures, courses, seminars and public engagements throughout the world.

If the pre-Santo Domingo Jon Sobrino was fully dedicated to the common project of his Jesuit community at the university, their assassination created a need for a rupture that emotionally healed him and theologically made him ask further questions about the globalized community of human beings, their values, their technology and their own position towards the victims, previously victims of the military regimes but after 1992 Santo Domingo the victims of globalization.

Sobrino went even further in linking throughout the journal *Concilium* the role of religion and of religious practitioners with a bonding of humanity in solidarity, peace and understanding after the sad events of 9/11 in New York and Washington DC. For the themes of global ethics and globalization opened discussions that connected those involved in *Concilium* who, when commenting on the events of 9/11, wrote:

> We appeal to all Christians with all the means at their disposal to forge bonds of solidarity, of peace and of reconciliation. Those who live in wealthy countries have a special obligation to track down injustice around the world, cry out against it, and, bit by bit, overcome it. At a time when the first impulse of governments is to focus only on the security of their own political system, economy and citizens, Christians have to remind political leaders that the funds to pay for this extra security must not be diverted from the small amounts

set aside to feed and to bring justice to the world's poor and oppressed.[63]

Sobrino stands within a globalized world of religion, in different shapes and forms, fundamentalist or otherwise main stream. Victims of the military regimes are changed into victims of an economic globalization that gives better economic ratings to the Latin American countries where the victims live but that has allowed the social agency of governments to be compromised by foreign economic institutions as has been the case of the government of El Salvador throughout its history. Within that process of globalization and particularly after 9/11 there is a globalized preoccupation with religion, its forms, its power and its deformities/anomalies. Religion associated with institutional forms, otherness, neo-colonialism or a wider sense of spirituality remains at the centre of the political realms of anxiety and profit. In the words of the Brazilian writer Mario Coelho 'the greatest dangers in the spiritual search are gurus, masters, and fundamentalism: what I referred to before as the globalization of spirituality'.[64]

For globalization as a process of internationalization has advantages for its citizens provided that the world is not perceived as one massive conurbation with all the problems attached to large urban areas and their inhabitants' loss of any sense of individual identity.[65] Globalization has advantages but creates victims because the market and the immediacy of economics remain at the centre, while theoreticians of globalization have subversively spoken of globalization as a natural development of Western civilization.[66]

For Sobrino globalization 'can refer to the universal spread of the market, to instantaneous communication across the planet, to the homogenization of cultural spheres, to hope for a new human *ekumene*'.[67] For Sobrino suggestions of Christian inspiration towards globalization do not solve the problem of human beings at the mercy of the system and of Christ as agent of redemption of this new context/system. Following from his Christological paradigm of Jesus as victim and those who suffer

with him as victims who help resurrect society, Sobrino argues
that the only ones that can bring salvation and redemption
within globalization are the victims of the system because they
are as much victims as part of the redemption of Christ towards
the system. The oppressed offer redemption to the oppressors as
far as they are crucified victims of the system on which they
depend.[68] Thus Sobrino writes:

> Globalization takes for granted that those who summon –
> bring together, 'globalize' – to salvation are those who hold
> power, economic power above all. Scripture opposed a very
> different and opposite summoning centre: the victims *sum-*
> *mon*. John's theology makes the crucified Christ the one who
> draws all things to him (see John 12.32; 19.37).[69]

It is through the victims that solidarity is shown and great
human efforts to alleviate poverty and suffering are recorded; it
is through the victims that a 'civilization of poverty' starts to
appear, a civilization in which all have their basic needs cov-
ered; and it is the victims who challenge an unhappy world
where the 'civilization of wealth' can rule, cohere and be considered the globalized norm.[70]

Utopian Bereavement

It is in this new globalized theoretical and locational argument
for the victims and from the point of view of the victims that
Sobrino articulates his own period of bereavement after 1989.
His writings seem to reproduce a second voice, that of his companion and friend Ignacio Ellacuría SJ. The older Sobrino, older
in age and in wisdom, affected by ill-health and sometimes frail
reflects upon his own journey and that of 'his family' asking
theological questions about the world to come and about his
own journey.

Within that journey Sobrino writes letters to 'Ellacu' as he
always called Ellacuría and in those letters he shares his views

of an ongoing hope, a hope that Sobrino has never denied of a better world seen from the point of view of the victims and therefore from the point of view of God and his Kingdom. He recalls how Ellacuría didn't like comments that he was a good man but he preferred to be told that he was just and clever. Sobrino remembers in a letter that Ellacuría didn't hate anybody, even when confronted in a public interview with the lies of the torturer and assassin Roberto D'Abuisson. It is in those letters that Sobrino draws his inspiration from Romero, the assassinated Jesuits and the two women who were at the Jesuit house that night of their annihilation and who were also murdered.[71] In his 'Letter to Jesus' on Christmas Day of 2005 Sobrino dialogues with Jesus of Nazareth and expresses his happiness that Jesus' parents are portrayed in the nativity scene, Joseph, one of the many working people of this world, and Mary, the good neighbour, dedicated to life and 'guardians of life', representing those who do not appear in the news, do not get an Oscar: they are not models, they do not score goals in a football match and they do not appear on the television. In that letter the globalized Sobrino recalls a letter he had just received for Christmas and the suffering of the poor in Africa, most probably the most neglected of the contemporary world, together with the poor of Iraq and Palestine.[72] It is there, according to Sobrino, that the Christ of faith and the social understanding of the historical Jesus meet.

Despite Sobrino's elaborate theological synthesis between the historical Jesus and the Christ of faith he was for years under theological investigation by the Vatican. In March 2007 the Congregation for the Doctrine of the Faith (CDF) led by Cardinal Willian Levada issued a Notification alerting the faithful about some errors in Sobrino's theology. The Notification focuses on two of Sobrino's works, *Jesus the Liberator* and *Christ the Liberator*, and while admitting that Sobrino 'does not deny the divinity of Christ', the Notification states that he fails to 'affirm' it with 'sufficient clarity'. Further, the Notification points to a much contested theological discussion and follows Pope Benedict XVI's understanding by suggesting that

Sobrino's works 'tend to exclude' Jesus' self-awareness of being divine. Sobrino had previously been asked to respond and to defend himself but he decided not to do so, and while having all the support from the Jesuits was forbidden to teach Catholic theology by the local Archbishop of San Salvador.[73]

It is in the next chapter and through the life and writings of Ignacio Ellacuría that one can gain a better understanding of the development of Sobrino's theological and personal interests, from concentration on the particular concerns of El Salvador to the concerns of a whole planet in need of redemption, from the victims in El Salvador to the victims of globalization, for it was the posthumous influence of Ellacuría that brought Sobrino to include his own victims among the crucified and the resurrected of this world.

2

Ignacio Ellacuría SJ

Ignacio Ellacuría (1930–89), a Jesuit and rector of the José Simeón Cañas University of Central America (UCA) of El Salvador, 59 years of age, was murdered by members of the Atlacatl regiment of the Salvadorian Army, a unit of which entered the compound of the Jesuit residence at the UCA at 1 a.m. on 16 November 1989.[74] The soldiers fired into the air and as they reached the Jesuit residence one of them threw a grenade into the building where the Jesuits were sleeping. Soldiers entered the building and shot two of the priests, Joaquín López y López and Juan Ramón Moreno, while they were asleep. They also killed the Jesuits' cook, Julia Elba Ramos and her daughter Celina, who had requested permission to spend the night at the residence because of the military curfew and the unsettled situation that existed within San Salvador. Three other priests, Amando López, Ignacio Martín-Baró and Segundo Montes, were dragged outside onto the lawn, and were joined by Ignacio Ellacuría, who slept in a separate quarter. The soldiers forced them to lie face down on the ground. According to a witness, Martín-Baró shouted at the soldiers and accused them of committing an injustice, but the four Jesuits were quickly shot dead.[75] Other accounts suggest that 'their brains were spilled out on the ground by their murderers', interpreted by Joseph O'Hare, president at that time of the Jesuit-run Fordham University in New York, as 'a chilling symbol of the contempt shown by men of violence for the power of truth'.[76] The soldiers burned university archives and threw grenades into the school of theology before painting rebel slogans on the walls accusing the rebels of murdering the

43

Jesuits. On the following morning a military truck with a loud speaker went around the archdiocesan offices announcing that Ellacuría and Martín-Baró had already been killed and that they would continue killing Communists.

Ignacio Ellacuría made a significant contribution to Latin American theology by his actions – his first step, and by his writings – his second step of discipleship. After his assassination a series of writings on his philosophy, political theology and his vision of a university for the poor started to emerge.[77] However, his main contribution to theology was made within the field of a theology of education, not a usual subject within liberation theology. His vision of a community of scholars, teachers and students who would live and learn the values of the Kingdom of God brought him international recognition and his martyrdom made his work and life part of the history of a Latin American theology built and written upon the God of Life and a preferential option for the poor and the marginalized within one's life, even unto death.

Theologian and Martyr

Ellacuría was born in Portugalete (Vizcaya), Spain, on 9 November 1930, one of five sons of the local optician and one of four sons who wanted to be Catholic priests.[78] Ellacuría studied at the Jesuit school of Tudela where he seemed to be reserved and intense and was not considered a possible candidate for the Jesuits. However, independently he applied to join the Jesuits and at the age of 17 entered the formation programme of the Society of Jesus (the Jesuits) at their novitiate house in Loyola; he was ordained as a Catholic priest in 1961.[79] During his novitiate the Jesuits decided to start a similar programme in El Salvador and Miguel Elizondo, the novice master, requested volunteers to go with him to El Salvador. Six novices departed from Bilbao on 26 February 1949 and after a month at sea they arrived at Santa Tecla (El Salvador).

Elizondo's personality made a great impression on Ellacuría

and on other novices who had Elizondo as their novice master. Elizondo had common sense and a deep spirituality centred on the Jesuit 'freedom of spirit', a call to be available to any mission assigned 'for the greater glory of God' – the motto of the Society of Jesus. Thus, while the Jesuit novices in Spain centred their lives upon norms and external practices of mortification that separated them from the world Elizondo designed a spiritual programme centred upon a personal spiritual growth with a very fluid timetable in which novices were even allowed to play games, particularly football, without their cassocks. Elizondo entered into dialogue with the novices and stressed the need for a spiritual availability at all times, particularly within the daily requirements of life with others. Throughout his life Ellacuría expressed his admiration for Elizondo and spoke warmly about Elizondo's life as a first-class example of a contemporary Jesuit.

In September 1949 the six novices made their vows of poverty, obedience and chastity and were sent to study at the Catholic University of Quito, where they followed two years of studies on the humanities and three years of philosophy. Ellacuría was an outstanding student with a critical mind who became very close to one of his teachers of classical humanities, Aurelio Espinoza Pólit. Espinoza had studied at Oxford University and was a world expert on Sophocles and Virgil; however, he wrote on many topics, such as Ecuadorian writers, past and present, and served as rector of the Catholic University as well as advisor on cultural matters to the Ecuadorian Government.

Ellacuría graduated in philosophy in 1955 and Espinoza advised him to gather a large library in El Salvador with all that was published about the country as Espinoza himself had done in Ecuador. Years later Ellacuría tried to gather all available materials through the UCA Florentino Idoate's Library and through the library of his own centre of research on contemporary issues of El Salvador. In Ecuador, Ellacuría met a Spanish Jesuit poet, Angel Martínez, one of the most important poets of Nicaragua. Ellacuría attended some of his lectures and poetry readings and for many years they corresponded; Martínez regularly sent unpublished work to Ellacuría in order to get his comments. Later, in 1957, Ellacuría published a paper about the poetry of Martínez in the magazine *Cultura* of the Ministry of Education of El Salvador, for Ellacuría had been very impressed by the synthesis of poetry, philosophy and theology achieved by Martínez and by his personal life in which poetry and life became one. The need for an honest expression, aesthetic and personal, and of the realities of life remained a challenge for Ellacuría who in his own life as a teacher and academic developed some of the attitudes of his masters, Aurelio Espinoza and Angel Martínez.

After his return to El Salvador in order to undergo his experience of regency, that is a period of teaching or pastoral work, Ellacuría spent three years in the Seminary San José de la Montaña. His duties included teaching seminarians scholastic philosophy in Latin; however, he also introduced them to the existentialist philosophers. During weekends he organized picnics and, on one occasion, a trip to a volcano, but he made an effort to acquire some classic works of literature in order to build up a small library so that the seminarians could read other books apart from popular paperbacks. During that time he wrote some papers on Ortega y Gasset, moral values and law for *Estudios Centroamericanos* and he also gave some public lectures.[80] In 1958 he returned to Europe and to the theological centre at Innsbruck where he completed his theological studies in 1962. Those were the years of a complex situation of ecclesiastical unrest before the Second Vatican Council and Ellacuría used to gather the Spanish-speaking students in his room at Innsbruck in order to plan changes and request more freedom for the student body. Ellacuría found Austria cold and distant, and his former teacher Aurelio Espinoza wrote him a letter alerting Ellacuría to the dangers of becoming Germanic in his critical thought.

From those pre-ordination years Ellacuría always remembered the lectures of one of the greatest theologians of the Second Vatican Council: Karl Rahner.[81] Other lecturers at Innsbruck included Hugo Rahner and Andreas Jürgmann. Ellacuría was ordained as a Catholic priest in Innsbruck on 26 July 1961. After ordination he took some holidays to see his family in Bilbao and decided to pursue the possibility of writing a doctorate on the philosophy of Xavier Zubiri, a Spanish philosopher. Zubiri did not answer his letters but finally when they met Zubiri agreed to direct his doctoral thesis and wrote to his wife that he had met 'a brilliant young Jesuit'. Zubiri's expectations were not only that he had found a disciple to share his own ideas but also that Ellacuría had the intellectual capacity to continue and carry out his own intellectual projects. Ellacuría pursued his doctorate at the Universidad Complutense of Madrid where he faced some problems owing to the fact that he was writing a doctorate on a philosopher who was still alive. Nevertheless, his thesis passed without problems but was not given a *cum laude* because of the animosity of the university authorities.

Having completed his third formation programme as a Jesuit in Dublin, Ellacuría made his final profession as a Jesuit in Portugalete on 2 February 1965 and in 1967 was appointed to the newly founded Jesuit University of El Salvador (UCA). With the ongoing reforms triggered by the Second Vatican Council Ellacuría became central to the changing vision of the Jesuits in Latin America (see Chapter 4) and he preached at a Jesuit Province retreat in December 1969 where he applied the principles of liberation in order to point to God's call for a changing commitment and lifestyle by the Jesuits in Central America. Ellacuría served as Delegate for Jesuit Formation from 1971 to 1974 but Father Paolo Dezza, one of Jesuit Superior General Arrupe's principal assistants, requested that Ellacuría be removed from those duties in 1974. Ellacuría expected the Jesuits in training to be critical in their studies; he made changes that were too quick for the Jesuit community and that divided them. One of those changes was the residency of Jesuit students outside the seminary at Aguilares and the opening of a full philosophical and theological programme of studies related to the programmes available at the UCA. Rome decided that Ellacuría was too independent and he was removed from all positions of authority within the Jesuit province. Even though such a measure must have been a heavy blow to his own personal ambitions as a Jesuit, Ellacuría retained a full commitment to the university where since his return from Europe in 1967 he had served as a member of the Board of Directors and head of the philosophy department. It was the influence of Ellacuría that had moved the general commitment of the UCA staff towards liberation and a commitment to the poor and those who were suffering within El Salvador.

Ellacuría had an intense personality and an independent mind that meant he always had a heavy work load and a complete commitment to whatever he was undertaking. Further, he was not part of any of the political groups, including the opposition to the military government, because he was too independent, sharp and intense.[82] His love of sports was an expression of his personal discipline; he played sports (*frontón*) every Wednesday and Saturday with Montes, Martín-Baró and Amando López and listened to the Spanish shortwave sports broadcast (Radio Exterior de España) everyday. Ellacuría was a keen follower of the football team Athletic of Bilbao and apart from the celebration of the Eucharist the time of the Spanish radio broadcast was the only time during the day in which he could not be disturbed. Regardless of those personal moments of enjoyment he was a very austere person, very careful with money, who always kept strictly to the purpose of any visits, and when he moved his possessions from the old to the new Jesuit residence he gave most of his books to the UCA libraries.

From the year of its foundation the UCA started to study and denounce unjust social structures, and in 1969 the Jesuit magazine *Estudios Centroamericanos* published a special edition on the Salvadoran–Honduran War. The articles in that issue showed that the war was a direct result of unjust landholdings and they were followed in subsequent issues by a series of criticisms of injustice within El Salvador. In 1970 the magazine was relocated to the university with Ellacuría as its central moving force. With such public influence and after his spell within the Jesuits-in-training team Ellacuría was destined to become rector of the UCA, and in 1975 he took Salvadoran citizenship, a requisite for any rector of a university in El Salvador.[83] In 1976 Ellacuría wrote an editorial in the magazine that criticized the position of the government vis-à-vis the landowners, and the government acted promptly and cut the government subsidies to UCA, while during the following months bombs were planted in the university campus. During his university life Ellacuría received many death threats and had to leave the country after the assassinations of the Jesuit Rutilio Grande in 1977 and Archbishop Oscar Romero in 1980.[84]

In 1979 Ellacuría became rector of the UCA during a year that saw renewed and sustained violence by the newly constituted military government and a year before the assassination of Archbishop Romero in March 1980. In February 1980 the Jesuit residence at the university was attacked and 100 bullets were fired upon its walls. After Romero's assassination bombs were planted at the UCA and a list of people to be assassinated included Ellacuría's name. Thus, he was advised to leave El Salvador at the end of 1980 and did so with the help of the Spanish Embassy, remaining in Spain until April 1982. In 1981 Ellacuría had continued his editorial call for a 'third way', that of mediation between the government and the rebels and in 1985 together with Archbishop Arturo Rivera y Damas he acted as go-between in the exchange of President Duarte's daughter for 22 political prisoners and 101 wounded guerrillas.[85] In 1984, together with Jon Sobrino, he founded the *Revista Latinoamericana de Teología*, a challenging project of theologizing in the midst of suffering.

The assassination of Archbishop Romero in March 1980 had a personal impact on Ellacuría. He didn't write much about those events but in his own personal life he started to cultivate and to speak about compassion and service. The efficient and clever Ellacuría was being slowly changed by the example of Romero and their previous encounters. If he had spoken before about carrying on his shoulders human realities, after 1980 his writings started making a direct connection with the crucified and suffering people of El Salvador who were not awaiting help but carrying with their strong faith the Jesuits, the work at the UCA and, finally, Ellacuría himself. This is the turning point of the academic and scholar who becomes a theologian of liberation and recognizes that it is within the suffering poor and marginalized that God lives and it is through them that God acts within the social and political realities of Latin America. Thus, the 'new' Ellacuría spoke in Barcelona on 6 November 1989 on the occasion at which he received the Alfonso Comín Prize, given to the UCA. Within a political context, he expressed the need to accept a tension between faith and justice and to commit both aspects of life to the needs of the majority of the population, after all a utopian necessity related to the values of the Kingdom of God. Further, in his last writings before his assassination ('Utopía y profetismo'), he concluded that there was the need for an ever new heaven in which a prophetic negation of a powerful and rich Church would lead to a civilization of poverty, with transformed human beings who would continue preaching higher things, that is, the future coming of a Saviour God, of God the liberator.[86] In his last writings it is clear that faith had brought Ellacuría to the grace of God so that the mighty and clever Ellacuría felt finally that others, the poor and the marginalized, were carrying him because they were closer to the God of Life.[87] Faith brought him to martyrdom because he opened himself to the poor of El Salvador who carried his coffin during his funeral and the Mass of the Resurrection for those killed before and after him.

Within that climate of personal change and personal conversion Ellacuría had been hopeful that the start of the Cristiani administration in 1989 could bring a more peaceful period to El Salvador.[88] After all, Alfredo Cristiani represented the most democratic part of the ARENA Party (Alianza Republicana Nacionalista).[89] Other sectors of the party had other ideas and the killing of Ellacuría, who had misjudged the threats towards the Jesuits during the previous months, was probably a tactical response from Roberto D'Aubuisson's militaristic policies at a time when the guerrillas had started a new phase of combat against the Salvadoran Government.[90] Ellacuría had opposed

that call for a new armed phase by the Farabundo Martí
National Liberation Front (FMNL) as he had always opposed
the complicity of the military with death squads and indeed any
kind of violence within Salvadoran society.[91] At that time he
was furious with the guerrillas because a new military offensive
would bring more and more suffering to El Salvador and his
intention had been to declare the UCA as neutral territory in
which people could find shelter and compassion. In early
November 1989 he had received in Barcelona a prize from the
Comín Foundation and, because of the escalation of violence in
El Salvador, had decided to return as soon as possible in order
to help with a possible mediation between the government and
the guerrillas as a new military offensive by the guerrillas had
been announced. Even when all the signs were there (members
of the Atlacatl Regiment searched the Jesuit residence on 13
November 1989), Ellacuría did not read them properly; or
maybe he did and decided to embrace his own death. Maybe his
awareness that the people of El Salvador had had no respite
from war and poverty made him into one of them, a tired and
introverted man who didn't seek refuge, as some politicians did
in foreign embassies, but who faced the end as he had faced the
beginning: with faith, with hope, and in the midst of very hard
academic work.

The Church and the Kingdom

Ellacuría was a Catholic priest, a Jesuit and a philosopher cum
theologian. Thus, his questions about liberation and the poor in
Latin America, particularly in Central America, arose from
within the Church, and, while he challenged the possibility that
the Church could ever be true to Christ when it was associated
with riches and power, he did not spend his emotional or intellectual energy challenging Church structures.[92] Others, such as
Pablo Richard, engaged the Church in a critique from within
vis-à-vis ecclesiastical structures and ways of preaching the
gospel of Christ. Ellacuría instead engaged with a central

concept that absorbed him during his lifetime: history in all its shapes, philosophical discussions on agency within history, theological discussions related to the salvific action of God within history and the possibility that moments in history were salvific, particularly when they connected the mission of the Church with the values and realities of the Kingdom of God. For Ellacuría, 'historic soteriology is a matter of seeking where and how the saving action of Jesus was carried out in order to pursue it in history'.[93]

Thus, in his contribution to *Mysterium liberationis*, the theological compendium on liberation theology, an entry later edited by Jon Sobrino, Ellacuría posed the following questions: 'What do human efforts towards historical, even socio-political liberation have to do with the establishment of the Kingdom of God that Jesus preached? What do the proclamation and realization of the Kingdom of God have to do with the historical liberation of the oppressed majorities?'[94] In posing such questions Ellacuría criticized the traditional distinction and dichotomy whereby grace comes out of a supernatural world and is injected within nature. Ellacuría did not dwell on the discussions between Augustine and Pelagius related to grace – those debates extended chronologically to the post-Reformation theological debates centred around grace and they are responsible for a traditional European treatment of a kind of grace from above that theologically is still separated from a biblical view of history and certainly a biblical account of the ministry of Jesus and his table fellowship with sinners.

Within his earlier work Ellacuría confronted the critique of Karl Rahner by political theologians such as Metz who suggested that Rahner's theology had nothing to do with the world and with a Church in the political and social world. Rahner's influence within the Second Vatican Council speaks of the contrary, particularly through his theological statements about a Church that is immersed in the world, and immersed in the sufferings and joys of the world as later stated by the council's document on the Church in the Modern World.[95] By the time that Ellacuría was writing his work *Teología política* (political theology) the dichotomy between grace and world had been officially broken within Catholic theology, and the growth of secularism in Europe had divided Catholic and Protestant theology between a Catholic theology immersed in the world and a Protestant theology that was still challenging the tenets of modernism and remained absolutely Christ-centric instead of centred within the Kingdom of God. The Christian liberation argued for by Ellacuría demanded a Church immersed in the world and in its politics but that fostered a belief that being political was not only political but demanded a liberation of the person and of society vis-à-vis the Kingdom of God. Thus, for Ellacuría, 'authentic Christian liberation is discovered and fostered in the liturgy, and only in the liturgy. Insofar as it is Christian at all, liberation must be comprehended and lived in and through the summons of a saving divine word.'[96]

It is within this early period of his writings that Ellacuría assumed the tenets of a Church that must move towards the world in El Salvador, towards the majority, towards the oppressed and the marginalized but with the Church at the centre, beginning and end of the Kingdom of God. The changes in his theology are clearly signalled and were remarkably striking as he continued his intellectual and personal association with the Basque philosopher Xavier Zubiri.

Ellacuría and Zubiri

It is possible to locate Ellacuría's philosophical studies within three periods that chronologically are dependent on each other:

1 the period before Zubiri's influence;
2 the period influenced directly by Zubiri's philosophy; and
3 Ellacuría's personal elaboration of a philosophical thought and rigorous work that depends directly on the context of El Salvador and is isolated with difficulty from Ellacuría's theological actions and theological writings.

Within the first period Ellacuría tried to find a connection between the work of Thomas Aquinas and the Spanish thinker Ortega y Gasset, both authors analysed within the realities of their context and their time.[97] During his second period, Ellacuría constructed his detailed doctoral thesis by analysing the concept of essence in Zubiri's philosophical work. Within that work Ellacuría declined to accept the distinction between physics and metaphysics by assuming that, going beyond individualism and positivism, physics becomes the metaphysical within the reality of every human being.[98] The physical side of reality then is not part of logical empiricism but it has two characteristics, one based on reality and the other based on metaphysics. Human beings can, sometimes, transcend the empirical and see a wide range of possibilities through a historic praxis or praxis of history.[99] Because of the centrality of Zubiri's influence on Ellacuría it is important to explore Zubiri's life and thought.

Xavier Zubiri was born in San Sebastián, within the Basque country of Spain, on 4 December 1898, and until he went to school his first language was Basque or *euskera*. When he was 17 years of age Zubiri entered the Diocesan Seminary of Madrid and he studied philosophy under Juan Zaragüeta. Two years later he met Ortega y Gasset who later directed his doctoral thesis submitted to the University of Madrid in 1923.[100] In 1920 Zubiri, a precocious intellectual genius, had received a licentiate in philosophy from the Higher Institute of Philosophy of the University of Louvain and a doctorate in theology from Rome. His doctoral thesis in philosophy was approved in 1923 at the Central University of Madrid and in 1926 he was awarded a chair in philosophy at the same university. In 1921 he was ordained as a deacon and later assigned to the archdiocese of Madrid.

Between 1928 and 1930 Zubiri visited the University of Freiborg where he studied with Husserl and Heidegger and the University of Berlin where he had the chance to attend the philosophical courses of Nicolai Hartman and where he met distinguished scholars such as Einstein, Schrödinger, Max Planck and

Werner Jaeger. In 1936 Zubiri married Carmen Castro in Rome
and became a layman staying for a period in Rome studying
oriental languages with A. Deimel. With the outbreak of the
Spanish Civil War Zubiri encountered distrust in Rome and
moved to Paris where he worked on physics with Luis de
Broglie, on philology with Benveniste and had the chance to listen to Maritain. From 1940 to 1942 he occupied the chair of
philosophy in Barcelona; however, he finally left his job because
of the official pressures on his work. Until 1942 Zubiri worked
on phenomenology and after 1942 he explored metaphysics,
culminating with his major book *Sobre la esencia* (1962).[101]

Even after Ellacuría moved to El Salvador Zubiri spent time
with him every year whenever Ellacuría was visiting Europe on
university business, and after Ellacuría completed his doctorate
Zubiri gave each of his writings to his disciple to read and to
critique in an honest manner. For the rest of his life and after
resigning from his chair at the University of Barcelona, Zubiri
taught private courses in philosophy, organized his writings
and chaired an international seminar that carried his name from
1971 until his death on 21 September 1983. Ellacuría took it
over after Zubiri's death and many of Zubiri's works were
published thanks to Ellacuría's efforts, including his master
trilogy on the theory of knowledge.[102] Ellacuría's admiration for
Zubiri's work arose out of the fact that Zubiri's philosophical
project carried a responsibility, an obligation towards an
honest response about the foundations of human life. In the
words of Ellacuría, it was pure philosophy but not only philosophy. Zubiri's project coincided with the philosophical project
of Ellacuría who before his death had completed a manuscript
on the philosophy of historic reality covering his favourite
philosophical subject, that of agency within history, asking
questions about the subject of history and about the possible
mover of all human events, past and present. There is no doubt
that Ellacuría was a theologian in El Salvador owing to circumstances but he remained attached to the deep and challenging
philosophical project that arose out of his doctorate and out of
the ongoing conversations with Zubiri.[103]

The influence of Zubiri on Ellacuría is very clear. Zubiri's intellectual rigour allowed him to develop an entire metaphysical system out of his view of a human being as a *sentient intelligence* located in reality. For Zubiri, the person is moulded by reality so that a personal human reality is connected with being situated in a real context. A person develops his own personal being through personal choice and by the appropriation of experience within a real context, so that Zubiri refers to a person as an *animal of realities*. Thus, a person is an *open essence* as opposed to a *closed essence* (a structure that operates in relation to rules of functionality). Zubiri's critique of classical metaphysics challenges the Aristotelian sense of reality, as autonomous and apart from context. Zubiri expands on reality as interconnected with structures of its own to some degree, structures of notes with *substantivity* rather than immersed in the classical notion of *substantiality*. Reality thus precedes being and leads to the *entification of reality*, an identification between reality and being, and a critique that Zubiri applies to the whole history of philosophy. Zubiri's work applied these new interpretations to theology and particularly to the Nicene doctrine of the Trinity, the Incarnation of Christ and the Real Presence in the Eucharist. It had all the potential of mediating the inherent contradictions of Eastern and Western theology with its discussions on the *filioque* and the *essence–energies distinction*.

Ellacuría applied Zubiri's ideas of reality and being and used them in order to interpret the contemporary situation of El Salvador in terms of a critical reading of reality and of the metaphysical contradictions posed by unjust social structures within Salvadoran society. After Zubiri's death Ellacuría felt a rupture with his master and was forced to develop his own writings which became more and more theological but informed by the philosophical edifice built by Zubiri. This rupture marks the start of a third intellectual period of Ellacuría's philosophical development that coincides with his own theological and personal conversion. Practical philosophy occupied a central place within this period of Ellacuría's intellectual life through ideas on political philosophy and philosophy within university life. His main writings of this third period are questions about philosophy, an ongoing analysis of the Central American social reality and his university courses on a philosophy of the historic reality.[104] For Ellacuría there is an ongoing historical dynamic where he is interested in the agencies within history so that for him history is not *factum* but *faciendum*. Reality's truth is not only what already happened but what is happening now and what is about to happen in the future.[105] If, in his political theology, Ellacuría had already explored the Kingdom of God, in these last years of his life he focused on the realities of the Kingdom of God among the poor of El Salvador and the possibility of mediation and integration between the worlds outside and within the university, a world that he felt was being supported and informed by the poor and the marginalized rather than by the abstract ideas of university professors.

Towards a University of the Kingdom

One of the most original contributions by Ellacuría towards liberation and a theology of the political was his insistence that a Jesuit university had a central role to play within society in order to support God's preferential option for the poor. At a time when only the most traditional Jesuits remained within rich schools and private universities throughout Latin America Ellacuría articulated a community of the Kingdom centred on the poor and those who suffer and he explained his vision in a visit to the Jesuit University of Santa Clara in California during 1982.[106] Ellacuría articulated this particular ministry in the following words: 'the university should be present intellectually where it is needed: to provide science for those who have no science; to provide skills for the unskilled; to be a voice for those who have no voice; to give intellectual support for those who do not possess the academic qualifications to promote and legitimate their rights'.[107]

Whether or not the UCA fulfilled that vision is a matter of

further study; however, it is clear that the theology and philosophy put forward by Ellacuría were directed by his own theological context that was not parish work but a university milieu. Historically, the period in which Ellacuría was rector of the UCA coincided with the assassination of Romero and direct persecution of the Catholic Church in general and of the Jesuits in particular. Intellectually, it coincided with Ellacuría's post-Zubiri period (1983–89). Ellacuría underwent a tremendous change in so far as his philosophical questions and his own personal conversion to the world of the poor and their compassion made him re-analyse not only his view of the university but also his view of the role of philosophy within an ethical and community project in which the centrality of reality overcame the balanced relation between reality and being.

As a result of his involvement with a university context vis-à-vis the socio-political reality of the poor in El Salvador, three aspects of philosophy, understood as liberation by Ellacuría, became central to his philosophical work and his way of life: to know about things, to know about the world and its direction, and to do philosophy as a way of life, as a historical and political project of acquiring freedom as liberation.[108] The systematization of academic thought through liberation and the life of academics constitute an important area of the history of theology in Latin America sometimes forgotten by commentators on politics or ideas. However, if Ellacuría was central to these developments within theology and academic thought, the Jesuit Juan Luis Segundo sj, subject of the next chapter, was probably the most systematic of all Latin American theologians, another Jesuit whose theological work has gone beyond the synchronic moment of theological reflection on a particular past social context.

3

Juan Luis Segundo SJ

Juan Luis Segundo (1925–96), a Uruguayan Jesuit, has been considered one of the most systematic writers and thinkers within liberation theology.[109] His context was the study of social realities, and in 1965 he founded the Centre of Theological and Social Studies in Montevideo, a venture that was closed down by the Uruguayan Government in 1971. His pastoral work and his ongoing context continued thereafter being linked to lay groups of educated Catholics and his arena of intellectual writings increased to the point that his works remain systematic collections of writings concerned with theological topics not addressed by other Latin American theologians and a challenge to any rethinking of pastoral work and ecclesial engagement at the level of urban parishes and lay reflection groups.[110] In the 1980s he became more and more enraged by the Vatican's criticism of Latin American theologies and he also engaged other fellow Jesuits through his enduring critical ability and methodology. If Gutiérrez can be called the founder of liberation theology, Segundo has been called the 'dean' of all other theologians.[111]

Jesuit and Theologian

Born in Montevideo, Uruguay on 31 March 1925, Segundo entered the Jesuits in 1941. His first studies of philosophy (1945–48) took place at the Jesuit Seminary of Colegio Máximo de San Miguel, near Buenos Aires in Argentina, a period during which he discovered phenomenology and existentialism, a discovery which was to lead him to a life-long engagement with the Russian philosopher Nicolai Berdyaev.[112] After studying one year of theology in Argentina, Segundo continued his theological studies at Eegenhoven (Louvain, Belgium), and he graduated with a licentiate in theology in 1956, having been ordained as a Catholic priest in 1955. During that period Gustavo Gutiérrez was studying in Lyons and both of them started a friendship of a lifetime.[113] While at Louvain, Segundo was also influenced by the systematic studies and lectures of Leopold Malevez and by the biblical studies of Gustav Lambert.

While at Louvain, Segundo enrolled on a course on the theology of grace given by Malevez, a scholar who gave time and intellectual care to Segundo. Malevez's influence on Segundo was so important that several years later Segundo wrote: 'On the intellectual and theological level, what I have always understood as my own "theology of liberation" began with him – a theology I amplified once I had returned to Latin America.'[114] Outside the university Segundo was influenced by the evolutionary ideas of the Jesuit Pierre Teilhard de Chardin, ideas that remained central to all Segundo's writings.

Further research followed at the University of Paris (Sorbonne) where Segundo prepared two doctoral theses on the philosophy of religion: 'Berdiaeff, une réflexion Chrétien sur la personne' and 'La cristiandad: una utopía?'[115] The first thesis was a study of Berdyaev and his creation-centred spirituality that challenged individualism and a two-tier Christianity, two spatial planes for Christianity, a very fashionable understanding in those days.[116] The university awarded him a doctorate of letters in philosophy and theology in 1961 and he returned to Latin America.

Liberation in Uruguay

After his return to Montevideo and in 1964 he founded the Centro de Investigación Acción Social, from 1965 to be known as the Pedro Fabro Centre for Theological and Social Studies, a centre that, using the methodologies of the sociology of religion, conducted studies on contemporary religion in Latin America. At the same time Segundo took active part in the magazine *Perspectiva de Diálogo*. However, Segundo became an outspoken critic of the Uruguayan Government and the research centre was closed down by the authorities in 1971.

The political situation in Uruguay had already become very difficult and the military coup of 27 June 1973 was only a slow development of a social situation of unrest in which violence from armed groups of the left and of the right dominated public life. Juan María Bordaberry won the presidential elections that preceded the military coup and he took over the government on 1 March 1972. However, parliament was unable to control the escalating violence and the life of the nation became ever more strained with crude verbal attacks and no dialogue between the different factions involved. Most of the violence was created by the Movimiento de Liberación Nacional (MNL or Tupamaros), a leftist-oriented urban guerrilla group that had appeared in 1965, responding to enormous economic problems and coinciding with other guerrilla groups that followed the example of the Cuban Revolution of 1959.[117] The right-wing paramilitary groups such as the Juventud Uruguaya de Pie (JUP) and the Comando Caza Tupamaros responded in a violent way to the Tupamaros and pledged to support the status quo within Uruguayan society. In 1972 the Tupamaros ended their cease fire to coincide with the presidential elections and, on 12 April 1972, 15 Tupamaros escaped from jail. On 13 April 1972, the armed forces and the police started attacks on political opponents, and the government declared a state of internal war that gave official permission for the persecution of political opponents. By February 1973 the military had challenged the appointment of a minister of defence and President Bordaberry had created a national security council (Consejo de Seguridad Nacional – COSENA) giving de facto, if not de iure, executive powers to the military and to the police. On 27 June 1973 Bordaberry closed down the Uruguayan congress and days later the trade unions were disbanded in order to reject Marxism publicly and to defend the nation from subversives.[118] By 1974 Uruguay had embraced the doctrine of national security together with other dictatorial regimes such as Chile, Brazil and Paraguay, and Bordaberry continued as president supported by the armed forces with an increasing violence against the opposition and a general internal war without democratic or human rights in place.[119]

In 1974, Segundo was invited to lecture at Harvard Divinity School, and his revised lectures became the classic work *Liberation of Theology*.[120] Later, Segundo lectured at the universities of Chicago, Toronto, Montreal, Birmingham, Sao Paulo and other Latin American universities, including the Universidad de la República in Montevideo. He remained in Uruguay throughout the military period, supporting writers and intellectuals, and he is mentioned in several publications as somebody who wrote in different magazines that tried to appeal to the conscience of a suppressed democratic nation. Thus, on 30 November 1979, the first issue of the magazine *La Plaza* appeared, with a contribution from the priests Juan Martín Posadas, Juan Luis Segundo and another Jesuit Luis Pérez Aguirre.[121] The magazine had reached a large distribution of 20,000 copies by February 1982 when, following the appearance of an article by Juan Luis Segundo requesting freedom for all political prisoners, it was closed down by the government, having published eight consecutive numbers; as a result it never appeared again.[122] The magazine that followed *La Plaza* with the name *Cinco Días* appeared for the first time on 28 October 1982 and had theological inputs by Juan Luis Segundo and Luis Pérez Aguirre.[123] Later, on 1 May 1983, and during the first public celebration of the day of the workers after the military coup, an occasion in which the Plenario Intersindical de Trabajadores (PIT) managed to gather 100,000 participants in front of the Palacio Legislativo, a manifesto read on behalf of all workers remembered that the first cry for freedom of expression and human rights on behalf of the workers had been triggered by Segundo through his article in *La Plaza*.[124] The persecution against the Church had silenced the Archbishop of Montevideo and for years any parish meeting required official permission from the government authorities after presentation of a full list of all those who were to take part in that meeting.[125] Years later, the report by the Uruguayan Peace and Justice Service (SERPAJ) uncovered a systematic violation of human rights and the use of torture, including sexual torture, against men and women during the period of the military's war against subversives.[126]

The military dictatorship in Uruguay ended with the election of President Julio María Sanguinetti on 25 November 1984 and his inauguration as president of Uruguay on 1 March 1985 with no participation by the leftist Frente Amplio.[127] Throughout those years and until his death on 17 January 1996 from an obstruction to an artery, Segundo continued publishing his thought and working with lay groups as chaplain.[128] After his death there were several tributes to his work within Uruguay, including a gathering in his honour promoted by Frente Amplio that took place at the Junta de Gobierno Departamental of Montevideo on 8 February 1996.[129] By his friends Segundo was portrayed as a courageous and astute priest who could have left Uruguay during the political troubles and could have lectured in any of the prestigious Jesuit universities of North America or Europe. Instead, he remained committed to a theological enquiry of suspicion in Uruguay. His friend Agustín Canessa has outlined Segundo's need to be in Montevideo, his personal joy and delight during a lamb barbeque with a couple of hours' conversation beside the barbeque together with friends.[130] His favourite foods were freshly cooked French fries with the barbeque; his favourite music included tangos composed by Discépolo and Cadícamo (Uruguayan tango), as well as pieces from the Spanish zarzuela; habitually, he wrote while listening to classical music, particularly pieces by Mozart, Beethoven and Bach.

History and Methodology

One of the central concerns of Segundo was the development of the necessary methodology for a theological interpretation of the Latin American context.[131] Thus, his change from a European educated intellectual to a scholar of liberation came about as a result of his dissatisfaction with a non-reflexive response to pastoral work and to situations of poverty and oppression in Latin America.[132]

If other authors, such as Gustavo Gutiérrez, show a remarkable continuity in their methodological analysis so that Gutiérrez, for example, uses his metaphor of liberation throughout his work over 40 years, Segundo's work evolves and changes from a philosophical investigation of hermeneutics in a more globalized context, as in *Liberation of Theology*, to a challenge against a non-changeable and non-adaptable use of Catholic dogma within the Church vis-à-vis Cardinal Ratzinger (later to become Pope Benedict XVI) and even criticizing the non-critical position of Jon Sobrino in relation to the development of the context in which the Ignatian *Exercises* were offered and guided through time with a first week of meditations without a proper Christological base.[133]

Thus, Segundo even asked questions about the possibility of closing a hermeneutical circle related to the Ignatian *Exercises*, a series of spiritual challenges that probably explain most of the actions and challenges posed by the Jesuits to unjust structures over the centuries (see the following chapter).[134]

If Sobrino seemed to have been criticized for not being critical enough, Teilhard de Chardin's language and critical thought, according to Segundo, seemed to have been permeated by the language and spiritual moments of the *Exercises*.[135] Thus, Segundo compares the theme of 'indifference to results' within the *Exercises* with Teilhard's realization of a process of human dehumanization whenever there is an indifference to results that, for Segundo, 'is untenable in the face of the central data of Christology'.[136] These comments may portray an angry Segundo, an angry Jesuit who has not managed to get his way with his much-wanted change in ecclesiastical structures. This is not so. Segundo was the most critical and theoretical of all Latin American theologians of the first generation. Thus his powerful mind continued asking questions about God, the world, the Church and the Jesuits that others located within a second phase of reflection because they had gone to live with the poor and the marginalized.

For a new generation of liberation theologians, the value of Segundo's contribution arose out of his engagement with the wider theological world as an intellectual who was constantly exploring new ideas and found them liberating not only for the cause of the poor and the marginalized but also for the liberator himself.[137] In more contemporary terms, his theology was a pastoral theology, a systematic teasing out of Christian tradition and biblical studies, searching not to close a theme of investigation but to assess it critically, keeping in mind the ongoing autonomy in thought and life of Christians in Latin America.[138]

Liberating Christianity

In 1962, long before his best-known theological works, Segundo published a book on the function of the Church in the area of the Rio de la Plata.[139] The book, which has not been translated from the original Spanish, shows that Segundo was already asking questions, even when related to functionalism, about the Church in Latin America and was already immersed in developing critical thinking on ecclesiology. In November 1962, Segundo gave a talk to students in Paris in which he outlined the characteristics of a closed Christianity in Latin America that needed to open.[140] Within that talk there were the seeds of a challenge to an established institutional Christianity, what later Pablo Richard associated with Christendom. In that talk there was also a challenge by Segundo on dogma as the essence of Christianity and the realization that within Latin America those who are not Christians are also honest people and good citizens. Within that talk one can see the genesis of Segundo's large engagement with freedom, agnosticism and institutional Christianity. His final analysis is crude but realistic:

> Every word of the Christian message has been used to sup-
> port the status quo of Christendom, but Christendom itself
> has been compromised by this attempt to maintain control
> of the masses, preserving Christian institutions by political
> means or through alliances with social conservatism.[141]

Segundo's awareness of the pastoral challenges faced by the Church and the need for the Church to be in the midst of social realities was heightened by the Second Vatican Council and certainly by the call made by the Jesuit Provincials in 1968 to rethink Jesuit institutions, their vocation and their service to the Church through the poor and the marginalized. Segundo worked within Uruguay, a small Latin American country in which European influences had created a very settled Christianity within a much-secularized state that needed reshaping and the relaunching of an ongoing challenge.

As a theologian Segundo remained critical and suspicious of theology throughout his life and he also challenged some changes within liberation theology that were taking place in the late 1970s. Thus, in a talk in Toronto in 1983, he surprised his audience by suggesting that there were two kinds of liberation theology. In Segundo's assessment of liberation theology Gutiérrez and others had developed a theology of liberation already ten years before Gutiérrez's seminal work was published and those developments coincided with the Second Vatican Council. However, the initial thrust of a written liberation theology was to influence the middle classes that were attending universities, then develop new insights into the usual systematic theological themes and later communicate those developments to the theologically uneducated masses. Instead and because of the difficult context of the military regimes and the conference of Medellín a new group of theologians decided to move towards the periphery and they started learning from the poor and the marginalized, as a result starting a second and somehow different project of liberation. For Segundo both groups made an enormous contribution to the development of Latin American theology but in turn they created a contradiction within the hermeneutics of the cross owing to the fact that the poor, for the most part, accept suffering as part of God's plan and deal with it through the so-called popular religiosity in their everyday life. The middle classes instead challenge injustice and appropriate the voice of the poor in their socio-political movements. Segundo's pastoral experience was of daily contact with educated lay people rather than with the general population, with whom Gutiérrez was familiar. Thus Segundo was able to identify the problems raised by the methodology used by liberation theologians and alert others to the contradictions of speaking of liberation theology as monolithic, a mode of thought in which theology is related to ortho-praxis rather than orthodoxy. Segundo concluded that the theologian of liberation does not advocate anything other than orthodoxy but that orthodoxy and the hermeneutical suspicion exercised by a theologian always require the use of the sciences of the past as well as those of the present in order to develop thought and ongoing critiques vis-à-vis theological methodologies for Latin America.

Segundo's insightful analysis was not taken further simply because most Latin American theologians did not have the possibility of stepping back from their contextual crises: the poor were being massacred by social injustice and military regimes throughout Latin America and the theologians themselves, exemplified by Gutiérrez, were under attack by the Vatican. As a result, instead of developing theological complexities and varieties of methodologies the theologians were forced to make a united defence of a single methodology against the accusations of a lack of orthodoxy and sometimes accusations of theological heresies made by Cardinal Ratzinger.

Segundo's contribution to the large theological work on liberation theology, *Mysterium liberationis*, was an essay on revelation, faith and the signs of the times.[142] One could say that this is an odd contribution by Segundo not because Latin

American theologians are not concerned with God's revelation or faith in God or with the signs of the times, an expression commonly used by the Second Vatican Council and later; it is an odd contribution because Segundo the theologian and the critical, methodological and severe Sobrino set or reset very clear methodological considerations for a theological model in which context took as important a place as theological methodology, and his essay seems to be doctrinal and without a context. Most of the other contributors stressed the contextual manner of God's revelation and the centrality of the poor and marginalized. Segundo located the Latin American experience of faith and revelation within a continuum rather than it being a rupture in that development, within the diachronic theological discussions about the process of revelation and of faith without making a direct inference from the biblical text but analysing the logical or illogical possibilities of relating to truths without God and without faith. The section on revelation within this paper starts with a short discussion on the truths about God that are at the same time truths about human beings, a kind of theological anthropology in the making but in which Segundo cites Denziger, the traditional repository of dogma, doctrine and 'Catholic truth'.[143]

His theological treatment of revelation and faith is not very different from that of other contemporary late twentieth-century theologians such as Rahner and his reliance on council documents and the tradition of the Church comparable to European systematic theology. However, Segundo's critical mind was at work when in the section on the 'signs of the times' he asked about the possibility and the basis of distinguishing between divine communications and any other merely human communication. In attempting to develop that problematic Segundo discussed briefly the formation of the canon and did not take for granted that the canon was supposed to be as it is now. Instead, because the canon of divinely inspired scriptures is the norm and the vehicle for divine communication, it is mandatory to problematize not only its use but also its formation. In that he challenges the absence of those discussions within established theological works by Rahner such as *Foundation of Christian Faith*.[144] Segundo praises the methodological criticism used by Andrés Torres Queiruga, who asked questions about the role of Moses in accepting Yahweh's intervention, in convincing the people of Israel of Yahweh's seriousness about his intentions and in creating 'Yahwism'.[145] The cult of Yahweh, 'Yahwism', becomes a following of a particular master, a learning experience, so that 'God speaks a human language, surely; but the divine revelatory word becomes such only when it is recognized, among so many other words, in the experience of the foundational liberation (in "Moses") and in the continuity of that liberation, which sustains Israel'.[146] Segundo concludes by arguing that the foundations of liberation are the first sources of a tradition of canonical communication; those traditions must be related to history, however, to the 'signs of the times' where the signs within the tradition 'are indications of the fact that history has meaning, and that it is reasonable to wager on that meaning'.[147]

Returning to his seminal work *Liberation of Theology*, it is possible to see Segundo's continuity of method and of an ongoing critique of any unification and acceptance of theological methodologies, be they liberationist or otherwise, that do not question the mere possibility and ways of doing theology and, following from Vatican II and particularly *Gaudium et Spes*, break any dichotomy between faith and reason, between faith and history and between canon/dogma and the possibility of theological changes within the Church, within society and within the world in general. While much has been made of Segundo's completion of the hermeneutical circle of suspicion by providing a changeable context, his question and his contribution in those Harvard lectures of 1974 remain with us as a challenge and as a manifesto. He wrote:

So there is an essential methodological issue to be faced by Latin American theology and, in general, by any theology that has liberation in mind as a goal. Was the original Christian message aimed at masses as such, so that it must be

69

thought out and propagated in those terms; or was it rather aimed at minorities who were destined to play an essential role in the transformation and liberation of the masses?[148]

In assessing the possible arguments for the masses and the small numbers, what Segundo would call the minorities, he returned to Ratzinger's comments on the rise of Christianity in relation to the idea of a little flock that triggers responses by the multitudes and that indeed started as a small community within a larger Roman empire.[149] Segundo concluded that liberation theology started as a hermeneutical process of the minorities but within a different sociological context than that of early Christianity: Christians are the majority of those living in Latin America and therefore Latin American theology can be, following Gutiérrez, part of the life of the masses because the masses are structured and unified within a larger socio-religious structure, that of the Church in Latin America. However, theological thinking remains part of a process carried out by a minority that is certainly influenced by the masses and by the practice of the majority.

But history is made of small incidents that change its course because actors and agents, and theologians, become engaged with events that challenge the way of the social, the way of understanding the divine and therefore the social, religious and intellectual life of theologians.

Segundo and Ratzinger

In 1983 and at the moment when liberation theology was finding new ideas after the Latin American Bishops Meeting in Puebla (1979) and the ideas coming out of Latin America were being discussed with African and Asian theologians the Vatican challenged the theological orthodoxy of Gustavo Gutiérrez. The Congregation for the Doctrine of the Faith (CDF) made ten observations on the theology of Gutiérrez, arguing that it provided 'extreme ambiguity' and that 'Gutiérrez accepts the

Marxist conception of history, which is a history of conflict, structured around the class struggle and requiring commitment on behalf of the oppressed in their struggle for liberation.'[150] Further, the CDF stated that 'the influence of Marxism is clear both in the understanding of truth and the notion of theology. Orthodoxy is replaced by orthopraxy, for truth does not exist except within praxis – that is, in the commitment to revolution.'[151]

That event not only saddened Segundo but also made him ever more conscious of the need to systematize theological methodologies in order to avoid misunderstandings and confusions, triggered on the one hand by the media that associated liberation theology with revolution after the 1979 Nicaraguan Revolution and triggered on the other hand by conservative theologians who, already unhappy about the changes in the Catholic Church after Vatican II, were trying to stop any further developments. Another Jesuit and theologian, Karl Rahner, also felt the need to defend Gutiérrez's work and, in a letter to the Cardinal of Lima Juan Landázuri Ricketts, he wrote:

> I am convinced of the orthodoxy of the theological work of Gustavo Gutiérrez. The liberation theology he represents is thoroughly orthodox and is aware of its limits within the whole context of Catholic theology. Moreover, it is deeply convinced (correctly, in my opinion) that the voice of the poor must be listened to by theology in the context of the Latin American church.[152]

However, Cardinal Joseph Ratzinger continued his admonitions of the theology of liberation and in March 1984 he published a paper, thus within the public domain, carefully constructing his case against this new Latin American theology.[153] In that paper, Ratzinger compared the development of liberation theology with the hermeneutical challenges posed by the rise of New Testament criticism; however, he argued consistently that he was referring to those theologians of liberation who have embraced a Marxist hermeneutics and the class struggle. The only theologian attacked directly was Jon Sobrino, and Ratzinger wrote:

> Love consists in an 'option for the poor', that is, it coincides with an option for class struggle. Theologians of liberation underline very strongly, in opposition to 'false universalism', the partiality and partial character of the Christian option; to take sides is, according to them, a fundamental requisite for a correct hermeneutics of the biblical witness.[154]

It is the last sentence in the paper by Ratzinger that prepared the way for a doctrinal attack on all Latin American theologians, including Segundo. Ratzinger wrote: 'If one thinks how radical this interpretation of Christianity that derives from it really is, the problem of what one can and must do about it becomes even more urgent.'[155] Foreseeing a possible ecclesiastical threat, the Board of the journal *Concilium* issued a statement in support of theologians of liberation, the most influential of them always associated with the whole theological enterprise of *Concilium* since Vatican II.[156]

The awaited doctrinal blow to liberation theology was published on 6 August 1984 and it was a blow not only because the document was a theological one of high calibre but also because it was the first Vatican document to deal particularly with liberation theology and its aim was to instruct the Catholic world about the dangers of such a theological movement as the CDF stated through its Prefect Cardinal Ratzinger:

> The present instruction has a much more limited and precise purpose: to draw the attention of pastors, theologians, and all the faithful to the deviations and risks of deviation, damaging to the faith and to Christian living, that are brought about by certain forms of liberation theology which use, in an insufficiently critical manner, concepts borrowed from various currents of Marxist thought.[157]

If Ratzinger had been uneasy about liberation theology and its influence, the *Instruction* had been endorsed and approved for publication by John Paul II.

While Leonardo Boff and Gustavo Gutiérrez responded publicly against the accusations by the Vatican, Segundo developed a full-text response to some theological aspects of the Vatican's criticism.[158] This text, published under the title *Theology and the Church*, is rather symptomatic of Segundo's theological training in that he not only apologizes for providing some personal stories within the text but also his response to critics was always systematic: he retired to his desk, read, reflected and wrote about any matter as if it were a new theological problem to be evaluated and expanded. However, as well as reading and writing he discussed many of those ideas with the groups he was journeying with.

In *Theology and the Church*, Segundo intended to evaluate the theological themes raised by the *Instruction* vis-à-vis the writings of Latin American theologians, but in doing so he produced a draft in which he wanted also to protect the authors. That would have contravened his golden rule of never writing without acknowledging authors and writers. As a result, the book became a more personal evaluation of the situation and the only book with a personal touch written by Segundo. Indeed, if one wanted to know in one single work what Sobrino stood for within the theological world this is the work to read rather than *Liberation of Theology*. Sobrino's argument is very clear throughout his examination of themes such as liberation and secularism, liberation and hermeneutics, the Church of the masses and the politically active Church:

1 the *Instruction* equates Marxism with a political party rather than with a philosophical system developed within Western civilization, and
2 the purpose of the *Instruction* is to halt and destroy any possible advancement of the Spirit as embodied within Vatican II.

For Segundo presumed that the *Instruction*, published before the 1985 Synod of Bishops, was sending a very clear signal to those within the Catholic Church who believed in a model of unity in diversity.[159] Therefore, Segundo was not concerned with developments within theology but he was concerned with the lack of theological and philosophical precision by the super-structure of the Vatican and the power over canon and dogma exercised by Cardinal Ratzinger.

Segundo remained committed to the theology of Vatican II and challenged the idea that Marxism was a popular move-ment; on the contrary, he always maintained that Marxism was for the educated and the middle classes and that the popular masses followed those who were advocating their rights and their good. Those most likely to be followed were not the politi-cians but the Christian communities because they were seen from the 1970s as part of society and as part of the struggle by the poor not for a new government but for a new and more just society. In a very personal way, Segundo challenged the intel-lectually ill-prepared *Instruction* but remained conscious of his own adherence to the theological principles that impeded him as a Catholic theologian to disassociate himself from the Church and with any ongoing implementation of Vatican II. He wrote:

> Fidelity to that magisterium does not allow me to treat the theology of the *Instruction* as heterodox. I heartily grant to others the right that is denied to me – to fashion, with that theological opinion, an enriching theological pluralism, like the one that Karl Rahner postulated shortly before his death. However, I am obligated by fidelity to the most solemn magisterium of the Church to deny that there is a transcend-ence proper to the individual that does not extend to the history wherein people seek to give to society more just and congenial structures.[160]

Critical Thinker

As if to emphasize his ongoing challenges to a society in which those who suffer seem not to have a place Segundo departed from his work on Christology after the publication of his challenges to dogma as a static formula without life.[161] Most of the criticisms he faced from more traditional theologians related to his use of contemporary thinkers and social theories in order to illuminate the theological response to the contemporary world. Those who criticized him preferred a closed theology, understood as faith seeking understanding with a strong association of faith with tradition and dogma within the Catholic Church.[162]

Instead, Segundo's reflections on suffering argued that God does not rejoice in the suffering of human beings as if to test how much suffering and pain they can take; suffering is the necessary experience of those who chose to follow God through the lives of those who suffer most, that is, the poor and the marginalized.[163] The redemptive characteristics of suffering do not relate to an individual process of endurance but to a self-immolation for the sake of others, as was the case of Jesus of Nazareth and his crucifixion and later his resurrection from the dead.

Segundo remains a Latin American theologian of the first generation, side by side with Gustavo Gutiérrez. He permeates the other generations and particularly those Catholic theologians still operating within the symbolic truths of the Catholic Church, however, because his systematic treatment of theology goes beyond a purely contextual theology. It is interesting that his theological writings on Christ, the human person, suffering, belief and revelation mirror the encyclicals of John Paul II and still relate very well to the central concerns of Benedict XVI. Segundo was correct when he argued that there were two kinds of liberation theologies, and indeed he is probably the only theologian of the first generation who raised the possibility of a monolithic Latin American theology as a problem, be it liberationist or otherwise. If, according to the theologian Pedro Trigo, his only weakness was that he never had the chance to live within the masses of Latin America, he made a different kind of contribution, an ever stretching and systematic critique not of others outside Latin American theology but of Latin American theology itself.[164] Segundo's approach to theology was realistic in so far as he didn't believe that any theology could be done without personal and social presuppositions and he critiziced the Dutch Dominican Edward Schillebeeckx for his 'naïve belief that the word of God is applied to human realities inside some antiseptic laboratory that is totally immune to the ideological tendencies and struggles of the present day'.[165] If Thomas Fox has called Segundo 'the Karl Rahner of liberation theology' it is because like Rahner he was concerned with the relation between God and the human person at a level that reflected the complexity of such interaction and the complexity of the human as much as of the divine. Segundo lived with an intellectual suspicion that made him into a prolific writer and a dedicated supporter of other educated people asking questions about their faith and their understanding within Uruguay.

Thus, the three theologians so far discussed, Sobrino, Ellacuría and Segundo, held many theological ideas in common but two facts stand the test of scholarship: three of them were members of the Society of Jesus (Jesuits) and three of them wrote about the *Spiritual Exercises* of St Ignatius of Loyola. The following chapter examines the impact of the Jesuits within Latin America and within Latin American theology, by asking questions about the religious context of the Jesuits in order to isolate common factors in their religious life and spirituality that made them into a real challenge to the powerful in Latin America over the centuries and made them central to theological developments in Latin America during the late twentieth century.

Part 2

Theological Challenges

4

The Jesuits

It is clear from the previous three chapters and from the social context of Latin America after Vatican II that the contribution by the Society of Jesus (Jesuits) to the development of Latin American theologies has been quite significant.[166] Following from Segundo's suggestion of two types of liberation theology, it is possible to argue that within a historical analysis of Latin American theologians more importance has been given to the Church's engagement with the poor and marginalized than to its engagement with educational institutions, the professions and the political parties that had some Christian adherence within them.[167] The Jesuits operated within those realms: educational institutions as well as poor parishes and settlements for refugees. Their contribution to Latin American theologies and to Latin American processes of liberation has been significant, not only by the fact that some of the most prominent theologians in Latin America have been members of this religious congregation but also because they were able to use their schools and universities for the production of discourses of liberation, social justice and ethical values. Thus, the Jesuits engaged themselves directly with civil society owing to the fact that through their educational institutions they were in daily contact with civil organizations, governments and Christian communities. However, it must be remembered that the engagement of the Jesuits within civil society in Latin America is not a new phenomenon. Already, during colonial times, Jesuit missionaries challenged the established social norms imposed by European civilization and the crowns of Spain and Portugal, and they were expelled from colonial territories for contradicting their political masters on matters of human rights, philosophy and their understanding of the role of Christianity within a common humanity.

This chapter explores the role of the Jesuits in fostering theologies of liberation since 1968 in Latin America by exploring the foundation, history and spirituality of the Jesuits, that is, their work among indigenous populations in colonial times and the centrality of the *Ignatian Exercises* within the formation and life of all Jesuits since their foundation in the sixteenth century.[168] This chapter outlines the fact that it is not possible to articulate developments within Latin American theologies without exploring the contribution of the Jesuits and that it is not possible to understand the actions and theologies of the Jesuits without understanding their thorough academic formation and their daily grounding in the *Exercises*.

Jesuits in Latin America

The Provincials of all the Jesuit provinces of Latin America met after Vatican II (1962–65) and before the Second General Meeting of Latin American Bishops in Medellín (Colombia, August–September 1968). In their meeting in Rio de Janeiro (Brazil, 6–14 May 1968), the national heads of the Jesuits reflected on their view of mission and their position in Latin America and decided to reiterate their involvement 'in the temporal life of humankind'.[169] Within the particular context of Latin America, however, their statement for their involvement within a movement to change unjust structures and to be with the people was very strong and very down to earth. There was no high theology within the document but a challenge to personal lives and community activities with a certain social and religious utopia. In a central passage of that document they asserted:

In all our activities, our goal should be the liberation of humankind from every sort of servitude that oppresses it: the lack of life's necessities, illiteracy, the weight of sociological structures which deprive it of personal responsibility over life itself, the materialistic conception of history. We want all our efforts to work together toward the construction of a society in which all persons will find their place, and in which they will enjoy political, economic, cultural, and religious equality and liberty.[170]

Within the document and in later educational practices, the Jesuits addressed a usual criticism of their academic institutions, particularly schools and universities: that Jesuit schools educated the children of the rich and that their universities reiterated that social paradigm. The document argued that all Jesuit institutions should foster the social gospel and that all students should be involved in practical activities in which they would experience different social realities.[171] The Jesuit Provincials called for a formation of consciences among those they taught and use of the media to foster those aims. However, the final call was aimed at all Jesuit superiors to implement those changes as soon as possible, even when some would take sometime. Moreover, there was also a call for a personal conversion with deep questions to each individual Jesuit working in Latin America:

Are we capable of responding to the world's expectations? Are our faith and charity equal to the anxiety-ridden appeals of the world around us? Do we practice self-denial sufficiently, so that God is able to flood us with light and energy? Does personal prayer have its proper place in our life, so that we are united with God in this great human task that cannot succeed without God? Can the Society keep within its ranks those members who do not want to pray or who do not have a real and personal prayer life?[172]

The response of the Jesuit communities in Latin America was swift and sometimes unsettling for parents and teachers of those students involved. Parents were told about the revised Jesuit

81

aims within their schools and, despite the many Jesuits who left the Society after Vatican II because of the changing times in which they found themselves, the Jesuit secondary schools maintained their academic excellence with the addition of summer work or activities of a social nature for pupils in their last years at school. Within universities, it was easier to comply with practical activities of a social nature as most university students were affected by a political climate of change, political awareness and political questioning. Thus, the Jesuits not only influenced the development of theologies, pastoral or otherwise, but also became involved in many activities related to the defence of indigenous minorities, political refugees and migrants.

In Chile, for example, Cardinal Silva Henríquez called upon the Jesuits to help him with administrative and counselling duties in the ecumenical enterprise of setting an office to help those persecuted by the military after the September 1973 military coup – the so-called Pro Paz Committee. A Jesuit, Fernando Salas, organized a group of social workers and served long hours at the house located in Santa Mónica Street 2338 which had been allocated to Pro Paz by the Archdiocese of Santiago. Two year later, in October 1975, Patricio Cariola, another Jesuit, helped to move four people wanted by the military authorities after a gun battle between the secret police and the leadership of the left-wing guerrilla group MIR (Movimiento de Izquierda Revolucionario).[173] Two men and two women were delivered safely to foreign embassies in the car of Patricio Cariola and later the two priests, Frs Cariola and Salas, wanted by the authorities, gave themselves in and appeared in court. They could only say that they had had to save lives in those cases where, if caught by the security services, those wanted would have been tortured and killed. What happened later when the two priests were brought to the Capuchinos Annex of the Santiago Prison was a moving testimony to the involvement of the Jesuits in a difficult period. As both priests entered the prison, under heavy escort and handcuffed, the prisoners lined up outside their cells and a long applause followed. When Cardinal Silva Henríquez heard the story in Rome, where he had gone to request the Pope's advice, he felt proud, and he wrote: 'they were my priests, the priests of my Church, the priests of the Church in Chile, that was their blessed madness'.[174] The British doctor Sheila Cassidy had also been influenced by the Jesuit activities; she too was arrested during this period, brought to a secret detention centre, tortured and later expelled from Chile.[175]

The contemporary relevance of the Jesuit apostolate and its mission of liberation from oppression was highlighted by the fact that Fr Alberto Hurtado, a Chilean Jesuit, was canonized (declared a saint) on 23 October 2005. Born in 1952, Hurtado joined the Jesuits in 1923 and, after studies in Chile and Europe, he became chaplain to university students all over Chile. His concern was to support the development of the whole person, and under his guidance the chaplaincies grew rapidly – from 1,500 students in 50 centres in 1941 to 12,000 students in 500 centres in 1944. In 1944, he met a sick and starving beggar who made such an impression on his life that he deepened his dedicated apostolate towards the poor, the unemployed and those without a home who lived under the Santiago bridges. He founded the Home of Christ, despairing that in a country where the majority were Christians there were people who were ill, homeless, and had to spend the cold winter nights without shelter, begging and waiting for others to help them. Fr Hurtado helped with the training of those poor and unwanted youth and was hated by traditional Catholics when he started asking questions about the reasons for poverty in society. Before his death in 1952 he had started an organization for workers at a time when workers belonged to the Chilean Communist Party and did not usually find a place within a very traditional Chilean Catholic Church.

The life of Fr Hurtado had a lot in common with the involvement in social issues by the Jesuits during colonial times, those who started schemes of inclusion, education and human dignity for the indigenous populations of Latin America who, after the encounter of 1492, had been enslaved and massacred by the conquistadors from Spain and Portugal.

The Jesuits of the Mission

The production of the film *The Mission* highlighted in a Hollywood-style film not only the sufferings of the Latin American indigenous populations through the colonial period of encounter between Latin American civilizations and European empires but also the work of the Jesuits in South America.[176]

The Jesuits first arrived in South America in 1550 and they preached at San Salvador de Bahia in Brazil and later in today's Paraguay. The first European settlements of Paraguay were started in 1554 within the district of Guayrá on the upper waters of the river Paraná. Above the cataract, now known as Iguazú, Don Ruiz Díaz de Melgarejo founded the towns of Ontiveros, Ciudad Real and Villa Rica.[177] Only a few years after their arrival in South America, the Jesuits in Chile, Peru, Argentina and Paraguay were already facing challenges by the colonial authorities because of their questioning of the treatment of indigenous peoples by the conquistadors. The Jesuits appealed to King Philip III requesting the protection of his indigenous subjects, a request that was granted by the king in 1608 giving the Jesuits the mission to convert the indigenous peoples located in the province of Guayrá. The Italian Jesuits Simon Maceta and José Cataldino arrived at the banks of the river Paranapané in February 1610 and founded the first *reducción* of Loreto, among the Guaraní, who had already come into contact with the Jesuits, Frs Fields and Ortega.[178] The contribution of the Jesuits was not only the protection of the indigenous populations whom, contrary to the beliefs of the slave traders, they deemed capable of Christian conversion and therefore being human beings with souls, but also the development of communal farms, schools and communities based upon the values of the gospel, for the indigenous populations a liberating experience, very different from their experience of the European presence within their ancestral lands.

Because of the large number of indigenous peoples that trusted them, the Jesuits had to start a second *reducción*, that of San Ignacio, founded in memory of the Jesuit founder. The success of the Jesuits was mainly owing to the fear experienced by the indigenous peoples of the *Paulistas*, Portuguese settlers of São Paulo, who enslaved Guaranís and bought them from the Spanish settlers. A policy of isolation followed, not only because the Jesuits had to show that they were not part of the colonial administration but also because the life of the missionary settlements was different from that outside them. Many of the indigenous people living in the *reducciones* left them because the orderly and semi-military life of the Jesuits was as hard as their own religious life modelled on a founder who had been a soldier and whose models were those of military personnel on the move, fighting evil as well as the Spanish settlers. Of the *reducciones*, Voltaire wrote:

> When in 1768 the missions of Paraguay left the hands of the Jesuits, they had arrived at perhaps the highest degree of civilization to which it is possible to conduct a young people, and certainly a far superior state than that which existed in the rest of the new hemisphere. The laws were respected there, morals were pure, a happy brotherhood united every heart, all the useful arts were in a flourishing state, and even some of the more agreeable sciences; plenty was universal.[179]

Thus, despite the fact that many of the indigenous peoples who were brought to the *reducciones* left them and that mainly women and children lived there, some of them driven there by violence and hunger, the Jesuits gave their best efforts to the missions and to the education of the Guaraní. The first Jesuits had to fight jungle and settlers to achieve their mission purpose, but once the *reducciones* became established colonial landscapes the Jesuits sent large numbers of priests and brothers to those isolated places. On 9 July 1717, for example, three boats arrived from Cádiz into the port of Buenos Aires, bringing the largest Jesuit group ever to arrive. There were more than 50 Jesuits from Spain, Italy, Germany and Switzerland. Among them, there were some very capable Italian artists and musicians, such as Domenico Zipoli, composer and organist, and

85

Gianbattista Primoli and Andrea Bianchi, both architects.[180]

It was clear that the indigenous populations were very recep-
tive to music and therefore every Jesuit settlement had a school
of music, and many first-class European musicians visited the
reducciones, sent by the Jesuits from Europe. Music was composed within the *reducciones* and two European periods of
music were central within the music schools: the polyphonic
music of the Renaissance and the era of the Baroque, initiated
by the arrival of the Jesuit Antonius Sepp in 1691.[181]

The end of the *reducciones* came about because the kings of
Portugal and Spain decided to negotiate lands and initially King
Ferdinand VI gave the seven towns of the *reducciones* to
Portugal. With Ferdinand's death in 1760, however, Charles III
once again listened to the plea of the Jesuits and maintained the
reducciones as possessions of Spain rather than Portugal. The
animosity against the Jesuits grew, however, as well as the
rumours that they had great wealth, that they intended to form
a Jesuit territory independent from the kings of Spain or
Portugal, and that they had 14,000 indigenous peoples as
prisoners within their territories. As a result, the expulsion of
the Jesuits was decreed, and an order given to groups of indigenous peoples to leave the *reducciones* and to return to the
forest, as all Jesuits were arrested and sent back to Spain by the
king's decree.[182] It is possible to argue that the Jesuits, who had
arms to defend the *reducciones* from the Portuguese, could have
resisted the advances of the small Spanish army and most probably would have succeeded, aided by thousands of indigenous
peoples. That never happened and the Jesuits were banished
from South America and indeed from all Spanish territories.

The expulsion of the Jesuits from the Spanish territories in
1767 created a double effect for the history of Latin America.
On the one hand, those Jesuits expelled had prepared the way
for a further colonization of the continent by their spatial and
communal arrangements within the *reducciones* and the Jesuit
lands; on the other hand, their dislike of Spain, as many Jesuits
were of mixed race between European and indigenous peoples,
created the beginning of ideas of emancipation in Europe that

later on were going to influence the formation of nationalist movements fostering independence from Spain.[183]

Much later, the Jesuit order was dissolved by the papal edict of Clement XIV in 1773, with a few Jesuits surviving in Poland and Russia under the protection of Empress Catherine II. By that time, the Society of Jesus had grown enormously and 'it was operating more than eight hundred universities, seminaries, and especially secondary schools almost around the globe'.[184] The Jesuits were restored as a religious order in 1814. It is worth asking what made the Society of Jesus expand so quickly and what made such an organized army of priests and religious so disciplined, then as now. The answer is twofold: a superb intellectual preparation with a clear personal commitment to God through the *Spiritual Exercises*. In the rest of this chapter, I shall explore the latter, which I would call the foundation for the liberation of each individual Jesuit and in turn of those who are affected by the ministry and influence of the Jesuits within the Church and within civil society at large, particularly in Latin America.

The Jesuit Way of Liberation

Referring to the first group of Jesuits and their identity, John O'Malley has argued that 'with the hindsight of over four hundred years, we see more clearly than they did that the *Spiritual Exercises* and the schools were the two most important institutional factors that, when taken in their full implications, shaped the distinctive character of the Society of Jesus'.[185] Others, such as Paul Crowley sj, have argued that the Jesuit emphasis on education must have theology as its central discipline and the *Spiritual Exercises* as a properly Jesuit approach to theology.[186]

There is no doubt that the *Spiritual Exercises* are central to the formation and the spiritual growth of a Jesuit not only because the *Exercises* were given by Ignatius to all his companions and followers but also because the spiritual movement within the *Exercises* makes a Jesuit now as it did in the past. The striking reality of the life of a Jesuit is that all Jesuits throughout the ages have had the experience of the *Exercises* and, from that experience of 30 days in prayer with the help of a director, they continue searching for Christ and for his will throughout every period of their lives. Any writing and conversation about the *Exercises* presupposes that the person has taken part in the *Exercises* as a personal retreat of 30 days rather than as a period of conferences and spiritual talks. In my own experience, having made the *Exercises* at Loyola Hall in Liverpool in the summer of 1985, the solitude of a whole month meditating on the scriptures and listening to God empties one of any intellectual constraint and brings a personal crisis of self, expressed during that period as a deep need of God's consolation and nothing else. Thus, David Fleming sj has argued that:

> What appears to be a rigidly structured approach, so meticulously ordered in hours of prayer and examination, in positions of prayer, in the use of food, sleep, penances, and so on, can only be studied with comprehension by someone who has had the experience of making the Exercises.[187]

The *Exercises* were written by Ignatius during his deep spiritual experience of conversion at Manresa, and, later on, those drafts were finalized and edited while he was a student in Paris. His reflections were not intended as a pious book to be read by others for personal inspiration but as a guide for spiritual directors of others who were seeking God and seeking a personal conversion. During his arrests and interrogation by the Inquisition, Ignatius maintained that he was guiding others towards God not towards himself and that the *Exercises* guided his own structuring of a deep reflection on his own experience of conversion.

Ignatius and the *Exercises*

Born in 1491, Ignatius, a member of a Basque family, enlisted himself in the army of the Duke of Najera, the rich and powerful viceroy of Navarra. In May 1521, the French Army attacked Navarra and the viceroy fled, leaving a small garrison including Ignatius among them. On 20 May 1521, a cannon ball smashed his right leg and damaged his left leaving him useless for battle; the French didn't kill him and sent him home to Azpeitia, 50 kilometres away.[188] It was during the long period of his physical healing that Ignatius underwent a personal conversion and decided that, when he was well enough, he would head for Jerusalem, that he would sell his possessions, and that he would live the life of a penitent and of a man of prayer. Once he was well enough, Ignatius departed for the Benedictine monastery of Monserrat in Catalonia, to him the first step of his journey to Jerusalem. It was at Monserrat that he spent a night in prayer before the statue of the Black Madonna, and he laid down his sword and dagger and changed them for a pilgrim's staff and a beggar's clothing. He followed the Benedictine practice of that time and took three days to write down his sins, made his confession and broke completely with his former life.

Ignatius stopped in Manresa, a small town near Barcelona, and for many reasons, including an outbreak of the plague, he remained there for almost a year. During those months, he searched for God, and the result of his own search became a large part of the *Spiritual Exercises*, a text that in the eyes of Ignatius could be helpful to others who wanted to guide Christians in search of conversion and deeper prayer as he had done with some people while at Manresa.[189]

The *Exercises* became a path to inner conversion but at the same time a marker of identity. For anyone to become a Jesuit it was not sufficient to have a vocation to the religious life or to the priesthood: they needed to pass through a rite of passage marked by the experience of God through the *Exercises*. Thus, over the centuries, Jesuit novices and already seasoned Jesuits have made the *Exercises* not only once but several times during their lives. In the contemporary life of the Jesuits, novices make the *Exercises* during the first spiritual steps of their training and once again during their tertiary period, a period of discernment and renewed apostolic zeal before their final religious profession as Jesuits for life, some 15 years or so later than their first profession after their novitiate.[190] The original text of the *Exercises* was edited and revised by Ignatius while he was a student in Paris years later in order to direct his first Jesuit companions through the same experience of prayer and conversion even before any of them took any religious vows and even before the canonical existence of the Society of Jesus was approved by the papacy.

The person making the *Exercises* usually retreats to a quiet place, in contemporary terms a Jesuit retreat house, where he is assigned a director and where he remains in silence throughout the four weeks.[191] The director acts as a spiritual catalyst, as an aide to the one making the *Exercises*; he suggests biblical texts for the periods of prayer and meditation and he listens to the movements of the soul, the feelings and the experiences of the one going through those weeks in God's presence.[192] It is God who directs the retreat towards his purpose and goal, not the retreat director while the retreat director should have the spiritual maturity to be able to speak of God and not to be afraid of moving with someone through 'a spiritual labyrinth'.[193] Thus, according to Barry, 'the work of the spiritual director now becomes one of helping the person praying to discern, that is, to figure out what is going on, what is God's voice, what not'.[194] The director faces as much a challenge as the person making a retreat and all Jesuits by the fact that they have made the *Exercises* could be potential retreat directors.[195] The challenges by the director during the *Exercises* are the same as those of a teacher or a theologian inasmuch as they must allow freedom for the people they are guiding in order to explore God's path and to move according to their experience of God. In summarizing the dangers faced by a controlling director of the *Exercises*, William Connolly sj has probably outlined the characteristics of a person who is certainly not an educated and discerning Jesuit:

The director of a personalized retreat must combat within himself five major enemies of the other person's freedom: the director's own desire to have others dependent on him; his fear that he may lose control of the retreat if the retreatant exercises freedom; the worry that he may not know what to do if the retreatant takes a path that he himself is not accustomed to; his desire to achieve results in the retreat; inflexibility in his own spiritual life, with the tendency to feel his personal spirituality threatened when the retreatant goes his own way.[196]

For one of the aims outlined by Ignatius in the *Exercises* is the attainment of freedom, the freedom to experience a deep conversion, the centrality of God in all things and detachment and indifference to other things, a feeling that comes out of that deep experience of God.[197] Each day of the four weeks is structured by four or even five periods of prayer, and towards the third week there is a period of prayer during the night.[198] At the end of the *Exercises* the person involved starts his Fifth Week, a long week that would last for the rest of his life or until he makes the *Exercises* once again.

The text of the *Exercises* starts with the 'Principle and Foundation', a set of presuppositions written by Ignatius at the start of his book which could sound like statements not to be taken for granted but they are very important as foundations for a common understanding of Ignatius's understanding of 'the truth about human existence'.[199] This 'Principle and Foundation' outlines the basic principle of Christian life lived to the full and within the Jesuit religious life and gives us a further clue as to the indifference displayed by Jesuits when faced with criticism about their involvement in politics within a world that does not perceive priests as part of a socio-political agency within a 'secular world'. Ignatius wrote:

Man was created to praise, reverence, and serve God our Lord, and by this means to save his soul; and the other things on the face of the earth were created for man's sake, and in order to aid him in the prosecution of the end for which he was created . . . It is therefore necessary that we should make ourselves indifferent to all created things, in all that is left to the liberty of our free-will, and is not forbidden.[200]

The emphasis in the *Exercises* is on movement: there is a movement of the Spirit that guides the retreatant towards God through a structured series of meditations from the Gospels and by which the retreatant is able to discern God's lead towards a life more oriented towards him or towards a different path in life within that same 'Principle and Foundation'.[201] During the First Week, the retreatant expands the intellectual knowledge of the 'Principle and Foundation' towards a more reflective dialogue with God in which he meditates on sin and on his own past life so as to prepare for a movement of the senses in which he can experience the mercy and love of God.[202] During the Second Week, the meditations point to the call by the King to work with him and serve in his army, thus to meditate on God's invitation to serve others by making the right choice between two standards and acquiring, by the mercy of God, the right kind of humility to serve and to centre one's life on the values of the King and of his Kingdom.[203] During the Third Week, the movement and emphasis is on staying with God, in a contemplative sense of requesting a small experience of that divine presence that would kindle the sentiments and the senses, with God at the centre of all. It is during the Third Week that retreatants are encouraged to pray during the night and when they awake naturally because they are called to do so. By the Third Week, the retreatants have become accustomed to the prayer routines and desperately seek some consolation in times when the standards of the Kingdom seem high and the body is tired from the interrupted nights.[204] The Fourth Week concentrates the senses on the love of God through contemplations on the Resurrection.[205] By the end of the *Exercises*, the retreatant starts the Fifth Week in which all practices of contemplation and prayer that were acquired during the four weeks in solitude will be carried forward into the rest of the person's life with time set aside for prayer and a sense of intensity that comes out of a full month in solitude and away from the ordinary life of work.[206]

It is possible to argue after this short exploration of the spiritual foundations of Jesuit life that the Jesuits have developed through the *Exercises* a tremendous sense of the centrality of God, thus a heightened sense of mission and a less dramatic sense of personal danger and discomfort. As it was during the time of the first 'soldiers' of the Company of Jesus, the *Exercises* help to develop a strong orderly sense of reflection and discernment that together with a challenging academic programme makes Jesuits able to discern social and political changes within society and to provide actions that could create the conditions for a life within the priorities of God's Kingdom and not of other peoples' kingdoms, governments or dominions.[207]

Contemporary Jesuit Priorities

The *Exercises* once again provide an explanation of why the Jesuits in 1968 related their own work on behalf of the Church and of Christ to a localized movement concerned with the poor and the marginalized. During the Second Week of the *Exercises*, the emphasis is on the two standards and the service of the King; however, three kinds of humility are discussed. The third degree of humility requires that the retreatant has before him the choice of being with the poor, not because of an exultation of poverty but because Christ chose to be with the poor and the marginalized. At that moment of the *Exercises*, the choice of work or location in society is not the question, but a full personal commitment to the person of Christ and therefore to the poor is preferential because that was the choice of Christ himself. William J. Byron has argued in very personal terms that the Second Week is crucial for that option for Christ and therefore for the poor, in the following words:

I regard the meditation on the Two Standards as a personal exercise in conscientization, the process of consciousness-raising, written about by Paulo Freire and concerned essentially with the dawning awareness of dominant values which can, in fact, be the oppressive forces. Once aware of the dominant values of Satan and of their oppressive, destructive force in my life and my world, I pray for the courage to choose and be chosen for the dominant values of Christ. I elect identifiable membership in a counterculture.[208]

If the Jesuits were clearly involved with civil society in Latin America during the period of the military regimes, their planning, pastoral objectives and mission work during the early twenty-first century still reflect the challenges of Latin America and the changes of Latin American society. The Jesuits' own ongoing discernment is not about their identity or their work, for Jesuits work in more or less any kind of ministry, pastoral situation or social context, but about the ongoing movement of the Spirit in their presence on behalf of God within society at large and within civil society in particular.

As an example, the first combined meeting of Jesuit representatives from Latin America and the United States that took place in Miami, Florida, 22–6 May 2004, explored a few common realities within an age of globalization and made a few choices akin to those made in 1968 within another context and another chronology. In his address to the participants, Fr Peter-Hans Kolvenbach sj, Superior General of the Jesuits, spoke of the interaction between all parts of the Americas in a technological age in which the North has more power than previously thought and the South has a considerable presence within the North through migration in general.[209] Kolvenbach recognized that the experience of the Church and of theology is very different in both hemispheres and sometimes faces a non-dialogical position of animosity and contradiction.[210] Thus, important themes of encounter were outlined by the Jesuit Superior General, among them justice and peace, education, closer collaboration with lay people and the already mentioned issue of migration.

Those who attended the meeting, mainly superiors of Jesuit

provinces in North, Central and South America, agreed to co-operate more closely on the matter of migration and the pastoral care of migrants following issues outlined in the document 'Migration in the Americas', a document developed by Jesuits and lay people over a couple of years before the Miami meeting. The Jesuits strengthened their commitment to migrants and refugees, a commitment that had institutionally started in 1980 with the foundation of the Jesuit Refugee Service. The Jesuit document of 2004 explored the need to know the facts, histories and social realities and to involve Jesuit personnel in their networks of support for refugees. However, particular emphasis within the document was given to the issue of 'advocacy', one would say a non-surprising Jesuit involvement with government and civil society that goes back a long way within the United States and Latin America, where Jesuits have even served in the US House of Representatives and the Sandinista revolutionary government of Nicaragua.

The five points outlined by the document are important because they constitute a fresh way of supporting the liberation of the poor and the oppressed and an ongoing commitment to their causes, their suffering and their marginalization. The document points to an exact understanding of Jesuit involvement in the United States and Latin America related to the cause of migrants and refugees:

1 Bilateral coordination would make advocacy more effective, for example, USA–Mexico regarding the Guest Worker proposals of President Bush.
2 Multinational presence in international agencies such as the United Nations, the Organization of American States and even the Vatican would strengthen their voice.
3 Multinational representation would allow them to speak in other continental migration forums, religious and secular.
4 Expertise in lobbying and advocacy work could be shared among them.
5 Together they could better facilitate cooperation among workers and labour organizations that are currently pitted

against one another, and instead promote labour rights such as just wage and working conditions throughout the Americas.[211]

The 'discernment of the Spirit' in relation to the *Exercises* today brings once again a Jesuit preoccupation with involvement with the poor and the marginalized and highlights a refreshed context for liberation in the name of Christ and his gospel. At a time when other Christian actors, such as the Bishop of Chiapas, Mexico, have highlighted the social injustices in the North of the Americas (see Chapter 6), the Jesuits, once again, have committed their members and their resources to the cause of the poor, the marginalized and the migrants. History repeats itself and governments worry today about these agents of liberation, as in the past the US President Reagan and the Republican Party worried about liberation theology and its impact among the peoples of Latin America and its 'subversives'.

The following chapter outlines one of those unfinished concerns with political disputes and social violence extended to the unfinished processes of social disclosure, where during the 1990s and into the twenty-first century the relatives of the victims of political violence during the military regimes, the victims of the so-called Cold War, remained signs and symbols of processes of liberation still to come, still to be unfolded in the public arena of the political dramas of Latin America for the new millennium.

5

Human Rights and the Disappeared

Throughout the period of the military regimes in Latin America and coinciding with the ongoing development of social processes of liberation and the formation of liberation theologies, there were thousands of victims of political repression. There were those arrested and tortured, and those who were never seen again, the disappeared, who in their thousands created a climate of ongoing injustice on their families who in most cases were never told about their fate and who searched for them for months and years without end.

The disappeared and their legal existence created one of the first points of close encounter and cooperation between theologians, the Church, the politicians and the State, because they constituted an ongoing sign of illegality on the one hand, and of social and personal sin on the other. Thus, the phenomenon of forced disappearance created a clear human and social bridge between those working for liberation within Christian communities and those who, upholding humanism and human rights, worked tirelessly to find the truth and to make sure that those atrocities would never happen again within Latin America.[212]

This chapter explores the historical processes that arose out of the phenomenon of forced disappearance, the theological challenges that will remain with us for many years and the fruitful cooperation of the faith communities and civil society in relation to human rights and a larger ethical order applicable to all human beings within Latin American society and globally. Most of the cases of forced disappearance remain unsolved and the perpetrators unpunished, while the questions about incommensurable suffering and social evil remain the same as those

questions about God and about society that have come out of
the history of Auschwitz, South Africa, Rwanda or the former
Yugoslavia. However, and despite that suffering, this chapter
asserts the presence of the God of Life within torture centres as
well as within Christian communities and throughout the whole
of civil society where the ethical social good is the normative
search and the normative way of life for all.

A Bodily Problem

The phenomenon of forced disappearance was widespread
throughout Latin America in the 1970s and 1980s and resulted
from a systematic attempt by totalitarian states to exterminate
opponents outside a framework of law and within the context of
the Cold War. The doctrine of the security state adopted by all
those totalitarian regimes triggered a war against communism
and against subversive elements within the State that was fully
supported by the United States Government. If the repression
started with the Brazilian military coup in March 1964, it quickly spread throughout the Latin American Southern Cone with
subsequent military coups in Uruguay, Chile and Argentina, and
intensified in countries such as Paraguay, El Salvador and
Guatemala. Throughout the Southern Cone the intelligence
services operated a common sharing of information and the
transfer of prisoners across borders through an international
network known as *Operación Cóndor*, coordinated by *Cóndor*
1: Colonel Manuel Contreras, Chief of the Chilean Intelligence
Services (DINA).[213] Specialized personnel serving within those
security services that kidnapped, tortured and made citizens
vanish, had been trained by US personnel in Panama and at the
School of the Americas (SOA) in Fort Benning, Georgia, in the
United States.[214]

The phenomenon was widespread and the numbers given in
contemporary reports fail to reveal the systematic dehumanizing processes of torture and abuse that went on within the walls
of secret detention centres, usually located within capital cities

and urban areas, that affected the victims' families, their friends and their work colleagues, imparting fear and despair in large parts of the civilian population.[215] In my opinion, the exact number of people who disappeared will never be known but working figures suggest, for example, more than 1,000 in Chile and 25,000 in Argentina.[216] The Christian communities were all affected as some of their members were taken away or they had to deal with different ecclesial experiences: support by some of the churches as was the case in Chile, or denial of their suffering, as was the case of the Catholic Church in Argentina. Over the years it was the Brazilian Episcopal Conference that was more active in publicly denouncing human rights abuses and in supporting a strong network of Basic Christian Communities who dealt with abuse, pain, guilt, and finally questions about suffering and about God himself.[217] Those communities not only alleviated suffering and created webs of human solidarity but also created a complete new understanding of the concept of Church and its role within contemporary society.[218]

A Case Study

One case is typical. By using the legal records that exist in Chile, it is possible to outline the process of arrest, torture and forced disappearance of those arrested, and their families' search for them, as well as the exile of other family members.[219]

On 10 July 1974, Bárbara Gabriela Uribe Tamblay and Edwin Francisco Van Jurick Altamirano (members of the Movimiento de Izquierda Revolucionario – MIR), who were husband and wife, were arrested together with Edwin's brother, Cristián Van Jurick (MIR).[220] Over the next few days, agents of the National Intelligence Directorate (DINA) brought eachof the prisoners back to their home one at a time to search for clues to their activities and their immediate political contacts.[221]

Bárbara Uribe came from a large family, and her parents (Enrique Uribe Vásquez – architect – and Teresa Tamblay) transmitted to their children their own sense of a problematic and unjust Chilean society.[222] Bárbara was described as a rebel student, loyal to friends, always acting as a leader among her peers in primary and secondary school. She studied at the Liceo 7 and the Liceo 11 of Maipú and decided not to attend university but to follow a secretarial course in order to become very quickly employable and financially independent. During the summer of 1971, Bárbara had taken part in community work in Talca, where students of the Universidad de Concepción, all close to the MIR, had also given their time and their youth to poor communities in need of hands to build schools, hospitals and roads.[223] Aged 17, Bárbara met Edwin during her work within poor communities, when both of them were secondary school students. Edwin's father was also an architect and Edwin studied at the Liceo Manuel de Salas. Against all odds and political turmoil, they married in December 1973. Since the day of the military coup, 11 September 1973, Bárbara had been involved in hiding the persecuted and she had organized pockets of resistance to the military within the Santiago shantytowns. Bárbara worked as a secretary after having studied at the Manpower School and, after her arrest, her home (she lived with Edwin's mother) and workplace were searched. Her husband Edwin had left his teachers' training in history at the Chilean University and worked for a Santiago editorial house. Several testimonies spoke of the strength of Bárbara who spoke to prisoners and met Edwin within different detention centres and took the conscious decision not to cooperate with the security forces and to follow Edwin's path to death.[224] While Edwin was moved to the Villa Grimaldi (a secret detention and torture centre), Bárbara arrived at Cuatro Alamos where witnesses spoke of her constant conversation, her memories of her husband and the fact that she sang through the window to other prisoners, determined not to give up names or information concerning the MIR. Bárbara was taken to an unknown destination on 2 and 3 August 1974 and she became one of 'the disappeared'.

Tamara Valdés, later in exile in Mexico, gave a long testimony about their life at different detention centres and the centrality of the DINA agent Osvaldo Romo in the detention and horrific torture of Bárbara and her sisters, and the torture of Bárbara's husband Edwin and his brother Cristián.²²⁵ Both were 20 years old. The couple were seen at 38 Londres Street by several witnesses, including Oscar Alfaro, Beatriz Kettlun Zaluk, Gabriela Mathieu, Viola Todorovic and Antonio Osorio. Bárbara's sisters, Viviana and Mónica, were arrested on 18 September 1974 and brought to the torture house of Irán and Los Plátanos Streets (the Venda Sexy) where Viviana was threatened with the same treatment that had been given to Edwin and Bárbara.

More recent testimonies suggest that, on 10 July 1974, Edwin Francisco Van Yurick Altamirano left his home at 9 a.m. and never returned for lunch; he was supposed to have met his brother Cristián at lunchtime.²²⁶ That evening, his wife Bárbara returned home from work at about 7 p.m. concerned about Edwin, and an hour later a man nicknamed 'Titín' arrived at the house, saying that he had a message from Edwin. He was accompanied by four other men. After her arrest and at 1 a.m. on 11 July 1974, Bárbara called her brother-in-law at a location in Echeñique Street, Ñuñoa, in order to alert him about what was happening. However, DINA agents arrested him after opening fire when he tried to escape. Cristián Van Yurick was taken to a pick-up and saw his brother Edwin blindfolded and handcuffed in another pick-up.

Cristián Van Yurick was taken to 38 Londres Street and interrogated in front of Bárbara, who was naked and was being raped by a DINA agent in order to pressurize Cristián to give them information. Cristián testified that he was also tortured together with his brother Edwin and that he remained for a month at 38 Londres Street and was then moved to the Villa Grimaldi, together with his brother. Those who tortured them at 38 Londres Street were Osvaldo Romo Mena, *Carabinero* Basclay Zapata, Army Lieutenant Miguel Krassnoff and Army Captain Marcelo Morén Brito. In mid-August 1974, a truck with prisoners, including Edwin Van Yurick, left the Villa Grimaldi. The DINA agents had spoken of 'Puerto Montt' or

'La Moneda', symbolic destinations of those prisoners to be killed, according to the testimony of former DINA agent Samuel Fuenzalida Devia. The practice of eliminating prisoners took several forms: some of them were thrown from helicopters into the sea while others were shot and buried on land.[227] Cristián Van Yurick also testified that by the end of August there was a crisis at the Villa Grimaldi (either on 26 or 28 August 1974) owing to the fact that somebody of some importance had rung the bell of the property at the villa.[228] As a precautionary measure the prisoners were divided into three groups known by letters of the alphabet. One group never returned, another group was set free and those in a third group were moved to either Cuatro Alamos detention centre or the torture house of José Domingo Cañas.

Cristián Van Yurick arrived at José Domingo Cañas and was asked about his brother Edwin. At this stage Edwin Van Yurick had been in a bad condition at the Villa Grimaldi, as DINA agents had driven a vehicle over his legs with the result that a leg was broken, became infected and had to be amputated. After September 1974, Cristián Van Yurick did not hear about his brother or sister-in-law and he remained a prisoner at several detention centres, Tres Alamos, Ritoque and Puchuncaví, until December 1976 when he was expelled to the United Kingdom.

In August 1974, and after a request from the British Embassy the Chilean Foreign Ministry stated that Bárbara and Edwin were under arrest pending an investigation, a fact that was later denied by the same ministry when requested to provide further information by the Santiago Courts.[229] In January 1975, the Foreign Ministry acknowledged that Cristián was a prisoner at Ritoque and that he had been able to receive visitors. Witnesses testified that Bárbara and Edwin had been prisoners at 38 Londres Street even after they had been listed among the disappeared.[230]

Theological Challenges

William Cavanaugh has explored the theological link between torture and the Eucharist, two bodily processes, one of destruction and brutality, the other of wholeness and completion, and has argued that:

> If torture is essentially an anti-liturgy, a drama in which the state realizes omnipotence on the bodies of others, then the Eucharist provides a direct and startling contrast, for in the Eucharist Christ sacrifices no other body but His own. Power is realized in self-sacrifice; Christians join in this sacrifice by uniting their own bodies to the sacrifice of Christ.[231]

During those years of military brutality, it was the body, the human body, that was at the centre of a theology that came out of action; for the State wanted to subdue bodies and their minds, the bodies of those who were challenging the integrity and objectives of the totalitarian states. Bodies were taken away in the middle of the night, were stripped naked and persistently beaten, burned and treated with electricity in order to inflict pain and fear so that the person would allow the State to find other 'subversive bodies' in order to prevent their action on a social body, the State. Those who were spared death by chance or State design returned to their social bodies and to the Christian communities only if they were welcomed, because psychologically they wanted to be alone in order to deal with their pain, their injuries and their shame. Torture destroyed lives, dreams and bodies; some lived in fear and left for other countries and other existences; most of them took years to recapture their worth and their dignity; others found it too painful and they took their own lives, never to return, never to heal.[232]

The difference between those healed and those who never healed was the possibility of a reintegration within the community, either a political community of similarly tortured people or a Christian community. Community values assured those who returned to a symbolic belonging that they had been liberated by their actions and that they should feel proud of those moments of honest assertion of the centrality of life and the right to live.[233] An example of this healing and of a liberating experience was that of the British doctor Sheila Cassidy, who managed to feel the welcoming spirit and the solidarity of the women prisoners after she had been kept in isolation. The women shared everything that was given to them, a practice that Dr Cassidy found difficult to follow, and therefore restored those who were tortured in isolation to the fold and the feeling of community solidarity.[234] Cavanaugh has suggested that this social experience could be compared to the experience of the disciples on the road to Emmaus, who were sad and suddenly felt the presence of the Risen Christ in the breaking of bread and in their sharing a meal together as a reminder of a eucharistic celebration (Lk. 24:13–35). However, there was a final twist to the tale of that story as the Christ that warmed their heart disappeared once again and the disciples only found an explanation later on: he was actually raised from the dead by his Father and was returning to him.[235]

For those who either died during torture or were killed by agents of the State, there was a further unknown destination. Their bodies were taken out of the secret detention centres and buried in unknown graves, or were loaded into helicopters and thrown into the sea.[236] Some of those bodies thrown into the sea were still alive; they were living human beings drugged and killed by falling into the deep waters of the sea, by immersion into the waters. Their fate was never disclosed to their families and therefore the families continued over the years living in hope of seeing them alive; they continued legal battles to request their appearance and only gave up after years of search and when it was made clear to them by a newly established democratic state that their loved ones were not prisoners and that the State didn't know where they were. They were presumed dead but for all legal purposes they were still alive.[237]

The relatives of the disappeared developed into social zombies, into people in a trance who didn't want to live their personal dreams any longer and couldn't do so because their only activity, physical and mental, during each and every day of their lives, was to search for their loved ones and to connect not with the State but with those who were also looking for their missing relatives. It is at this stage that some of them were welcomed by the Church and remained hopeful with the help of the Church, and others were rejected by the Church as mixing their pious ritual obligations towards God with the wrong political and social affiliation. In Chile, for example, most of the relatives of the disappeared were not members of the Catholic Church but later paid homage to a Church that was with them in time of trouble. In Argentina, the Catholic Church worked closely with the totalitarian State and ongoing legal cases have revealed the involvement of military chaplains in the secret detention centres, not only justifying kidnapping, torture and disappearance in the name of Western civilization but some of them being directly involved in those grave abuses of human rights, certainly never willed by God and unacceptable in Christian ethics.

Integrated Approaches to Liberation

In the case of Chile, Brazil and El Salvador, it can be argued that one of the strengths of the new democratic regimes in Latin America after the military regimes was the fact that those who previously were not part of the Churches, such as the members of some left-wing parties and coalitions, worked through the churches within the period of totalitarian regimes. There was a movement from the civil and political arenas towards the Basic Christian Communities and after the return to democratic rule there was a movement in the opposite direction. Fewer people took part in the life of churches and parishes but there was a renewed understanding of the centrality of Christian values understood as human rights.

After a few years of democratic bliss and when citizens started asking further questions about social and economic poli-cies within democratic regimes, human rights were understood as central to society and the need was expressed of having fully united and reconciled societies. A crude political analysis asserted that the possibility for totalitarian regimes arose out of a sectarian attitude by all parties within the democratic mechanisms that already existed, and the increase of social and political violence provided a self-justification for the military to intervene. 'How to achieve reconciliation in divided and wounded social bodies?' It was a question that very few attempted to answer and those who tried were actually part of the wounded body in which reconciliation seemed difficult to achieve. The Truth and Reconciliation Commissions searched for historical narratives and information about past human rights abuses but didn't have the power to do more. Thus, the wounded social bodies were confronted with several options:

1 reconciliation without truth, that is, a *tabula rasa* situation where the past was forgotten and a nation moved on;
2 reconciliation with truth, that is, an ongoing investigation into human rights abuses without a period of termination of judicial investigations; and
3 legal reconciliation in which the State can move on and the social body can also move on but with the proviso that families can pursue judicial cases against the perpetrators of human right abuses.

All Latin American states attempted a bit of each one of those options with more emphasis on a legal closure by those who were part of the military regimes and a larger emphasis on truth rather than reconciliation by those who were the victims of the totalitarian violence.

This is an area of theological praxis where the first generations of theologians failed to engage themselves with a larger theological discourse. Most contemporary approaches to reconciliation, truth and the past sufferings of people have come from Jon Sobrino sj (see Chapter 1) and José Comblin. Comblin, a Catholic priest who experienced the totalitarian regimes of Brazil and Chile, argued in the mid-1980s that there were enough elements within the Old and New Testament and within the modern philosophers as to suggest that reconciliation is always a possibility. However, he pointed to two important questions regarding religion, expressed as theology and politics. In the political realm, he asked about a possible reconciliation between diverse political parties that didn't have the same project of nation, and he requested an agreement on a just social project in which all citizens have concretely the same rights as well as the same obligations. In the theological realm, he questioned the possibility of social and national reconciliation without a servant Church that forgets her privileges and that acknowledges her past involvement in processes of conquest, colonialism, servitude and oppression towards the Latin American indigenous populations. Comblin writes:

> Yet to the extent that the Church bears an immense responsibility in the formation of Latin American culture, and a responsibility which she has publicly acknowledged, the problematic of Latin American society is also a problem for theology. What then in the Church would permit the development of such a society? How is it possible for a Christian Church to be at the base of such an unjust and oppressive society? What are the basic principles which enable us to comprehend that the Church has produced such a phenomenon? This is a theological problem.[238]

Indeed, this is an area where theologies of liberation have not managed to have the impact that European political theologies previously had in the climate of change of the 1960s and within a post-Vatican II climate. The options seem to be many within a general apathy towards the possibilities of political systems achieving the autonomy of the past vis-à-vis processes of globalization and the market as all-embracing and all-enslaving.[239] Is it possible to argue that the nation-state has already died with the conflicts in Iraq? What it is not possible to assume is a theological model in which the State is unified and orderly, as it was constructed by mediaeval scholastic theologians who were writing before the Reformation, before the opening of new worlds and before the encounter of civilizations in 1492.

I return here to the centrality and importance of the God of history and his continuous intervention within the lives of the poor and the marginalized, a less tangible and recognizable intervention within the lives of those fully engaged with the markets and the absence of God. The boundary of my engagement within theology and politics is clear: democratic systems of government can change, and through change God walks with his people. Much more engagement by those on the ground in Latin America is needed vis-à-vis the world situation after the 2003 invasion of Iraq because the signs are that history repeats itself and that the mighty US empire is exporting its own understanding of the worth of human beings through force, an escalation of the arms race, a proliferation of nuclear weapons and a failure to comply with international law, international agreements regarding torture, abduction and justice, as symbolized by the ongoing expansion of Guantánamo Bay and the abductions by US personnel of suspects within a climate of a 'War on Terror' that has overrun the possibility of a globalized ethics and a globalized reconciliation among peoples and nations of the world.

A Globalized Ethics

Those groups of the relatives of the disappeared that existed within different Latin American countries organized themselves into a Latin American large umbrella organization in the 1980s and worked very closely with other human rights groups within civil society in order to lobby the new democratic states for a complete condemnation of forced disappearance, for a full condemnation of torture and for further legal investigations into the fate of their loves ones. Several countries appointed national commissions to investigate the truth of the military repression of those years and most countries relied on the help and the authority of the churches in order to support those national efforts for truth and reconciliation.

Theologians of liberation had already explored the strength

of globalized ethical principles that also applied to Latin America and as a result the churches and the State assumed together the trope of 'human rights', a term despised by the totalitarian regimes, as a working model for any Latin American society within the twenty-first century. As a result, the churches assumed, and in some cases were pushed into, a position more peripheral to that which previously they had held. The churches supported the efforts by civil society regarding human rights but at the same time the Church opposed those State developments that contradicted assumed Christian principles related to birth control and the end of one person's biological life. The Christian communities remained at the centre of social and pastoral action that created theological narratives, but the concerns changed from human rights abuses to ecological issues, redistribution of wealth, global economic policies, local education and health matters. Despite those alliances the issue of the disappeared remained and still remains fully unresolved within the Latin American states, with certain political factions satisfied that some economic reparation was given to the relatives of the victims and with other groups hoping that with the passing of time the problem will be forgotten.

The contemporary and very strong lobby for human rights constitutes a very rich place for theology as it is within those social movements that human rights and theology have encountered each other. In the contemporary way of speaking, different kinds of ethics divide the world; however, the language of human rights as a universal ethical language makes for a very cohesive understanding of the rights of the human person that within a faith community have been given by God to every human being. Even those more sceptical of Latin American theology, such as Pope John Paul II, spoke about a globalized combination of shared understandings that combine Christian and humanistic understandings of the human person within contemporary society, stating that: 'Social, legal and cultural safeguards – the result of people's efforts to defend the common good – are vitally necessary if individuals and intermediary groups are to maintain their centrality.'[240] Other calls to develop a so-called 'global ethics' took place at the 1993 Parliament of the World Religions in Chicago in response to a global crisis of human rights abuses, a much-needed call summarized by Konrad Raiser in the following analysis:

> The flagrant violation of human rights in all parts of the world shows that the present international order is more a community of interests of the powerful, and is not primarily orientated on protecting the living conditions of ordinary people. Human rights still remain an ideal without the character of a binding obligation, and their universality is increasingly put in question.[241]

But a note of caution on pessimism: it is clear from the declaration of the Parliament of World Religions that the major religions of the world provide an ethical framework that can constitute a central backbone for the utopian creation of a better world. Within the contradictions between the religions and their beliefs about human rights there is a common recognition that human beings, not the markets, not something else, are at the centre of God's plan and God's action in the world.

Returning to Latin American theology and the disappeared, it is possible to draw a parallel between the associations of relatives of the disappeared and the concern for common universal human rights stressed by the Parliament of World Religions in Chicago. The general questioning of and reminder about passivity in the implementation of legislation and political systems that uphold human rights remains a common concern. Further, as the relatives of the disappeared, mostly women, represent a powerful force within the ongoing strengthening of civil society in a general climate of the death of the nation-state the theologies of liberation arising during the 1990s represent a clear supportive and contextual statement of the Parliament of World Religions. Thus, concerns for the environment as not owned but entrusted to humans by God, concerns for the rights of women as part of that human centrality within creation, and concerns for an ongoing liberation from oppressive structures, be they ideological, symbolic or political, in the name of a divine manifestation are represented by the emergence of liberation theology in the 1990s (see the chapters on Casaldáliga, Althaus-Reid and Petrella within this volume).

The relatives of the disappeared and their milieu remain within the early twenty-first century as a place where God is speaking because their voices and actions remind us of the need for the liberation of many human beings in Latin America. The theological questions posed by the relatives of the disappeared are the same that have been asked so many times about the location and action of God within the atrocious period of annihilation of 6 million Jews by the Nazi regime in the 1940s. 'Was God in Auschwitz?' 'Is there still the possibility of believing in a God after Auschwitz?' 'Would there ever be human dignity and reconciliation after Auschwitz?' There were those who answered 'no' to those questions within a post-holocaust theology but there were many who answered 'yes' as well.[242] Those were questions and answers not only about location but also about faith in a liberating God.

Let me put the same theological questions to the historical facts of a more contemporary detention and torture centre in the hills of Santiago, Chile, the infamous Villa Grimaldi. Was God in the Villa Grimaldi? Is there the possibility of believing in God after the Villa Grimaldi? Would there ever be human dignity and reconciliation after the Villa Grimaldi? My answer is 'yes', and I painfully answer with bodily knowledge of what went on in that camp of death where human beings were forgotten, where others were kept in kennels and treated as dogs, and where honest human beings were forgotten, mutilated, burned, electrocuted, raped, and made to disappear with no name, with no rites and with no family around them. My answer within a contextual framework of a Latin American theology of the disappeared is a big YES, many times 'yes', always and unequivocally 'yes'.

The liberating God of history was in the Villa Grimaldi, not as an all-knowing God who was watching what he already knew. The liberating God was not predestining those who were there, mostly atheists and agnostics, to eternal damnation or salvation, counting their suffering and their sins as the Egyptian Gods did. The liberating God of Latin America was there as *el Dios de los pobres y los oprimidos*, the God of the poor and the oppressed. He was there naked on the *parrilla*, on the metallic structure that acted as an electricity conductor, being himself crucified, interrogated and scorned. He was there as one of the criminals and subversives, the ones loved by God and those who like the prostitutes of the Gospel most probably entered Heaven before clean, legalistic and altruistic men and women of this world and of Chilean society. The God of history was there in the Villa Grimaldi when prisoners sat outside on a bench smelling the fragrance of the roses that reminded them of their loved ones and of their decency as human beings. He was there, he was killed and his body made to disappear because that was the fate of the Son of God himself.

The relatives of the disappeared have the privilege of having made their sons and daughters alive within the historical narratives and the social memory of Latin America because, as Archbishop Romero had, they rose among the people that loved them and they rose in the theological narratives of those theologians who accompanied them, some of whom died in the horrors of the Villa Grimaldi and many other camps of horror.[243] Gutiérrez has spoken of the God of Life and has spoken of the God who lives in history, that God is not dead just because the military regimes wanted him dead or because the post-Vatican II Church has become more traditional and more pious.[244] God continues walking with the churches and with civil society within Latin America and continues his incarnation within the poor and the marginalized, within those in prison and the hungry, within those with HIV/AIDS, within those trafficked for sexual and economic purposes, within those who are the victims of a globalized collapse of human rights, and within those who still beg in the streets, without a name, without a social identity and without a future.

The relatives of the disappeared remind us that there is a close connection between the God of believers and the system of human rights defended by many sectors of civil society. If, during the period of the military regimes, sections of the Church defended those who had had their human rights abused there is the possibility of an ongoing continuity between the Latin American theology of the twentieth and that of the twenty-first century. The relatives of the disappeared remind us that the involvement of Christians with those organizations was not made through a common belief or a common understanding of God but that it was a commitment of service by Christians in the name of the God who was and remains Lord of History and Lord of all political processes.

A contextual example of this common understanding and of the churches' service to civil society is highlighted in the next chapter: the role of the Church in the indigenous uprising in Chiapas, Mexico, during 1994.

6

Chiapas and Governance

In the two previous chapters, I have argued that the social and religious base of all Latin American theologies has been, and always will be, the social movements for equality and human rights within civic society. If, and only if, some systematizing of theology in Latin America could have given the impression that academics and intellectuals were driving social processes, the example of the Jesuits throughout Latin America (see Chapter 4) and of the ecclesial support groups for the persecuted and the politically suppressed (see Chapter 5) could be seen as following the directives by Vatican II in which the Church became a servant church, ready and willing to be misunderstood for the sake of those whom Christ loved, the poor and the marginalized, the persecuted and those without jobs, housing or human dignity.

If a first generation of Latin American theologians commented on the possibility of a Christ who loved the poor and a Church that would follow that example, they did it within a socio-political context in which the Church occupied a social role that was vacant owing to the increasing numbers of military regimes and the Cold War, with all its sinister implications for a global war on Communism carried out by elements of the Latin American armies that murdered, raped and located themselves above any scrutiny by civil society.

The socio-political context changed with the end of the Cold War and the collapse of the Eastern Bloc and the Soviet Union. As previously explored in Volume I, the five-hundredth anniversary of the encounter between Europeans and indigenous populations brought new questions about the Latin American nation-state, and theologians such as Leonardo Boff and Diego Irarrázaval articulated narratives of ecclesial communion with nature and God through increasing processes of inculturation and challenges to global warming and the possible destruction of the planet.

It is within that climate of theological development after 1992 that the utopian dream of democratic nation-states was challenged by an indigenous armed rebellion in the Mexican province of Chiapas, where on 1 January 1994 an organized indigenous army, the Zapatista National Liberation Army (Ejército Zapatista de Liberación Nacional, EZLN) took over San Cristóbal de las Casas and six other towns by force and challenged the status quo of social inequality provided by the Mexican State. The Zapatista movement used indigenous symbols and aspirations for justice and equality in order to foster successfully a sense of a new challenge against the oppressors, the Mexican State, a descendant of an earlier oppressor, the Spanish empire.[245] The response of the local bishop was clear; he supported the demands of the rebels and mediated in an ongoing armed conflict that was very soon reported by the international media. In doing so, Bishop Samuel Ruiz García articulated an ecclesial response to a new development within the changing umbrella of liberation theology, in particular, and of Latin American theology, in general. In doing so, Ruiz opened the possibility of an ongoing theological reflection out of actions that supported civil society and social movements that have in the past 15 years challenged the plausibility of neo-liberal states that claim no obligations towards their citizens in the name of globalization and arising market economies without a face and without a name.

Chiapas as a Theological Context

It is within a particular social context that theological questions are asked and where the God of Life operates. Chiapas had already been conquered by the Spaniards in 1520, when, later, in 1712 a large contingent of 6,000 Indians arose against

them.[246] Over the next centuries, most of the indigenous populations 'converted to Catholicism' while keeping their indigenous traditions and surviving the upheavals of the Mexican
revolution and the subsequent problems between Church and
State. The development of land ownership by a few and the
importance of coffee-growing within a region meant in practice
that social unrest because of poverty, unemployment and neg-
lect remained part of a forgotten land in which feudal systems
with their racial undertones of humiliation towards the indigenous population remained in operation and a social reality
within a twentieth-century democratic Mexico.[247] The EZLN
restored an indigenous narrative of land and cosmos that
connected their own quest for social agency with the richness of
the Mayan cosmology and an indigenous quest for social and
cultural identity within a globalized and culturally impover-
ished world dreaming of post-modernity and neo-liberalism.[248]

At the time when the nucleus of the EZLN moved to the
mountains of Chiapas in 1983 it was still a territory in need of
land reform. The whole of Chiapas includes 75,600 square kilometres or 3.8 per cent of the total land in Mexico, and within
the four million population of Chiapas one-third is indigenous,
belonging to nine ethnic groups, each one with its own language: Tzotzil, Tzelbal, Tojaolabal, Chol, Mam, Zoque, Mixe,
Kakchiquel and Lacandon.[249] The illiteracy rates are close to 37
per cent in men and 63 per cent in women. The levels of malnutrition reach 66 per cent of the population and 80 per cent of
the Zapatista territory, known as Los Altos de Chiapas. Seven
out of ten indigenous homes do not have electricity and nine out
of ten do not have water. Chiapas produces 28 per cent of
Mexico's meat but 90 per cent of all indigenous households
cannot afford to buy meat. Wages are three times lower than
the national average, and infant mortality (66 in 1,000) double
the national average. In a population in which 60 per cent are
less than 20 years of age, one-third of deaths are due to curable
infectious diseases.[250] In summary, Chiapas remains a poor and
undeveloped area where the Mexican State has not managed to
look after its own citizens.

It was within that poverty and destitution that Bishop Ruiz managed to develop systems of support for the local population and also for 44,000 refugees escaping from the violent conflicts that were taking place in neighbouring Guatemala. There is no doubt that in his 40 years as a bishop of the diocese of San Cristóbal (1959–99) Ruiz applied the post-Vatican II model of the servant church.

A Bishop for Liberation

Bishop Samuel Ruiz García was born in the city of Irapuato, State of Guanajuato, on 3 November 1924, and in 1949 he was ordained as a Catholic priest. In 1952, Ruiz became a lecturer at the seminary in León and later its rector; in 1959, Ruiz was appointed bishop. Between 1962 and 1965, Ruiz participated in all the sessions of the Second Vatican Council, in the first Latin American Missions meeting in Meigar and in the Second General Meeting of Latin American Bishops in Medellín (Colombia) in 1968. Between 1965 and 1970 Ruiz served as President of the Episcopal Commission for Indigenous Peoples of the Mexican Bishops and in 1970 he was appointed President of the Department of Missions of the Latin American Episcopal Conference (CELAM). In 1974, he also fostered the beginnings of the National Indigenous Congress of Mexico that promoted collaboration between the diverse indigenous groups of Mexico.

His main thrust towards the Church's support for human rights in Chiapas came about in 1988 through the foundation of the Centre for Human Rights Fray Bartolomé de las Casas, an organization which, under his leadership, analysed and condemned all human rights violations against indigenous peoples and peasants in Chiapas. International recognition for such a project was given in 1992, when Bishop Ruiz was elected President of the Secretariado Internacional Cristiano de Solidaridad con América Latina (SICSAL), an organization that aimed at supporting marginalized peoples and post-conflict resolutions within Latin America. Immediately after the Zapatista rebellion,

Ruiz served as President of the National Mediation Commission (CONAI), a public body that aimed at peace and reconciliation between the Zapatista Army of National Liberation (EZLN), the Mexican military, the Mexican Government and the indigenous peoples in Chiapas.

Between 1994 and 1996, Bishop Ruiz was nominated three times for the Nobel Peace Prize, the maximum number of nominations allowed by the Nobel Prize Committee. That international recognition came about because of his continuous work for human rights in the midst of threats and attempts on his life. Other prizes received by Bishop Ruiz include the Martin Ennals Award for Human Rights Defender (1997), a prize given by leading non-governmental organizations, including Amnesty International, Defence for Children, German Diakonia, Human Rights Watch, HURIDOCS, International Alert, International Commission of Jurists, International Federation for Human Rights, International Service for Human Rights and World Against Torture. In 2000, UNESCO awarded Bishop Ruiz the Simón Bolívar Prize, a prize awarded every two years to an individual who 'has contributed to the freedom, independence and dignity of peoples, as well as to the strengthening of ties of solidarity between nations'. In 2001, Ruiz was awarded the Niwano Peace Prize, a prize awarded annually to 'an individual or an organization that is making a significant contribution to world peace through promoting inter-religious cooperation'.[251]

Theological Narratives of Liberation

After his retirement owing to age in 2000, Ruiz started a series of public lectures throughout university campuses and public institutions that as 'a second step' consolidated his theological thinking on a theology of action that he had already put into place in Chiapas as 'a first step'. For example, on the sixth annual University of Alberta Visiting Lectureship in Human Rights and on 26 February 2004, Ruiz reiterated the theological connections between assisting the poor and the gospel of

Christ, between serving the persecuted and the gospel of Christ and between the work for human rights and the work of the Church.

That practice and discourse on human rights among pastoral bishops of Latin America who had been influenced by the Second Vatican Council and the meeting of bishops at Medellín was nothing new. However, what was new was that Ruiz's support for liberation processes took place within an established democratic state, Mexico, and within a new wave of pastoral concerns for indigenous peoples in Latin America. As had been the case of Archbishop Oscar Romero of El Salvador (see Volume 1), Ruiz converted to the poor and found the Christ of faith within the faces and lives of the poor and the marginalized of Chiapas. There is no doubt that when the EZLN took over San Cristóbal de las Casas, Ruiz could have either condemned that forceful act or could have indicated that the Church had nothing to say to a localized conflict between indigenous peoples and the Mexican Government. Indeed, his position was even more radical because he operated within Mexico where the Church and State remain separate in public life and where even clerics cannot by law wear ecclesiastical clothing, even though this is done in practice.

Ruiz has in his public appearances pointed to a universal indigenous struggle and he has linked the struggle in Chiapas to such globalized phenomenon, defending the right of the Church to support oppressed indigenous populations. When accused of preaching the 'theology of liberation', as was the case in Toronto in 2003, Ruiz asked a cunning question: 'Is there a theology of slavery?'[252] Over the years, Pope John Paul II asked him twice to resign and Ruiz had to take strong criticisms from the then Prefect of the Sacred Congregation for the Doctrine of the Faith, Cardinal Josef Ratzinger (currently Pope Benedict XVI).

Ruiz's conversion to a more liberationist view has been expressed by him in the following words: 'My way of thinking changed. From having a vision of churches filled with indigenous peoples singing, I started seeing communities oppressed by society and structures . . . The Mayan people endured threats and physical violence for speaking their own language. Many were used as beasts of burden by their bosses, even carrying them on a chair if there was too much mud on the pathway.'[253] While condemning violence, Ruiz argued that the Zapatista were pursuing a just cause.

His mediation between the rebels and the government worked well after Ruiz had had an open conversation with the Mexican Government representative, Dr Manuel Solís. Ruiz told Solís that both of them were like drunks, to which Solís replied that he did not drink at all. Ruiz continued explaining and told Solís that they were like two drunks who needed each other in order to continue walking down the street. In Ruiz's words: 'We're like two drunks because if two drunks walk together, they need to hold each other up. You need the moral force that I represent and I need the political force you represent.' From then onwards the mediation talks were easier because the EZLN implemented peace accords through the local communities and trusted that Ruiz's mediation was bringing peace to the region and better living conditions for all.

Even though the peace talks started 11 days after the Zapatista uprising, the talks and reforms within Chiapas have until today been marked by violence, unrest and attacks on Bishop Ruiz and the Church.

The Chiapas Uprising

Subcomandante Marcos and other members of the EZLN arrived in Chiapas in 1983 in order to explore the possibility of armed struggle against the landowners and against the Mexican State.[254] However, most of the indigenous organizations and Christian communities believed in a peaceful solution to the social problems of the area. In 1985, the EZLN had only 12 members. Within a few years the EZLN, named after Emiliano Zapata, the Mexican leader of the 1917 revolution, was receiving more support from indigenous organizations and the Christian communities. Three important developments took place that can explain the fast growth of the EZLN: the central government's passive response to the international collapse of coffee prices in 1989 (coffee crops remain very important for employment within Chiapas); an amendment to the Mexican Constitution in 1992 that made peasants more vulnerable by halting the ongoing agrarian reform; and the political discussions that were paving the way for Mexico to enter into a trade agreement with the United States (NAFTA), an economic choice by the Mexican Government that in reality would allow all American cheap imports into Mexico and would damage local industry and employment opportunities.

In 1989, a majority of the settlements in Las Cañadas invited the EZLN to enter and to recruit from within their communities. By the end of 1992, military training was on its way under the Zapatista cry 'We, the dead of hunger, the ones with no name, the ones with no face', for the EZLN maintained an egalitarian structure by covering the faces of their commanders with a ski mask, so that people would not follow individuals but the EZLN as a group that represented the oppressed and the marginalized. The EZLN didn't want political power or to change a particular way of government but they wanted to secure basic rights for the people of Chiapas.

The uprising took place on 1 January 1994, on the same day in which the NAFTA agreement came into effect, and in his first sermon at the Chiapas Cathedral Bishop Ruiz reiterated his support for the indigenous populations of Chiapas by analysing the situation in the following terms: 'But our brothers and sisters living under oppression have given up hope . . . They have made a call, a scream, about their condition.' On the day of the uprising, a masked commander, Marcos, had declared at the municipal presidency of San Cristóbal de Las Casas on behalf of the rebels: 'Today the North American Free Trade Agreement begins, which is nothing more than a death sentence for the indigenous ethnicities of Mexico, who are perfectly dispensable in the modernization program of Salinas de Gotari' and 'Don't forget this: This is an ethnic movement.'[255]

The fighting did not last very long as the international media showed images of Zapatistas, hand-tied, being carried as prisoners of the Mexican Army and there was a general condemnation of Mexico's inability to cope with social demands even on the day when they were joining NAFTA.[256] Bishop Ruiz offered to mediate a ceasefire and the Mexican Government offered pardon to those who had risen in arms against the State.

By the time that the negotiations started, the Zapatistas had elaborated 34 demands that included an agrarian reform, improvements in education and health, and the autonomy of indigenous communities, plus the recognition of the Zapatista combatants as an army. Government envoys and the Zapatistas met at San Cristóbal Cathedral in the presence of Ruiz and agreed on a ceasefire that lasted until the end of the year. By that time, the Mexican Army had started building up numbers in the region and by December 1994 the Zapatistas responded by blocking roads, taking other towns and declaring that war was imminent. The response of Bishop Ruiz, then in his 70s, was to start a hunger strike that lasted for two weeks until the parties returned to the negotiating table.

Despite the efforts by Ruiz, the international finance community put enormous pressure on the Mexican President Ernesto Zedillo to end the crisis and a week after Ruiz ended his fast a leaked memo from the Chase Manhattan Bank showed that the bank perceived the elimination of the Zapatistas as a must in order for the Mexican Government to keep its financial promises. As a result, the Mexican Army entered rebel territories in February 1995 and, following orders to hassle dissident groups, an army patrol entered and searched the human rights office of Ruiz's diocese. During the night raid, the soldiers found a group of human rights workers in the office as well as a group of Americans, members of the Servicio Internacional para la Paz (SIPAZ), non-violent guards of peace, who had travelled to Chiapas after Ruiz had called on humanitarian organizations to assist the peace process in the Chiapas region. The visiting Americans were all ready with their pads and pens to record events at the human rights office and dispatch news back to the

United States. The soldiers carried out a quick search and then left, returning an hour later to ransack the office after the visiting Americans had been taken to safety.

At the level of the local indigenous communities, the Zapatista takeover was supported by the replacement of municipal authorities belonging to the official Mexican party. Those authorities were replaced by communally elected leaders and by 1996 'autonomous municipalities' were created following the amendment to the first paragraph of Article 4 of the Mexican Constitution which gave legal parameters for indigenous towns to organize their own forms of government.[257] After the process of strengthening the indigenous communities, there were more than 2,000 occupations of idle land that belonged to private ranchers; it is presumed that they pressurized the Mexican Government to act in order to protect their economic interests and the future international investment in Chiapas.

By August 1996, the peace talks had collapsed completely as it was clear that the Mexican Government did not have the will to seek reform and to allow for indigenous autonomy. After that Chiapas became part of a strategical phenomenon known as 'low-intensity war' and the conflict continued with an absence of dialogue between the parties. The Mexican Government implemented institutional peace within the region by fuelling the paramilitary groups, while the Zapatista kept some control of ethnic unrest and managed to stage demonstrations and marches in Mexico City. The new Zapatistas discovered the power of civil society and in their public actions triggered a wider political debate related to the ills and perils of government intervention among indigenous communities.[258] International activists for indigenous rights and against poverty and oppression supported the Zapatista cause and very quickly the Zapatistas had support groups and individuals who stayed in Chiapas for short periods of time in order to show international solidarity with them, a utopian resemblance to the international solidarity shown by political activists with those fighting Franco in the Spanish Civil War or those who worked for the government of Allende in 1970s Chile in order to support a political experiment in socialism.²⁵⁹ In the rest of this chapter, I do not intend to predict what could happen to Chiapas in the future. My aim is to analyse the possibility that all the social unrest and violence are part of deep-seated sinful social structures which are fuelled by greed and self-gratification. These are criticized by Latin American theology and by practitioners of the values of the Kingdom such as Bishop Ruiz.

Liberation from Structural Sin

One of the main messages proclaimed by the Latin American Bishops at Medellín (1968) and Puebla (1979) came from their inclusion of the term 'structural sin'. The bishops recognized that within the salvific and theological context of Latin America there were social structures that were sinful because they discriminated among God's children. Those structures of social sin maintained poverty and underdevelopment and allowed a few to have the goods of the earth in the name of discrimination on account of race, class and social privileges. Liberation from sin included a personal conversion towards the God of Life as well as a communal conversion towards an egalitarian, more inclusive society where the values of the Kingdom were to be realized.

Bishop Ruiz summarized his challenges to the situation in Chiapas in the same manner and, in a clear analysis, he understood most of the problems of society in Chiapas as arising from racism, whereby the voice of one white person was and still is more important than the voice of a thousand indigenous peoples. It is a fact that, from the beginning of his pastoral work in Chiapas, Ruiz asserted the beauty and creativity of indigenous cultures and challenged the lack of opportunities through the lack of land for the majority of those living in Chiapas. From the beginning, he announced that the Church's resources would be at the service of the indigenous peoples and he fostered the organization of peasant indigenous cooperatives, reflection groups and support mechanisms, particularly within

the area of Las Cañadas, a number of settlements at the
Lacandón rain forest near the Mexican border with Guatemala.
The book of Exodus was translated into the Tzeltal language
and a message of hope and deliverance from oppression arose
out of the connection between the biblical text and the context
of land shortage, violence and oppression within the region.
The ideal deliverance wanted by Ruiz never happened but he
triggered a unique development within civil society: the anthropological egalitarianism of Maya wisdom, the community's
empowerment by the Church and the political goals of those
who wanted change met in a powerful grass-roots organization,
a clear example of the power of civil society against the structures of sin.

It is important to reiterate that Ruiz's support for civil society
was different from that of other ecclesiastical responses to crisis
throughout Latin America, for example, Romero's leadership
role through the Christian communities in El Salvador or Silva
Henríquez's creation of human rights offices in Chile. Ruiz
didn't bring people to the churches but made sure that those
who were committed to the Church did everything they could to
take part and support efforts by civil society within a tense and
difficult situation. His discourse is reminiscent of that of African
theologians who have asserted the centrality of community to
such an extent that they have correlated individual salvation
with the salvation of the whole community. If Ernesto Cardenal
or Pedro Casaldáliga stressed the contribution and creativity of
indigenous communities in Nicaragua or Brazil, Bishop Ruiz
located those indigenous communities and their cosmologies at
the centre of a process of conversion, change and liberation for
them and for all Christians in Chiapas.

Before the Zapatista uprising of 1994, Ruiz had become
aware that the number of guerrilla fighters had increased and
that many of them came from the Basic Christian Communities.
Ruiz spoke to many Zapatistas warning them of the conse-
quences of an armed rebellion and the start of a 'spiral of violence', a term coined by Dom Helder Camara in Brazil, a term
that asserted the fact that once violence is used in order to solve

conflict it can only escalate, it cannot solve a social problem. Ruiz remained torn between his condemnation of violence and his support for self-determination. Thus, his mediation between the Mexican Government and the Zapatistas was perceived by landowners and the traditionalists within Mexican society as support for the Zapatistas and Ruiz was labelled 'the red bishop'.

If his actions of mediation and support of the Basic Christian Communities meant anything, it was because the Catholic Church led by Ruiz in Chiapas chose not to take a central position within the conflict but a middle one in which the main actors were the Zapatista and the Mexican Government while the Church supported those affected by the conflict. In that sense, Ruiz chose to locate ecclesiastical tiers within civil society, within groups of citizens with a certain idea of the common good who associated together in order to serve society as a community. Ruiz did not locate himself within the usual power struggle of Church–State relations but within the concerns of groups of citizens with different ideas about history, the conflict and possible future solutions. By the year 2000, the year of his retirement, Ruiz had given way to a new local bishop and Mexico had a new president. After the elections of 2 July 2000, Vicente Fox took over as Mexican president marking the first election in 70 years of a candidate who didn't belong to the official party (PRI). Later, on 21 August 2000, Pablo Salazar Mendiguchía, candidate for governor for the Alianza de Chiapas, was elected Governor of Chiapas, representing a coalition of seven opposition parties. Politically, it was the first time that the corporate system of an official party, the government and the state of Chiapas were not ruled by the same people, all allied to financial interests and landowners in Chiapas. However, the situation remained tense and violent with many social problems to be solved but with the sense that civil society had been strengthened by the ministry of Bishop Ruiz. The challenge remained in the possibility of changing the structural causes of inequality and, as poignantly expressed by Aída Hernández, 'civil society has the responsibility to pressure these new authorities to make good on their campaign promises in order to put an end to the violence that has left Chiapas' indigenous population with so many dead and so much suffering'.[260]

For Ruiz, part of that social unrest and violence came from the international pressures put by financial institutions on the poor. Thus, on 23 September 1999, 100 days before the start of the new millennium, Ruiz congregated thousands at the Basilica of Guadalupe in Mexico City and supported the foreign debt cancellation coinciding with a conference hosted on the same day and on the same topic by Pope John Paul II in Rome. John Paul II had called for a greater investment in human beings through education and health, a cry echoed by Ruiz in Mexico at the start of a pilgrimage to Jerusalem, with a group of indigenous peoples. At that time, the statistics on Mexican poverty were staggering: between 1989 and 1999 the number of Mexicans living below the poverty line rose from 39 per cent to 43 per cent so that two-thirds of Mexicans lived in poverty. Wages were 20 per cent lower than in 1994 and the amount of profit by Mexican millionaires exceeded the government expenditure on education, health, urban programmes, ecology, water programmes and public social investments all together. Ruiz linked with organizations such as the Cry of the Excluded Movement, indigenous rights, human rights and Church organizations to request debt cancellation, as he declared that not even Chiapas could ever pay its debts to Mexico City.

It is a fact that not all civil society in Chiapas supported Bishop Ruiz and that Catholics remained divided between those who followed Ruiz and those more conservative who were not happy with his stand on land, human rights and temporal matters. Over the years, there was an increase in conversion to Protestant groups that preached an individual gospel of conversion rather than a communitarian response to biblical challenges. Thus, in some villages, Bishop Ruiz could not celebrate Mass at particular churches because of the threat of reprisals by local paramilitary groups supported by land owners. Since 1994, 40 Catholic churches or chapels have been burned, destroyed or closed by opponents to Bishop Ruiz and, by 1998, 14 chapels remained closed to the public. In November 1997, Bishop Ruiz and his entourage suffered an ambush on a dirt road and three Bible teachers suffered bullet wounds. Therefore, despite the possibility of building peace in Chiapas, the Catholic community remains deeply divided between those who support reform and those who maintain a colonial traditional religious practice; for the latter, they remain divided by the words of Bishop Ruiz who, during a visit to a village that opposed the social reforms that he outlined, stated: 'Jesus tells us the path we must take should be different from the path of the powerful, the people who build their own strength by taking away what others have.'[261]

A Theology of Chiapas

By now it must be clear to the reader that God acts within the history of humans and that the salvific events that marked his intervention for liberation and his preference for the poor and the marginalized are also present within the struggle by the Christian communities in particular and by civil society in Chiapas. The general situation of violence and the 'cycle of violence' increased with the Zapatista action; however, it was exacerbated by the Mexican Army and the increasing repression against the indigenous communities and particularly the women of Chiapas.

On 22 December 1997, 32 women and 13 men of the Tzotzil community were brutally murdered in what became known as 'the Acteal Massacre', by paramilitary forces linked to the official party, the Revolutionary Institutional Party (PRI).[262] The brutality of the killings and the despicable acts against the unborn provided a chilling reminder of the horrible crimes that human beings can commit in the name of peace and stability, and the actual desecration of women's bodies resembled the methods for spreading fear used previously by the Guatemalan Army and those trained at military camps in the United

States.[263] However, the fact that more than 30 paramilitary groups roamed freely within Chiapas while Bishop Ruiz was trying to mediate a ceasefire speaks of a low-intensity war in which, as in many other places, civilians and particularly women, are especially at risk.[264]

The situation of the indigenous populations has not improved, threatening their cultural existence, while the presence of 60,000 federal military troops, located at 30 military centres, has meant in reality that the notion of economic growth and competition for markets has not reached Chiapas. The budget of those soldiers was calculated at 200 million dollars while the situation of conflict and violence had created by the year 2000 a situation where 21,000 displaced citizens lived within 13 municipalities of Chiapas. In summary, there is one member of the army per ten civilians in Chiapas. Those belonging to support groups for the Zapatista experienced persecution and most of them were women, owing to the fact that 40 per cent of the 25,000-strong Zapatista Army were women.

The context of this crisis resembles that of neighbouring Guatemala in the 1980s, when in the name of peace and development the centralized government annihilated indigenous populations, tortured and raped, with the excuse of fighting a war against insurgents and their sympathizers, probably most of the population of Guatemala who wanted some basic human rights and a better future for their children. The responses of the Church in Chiapas have been consistent with that of a servant church that accompanies, comforts and provides the tools and means for education, supports communal gatherings and analyses the social context in order to provide basic sociological facts of what is happening. However, with the retirement of Bishop Ruiz, the task of theologizing has been left practically in the hands of Christian communities and of women, because they take daily the first step of acting in solidarity with others, while, in a second step, they reflect around the Eucharist on the possibilities of realizing the Kingdom within a situation of poverty, displacement, persecution and hunger.

Bishop Ruiz created a new model of involvement by the

Christian communities in that he took them out of their bases and allowed them to become the periphery rather than the centre. This process is reminiscent of that lived by Leonardo Boff with the movement of those without land who with the support of the Brazilian Basic Christian Communities created a theology of peripherical issues in which the God of the periphery chooses to dwell among those who are not necessarily linked to the Church. It is interesting that Archbishop Romero had these kinds of discussions with some of his priests who were living with guerrilla groups. Romero never allowed himself to move out of the centre, as Pedro Casaldáliga did, but he allowed the possibility that the periphery had something to offer, and I wonder whether he would not have been assassinated if he had eventually moved to the periphery.

Bishop Ruiz's theological model remains very similar to that advocated by those articulating the place of the Christ vis-à-vis the world religions, for example, Paul Knitter. Instead of arguing for an exclusivist approach, Knitter argues for a non-traditional, theological mode of existence, in which the Christ, the ultimate centre of all theological action and discourse, can choose to move somewhere else and not necessarily consider the Church as the only vehicle and indeed place for salvation. Thus, God can choose to save within Hinduism or Islam because it is part of his attribute to save and to love within that larger reality of the Kingdom of God which is certainly larger than the Church. Ruiz accepted the mysteriousness of God's actions so that, without understanding the reason behind it, he was able to journey with the people of Chiapas, considering them to be agents of their own destiny. Ruiz provided the tools and the physical space for the Christian communities and involved them in a utopian Christian pilgrimage towards love and towards God that could not exclude others, and therefore the Christian communities, while condemning violence, loved and supported others, even the Zapatistas. The context and analysis of the local situation was very clear: God does not support oppression and injustice, thus he could not support the feudal possession of land, the violence exercised by the army, the intimidation and crushing of indigenous populations or the murders and rapes carried out in the name of security and peace.

The Christ of Ruiz is a Christ who opts to be on the periphery and decides to remain with those who suffer, even when it would be easier to step out of the human mess of violence and greed. The Christ of Ruiz, as that of Leonardo Boff, is a liberator because he allows those who suffer to be loved and to be supported; he gives them the dignity and the humanity that racist voices deny them by suggesting that indigenous populations are less able to be human and that they are lesser beings within society. The Christ of Ruiz is a Latin American Christ because, in the fullness of a cosmological revelation that applies to all and that embraces all, he remains as he did on the periphery of Galilee, with those who seek justice and seek peace in the midst of history. History and politics meet because the situation of Chiapas brings us back to the same dilemmas faced 500 years ago by the Conquistadors and the indigenous populations during the European genocide of the periphery, at that time a global periphery. If characters such as Bishop Bartolomé de las Casas spoke against the annihilation of the indigenous periphery, they achieved centuries later what they wanted: the periphery of Latin America has become the place of theological thinking because it is the Latin American continent that houses the majority of Christians in the world and remains peripheral to the normative and oppressive discourses of a consumerist God who seems to love the individual and does not ask for risks or peripheral dreams. That God rejected by Las Casas and Ruiz is still the God of war and the God of thunder, the God of the Old Testament, to be superseded by new things and new understandings coming out of the gentile world and of the situation in Chiapas.

For it is in Chiapas that the dialogue and cooperation between theology and civil society reaches a high moment, a moment that has been present in the spirituality of the theology of Pedro Casaldáliga, subject of the next chapter. It is in Chiapas that one can find the fruits of a Latin American theology of liberation for the twenty-first century because it is in Chiapas that the God of Life has chosen to accompany the poor and the oppressed within the advent of the new millennium. For it is in Chiapas that the God of history does not condemn the possibilities of civil society, on the contrary, the God of all sustains women and their civil organizations in a search for new ways of acting on behalf of the God who has a preference: the poor, the oppressed and the marginalized. The constraints of the male God of Europe unleashes the power of liberation and salvation within the context of the Maya bipolar unity of the male and the female and by the power of Latin American women, after all the majority of Christian practitioners within the continent. Thus, it is becoming obvious through this theological investigation on context that a *theology of the periphery* supplies the continuity between the old and the new, between theological generations and between chronological centuries.

In the next chapter, I explore the theological aesthetics and spirituality of a theologian of the periphery, Pedro Casaldáliga.

Part 3

Contemporary Issues

7

Pedro Casaldáliga

The theological narratives arising out of the commemorations in 1992 of 500 years of Christian presence in Latin America brought the work of Diego Irarrázaval into the forum of a possible further encounter between indigenous perceptions of the world and of the divine and Christian narratives that could describe in a hermeneutical manner the presence of God, past and present, and the future work of God, within Latin America.[265] More attention has been paid to the systematic conceptualization of inculturation than to the contextual liberalization of the social actions and social aesthetics of the process in relation to the indigenous populations and the actions of God.

Pedro Casaldáliga becomes part of the last structural section of this book, a section that examines some of the present continuities between the generations but more forcefully argues for a process of theological rupture, rupture that through a dialectic comparison and a hermeneutical departure from Gutiérrez or Dussel explores new avenues for the twenty-first century. Casaldáliga represents continuity because he served as a bishop of the Catholic Church throughout the whole formative period of liberation theology and at the same time retired at the time when new globalized works on the environment, Amazonia and the warming of the planet became central not only to theology but to the governments of the powerful nations as well. Casaldáliga brings the freshness of the periphery to Latin American theology; he remained in his rural Amazonian diocese and he remained in the contemplation of God and his creation, writing poetry and enjoying the journey with his people. If Latin American theologians seem angry commentators on social realities, Casaldáliga brings spirituality and the joy of conversation with God into theology so that theology as faith seeking understanding arises out of spirituality; in the case of Casaldáliga, out of a spirituality of liberation.

The Brazilian Context

Brazil was the first Latin American country to promote the formation of the Basic Christian Communities, the reading of the Bible at all levels and the involvement of the Catholic Church within the ongoing social realities of ordinary people; however, the 1964 military coup focused most of the Church's attention on a repressive situation rather than on a creative one. It is difficult to know, for example, if the Brazilian church would have grown so much after Vatican II and Medellín without that experience of a military dictatorship but certainly Brazilian Catholics were more active in socio-political life than those of Argentina or Chile at the time of Vatican II and therefore at the time of the military coup.[266]

In March 1964, a military coup supported by civilian conspirators deposed President João Goulart and started an authoritarian system of government whereby the president was designated by the army and approved by the Brazilian congress.[267] The system, with periodical moves from mild liberalism to further authoritarianism, was to last until 1985 when the first attempts were made to pass legislation that allowed the direct election of the Brazilian president and the control of the budget to be restored to the national congress.[268] Therefore the most seminal years of Boff's theological thinking took place while the Brazilian State was arresting and torturing dissenters and within a continuous political game of considerable violence between the police, the guerrillas and some right-wing paramilitary groups. Brazilian security and interrogation advisors were provided to other emerging military regimes, such as the Chilean military in 1973, and Brazil also supported the work of the Southern Cone intelligence forces through the Operación Cóndor.[269]

Casaldáliga was part of a very active Catholic Church with prominent personalities such as Cardinal Evaristo Arns (São Paulo) and Archbishop Helder Cámara (Recife and Olinda), and he became part of a revered generation of Brazilian bishops.[270] The Brazilian Basic Christian Communities united in a large movement, known as the 'popular movement', asked questions not only about social, economic and political participation in Brazil but also about the democratization of the Catholic Church and the creation of a 'popular Church'.[271] Within those challenges, large sectors of the Brazilian church's hierarchy became active in politics and, as was to be the case in Chile, the Catholic Church in Brazil became one of the few voices of dissent towards subsequent authoritarian regimes.[272] Thus, over a period of 30 years from the formation of the National Bishops' Conference of Brazil (CNBB) in October 1952, the Catholic Church changed its view of the world and chose to be politically involved in the name of the gospel.[273]

With the end of the military regimes, the Basic Christian Communities became involved in national movements that supported the landless, the problems of recuperation of the Amazonian forest, and the preservation of ecological areas threatened by multinational corporations and their enormous overexploitation of natural resources that had previously been privatized and sold to multinational companies by the military. Casaldáliga was part of that ecological crisis because he lived in a diocese that was part of the Brazilian Amazonian basin and his pastoral concerns involved the daily lives of the indigenous community vis-à-vis growing urban centres that resembled colonial enclaves of transient populations and forgotten worlds. Casaldáliga's preoccupation with Latin America came out of his own involvement with the world of the Amazon and over the 2000 jubilee year the Amazon became part of the preoccupation of a universal humanity concerned not about others' welfare but concerned with its own survival as a species. In the words of Casaldáliga 'the inventory of iniquity' by transnational corporations includes the destruction of the Amazonian forest:

'The beautiful mother Earth', as Francis of Assissi would say, is being brutally violated. Its products are no longer natural, they are transgenic. And just in our Brazil, in only one year, 16,838 square kilometres were deforested. And in Amazonia the equivalent of seven thousand football fields of trees are cut down every day. One fourth of the surface of the land is under the threat to become a desert.[274]

Those concerns, social, religious and political, shaped the life of the young Claretian priest who arrived in Brazil at a time when a new world and a new society was being shaped not only by the conflicts of the Cold War but also by the hopes of a new socialist utopia throughout Latin America and within the Catholic Church.

An Amazonian Bishop

Pedro Casaldáliga was born in Balsareny, Catalonia, Spain in 1928, the son of a farm worker. He was ordained as a priest in Montjuich, Barcelona, on 31 May 1952. A member of the Claretians, he served as Catholic bishop of the diocese of São Félix do Araguaia, Brazil, from 1971 to 2004.[275]

Why Brazil? At the Claretian Congregation general chapter of 1967 members of that religious congregation evaluated their own response to the recently concluded Second Vatican Council (1962–65). As a result, Casaldáliga was given the option of going overseas, either to Bolivia or Brazil. Following the advice of the Claretian Superior General Peter Schweiger he opted for the latter and on 28 January 1968 Casaldáliga arrived in Brazil, in a year in which the Latin American bishops met at Medellín (Colombia) and the Institutional Act (A15) cemented the military regime in Brazil. In July 1968, he arrived in São Félix do Araguaia during one of the fiercest periods of political repression and over the years he helped to start a Pastoral Commission for Land (Comissão Pastoral da Terra – CPT) and an indigenous missionary council (Conselho Indigenista Missionário – CIMI) within a territory in which social conflicts over land are usual and quite violent.[276] His diocese, located within the Brazilian state of Mato Grosso, was the size of Catalonia and had 120,000 people living in the territory.

There is no doubt that Casaldáliga loved his pastoral work in Brazil and he became a Brazilian not by birth or adoption but by social experience.[277] Casaldáliga, the poet, addressed many poems, songs and letters to Brazil, as a diverse group of people, as a fervent mass of dancing human beings who live in noise and in community. Towards the end of his service as a bishop, for example, Casaldáliga wrote:

> You, Brazil, have a clear call to give a lead; not, of course, in the sense of being a leading power, but of leading in service in solidarity, of setting a coherent example, of providing brotherly encouragement, in our America most specifically but also to a certain extent in relationship with other countries of the so-called Third World, especially with certain African peoples (from whom you also derive and to whom you should return in solidarity). To do so, your first task is clearly to become more Latin American yourself. You often feel yourself to be somehow set apart, like a sort of autonomous continent. Never forget that you are America, my Brazil – Latin America, Amerindia, Afro-America, and our America![278]

His first pastoral letter, dated 23 October 1971, provided a full evaluation of the social conflicts within his diocese and included a call to all to increase their Christian commitment to the gospel through justice and peace work in the context of the private ownership of land and social conflict vis-à-vis the need for agrarian reform.[279] Throughout his episcopal life, he lived very simply in a house that resembled every other house, usually open to the passer-by and to the people around him. In 1976, he survived a serious attempt on his life when the bullet aimed at him killed the Jesuit priest João Bosco Burnier who was beside him. That incident was to mark the life of his diocese and yearly a diocesan pilgrimage departed to the place where Burnier had been killed, a place that became a place of memory, martyrdom and devotion for all the victims of the political violence within the diocese.[280] In his own assessment, Casaldáliga recognized that the difficulties between him and the local government were a product of the fact that he lived close to the territory where the guerrillas of Araguaia operated. The Brazilian Army, Air Force, Navy and police carried out four major war operations against the guerrillas by surrounding the territory occupied by Casaldáliga's diocese and by arresting people, some of whom were tortured. Many of them were members of the Basic Christian Communities, and Casaldáliga denounced the military operation. As a result, the Brazilian Government tried to expel him from the country five times. However, Pope Paul VI was very clear in this matter and told Mgr Paulo Evaristo Arns to let the Brazilian Government know that any hostile act against Casaldáliga would be considered as an attack on the Pope and the Vatican. Casaldáliga did not have to leave the country but he was kept under house arrest.

After the military regime ended in Brazil, Casaldáliga had to deal with the land owners and the increasing privatization of lands, a product of the free-market economy embraced by Brazil. There were many warnings that if he continued interfering something very serious could happen to him. It never did: in the words of Casaldáliga 'because his hour had not come and God wanted him to mature as a human being'.[281]

In 2003, he sent his letter of resignation to the Pope, as expected of all Catholic bishops who reach the age of 75, having been diagnosed with Parkinson's disease and high blood pressure.[282] His episcopal succession was made conditional on his settlement as bishop emeritus outside his diocese in order not to interfere with the new bishop who was to be appointed, a fact that was challenged by the pastoral council that also complained about the fact that they didn't have any say in the appointment of a new bishop. At that moment, Casaldáliga's dream would have been to visit Africa and to pray with Africans in solidarity with the rest of the world, but his health did not allow him to go. Nevertheless he made a conscious decision to remain in Brazil and not to return to his native Catalonia.

The episcopal succession was a difficult moment for all because the general suspicion, aided by the contemporary experience of the appointment of traditional bishops all over Latin America, was that John Paul II would appoint somebody with a very different idea of the pastoral priorities and engagement of the Church with contemporary society. After many letters, challenges and misunderstandings, John Paul II appointed a Franciscan Friar Leonardo Ulrich Steiner as new bishop of São Félix do Araguaia. Casaldáliga called the new bishop 'a true Franciscan, fraternal, open to dialogue, interested in the people' and that settled the matter.[283] Casaldáliga remained near the banks of the river Araguaia supporting in his old age the life of those around him.

A Passion for Utopia

One of his few public appearances outside his pastoral work, as Casaldáliga preferred to pray, to write and to share with the people of his diocese and to remain 'on the red soil', was on 24 October 2000.[284] On that day he was awarded a doctorate *honoris causa* by the State University of Campinas in Brazil.[285] After the award was conferred, he gave a lecture that summarized his own life and his own gratitude to those who had worked with him over many years. On that occasion, he spoke of his passion for utopia and suggested that passion was the only possible reason for the important university degree awarded to him.

For Casaldáliga described himself as out of fashion, in a contemporary world of pragmatisms, productivity, full-market economies, and postmodernity. His passion, he commented, was always the Kingdom of God, as it was the passion of Christ that coincides with the aspirations of all humanity for a fully human life, an authentic life that is fully happy.[286] The utopia of God and his love is to proclaim a place in this world for all and a place for all in the next world. If only 20 per cent of people have access to world commodities and the majority are excluded, Casaldáliga's utopia was to proclaim once and again that God wants all to have a place in the universal history that comes out of the here and now. Citing the work of Marciano Vidal on a universal ethics, Casaldáliga pointed to three ethical ways that prepare the Church and every Christian for a new millennium:

1 a pure vision, meaning the possibility for every human being to appreciate reality without self-interest and without prejudices;
2 a compassionate empathy, meaning an ongoing solidarity with the weak of this world; and
3 a simple lifestyle, in order to create alternative values to those of the complex contemporary world.

The twenty-first century manifesto for all is the Sermon on the Mount, where those who are blessed are those who follow human attitudes that are very different from the contemporary canon of profit, self-importance and of a world considered real and tangible in which God and the Kingdom of God do not have a place, a time or social influence.

Casaldáliga in his acceptance speech at the University of Campinas proclaimed once again the possibility, not a passive one, of proclaiming hope against all hope, without a religious passivity or a belief in electoral and political promises. Thus, this challenge, he maintained, is not for those who are satisfied with the neo-liberal McDonald's or those who have packed their flags and gone home defeated. Playing with words and the Brazilian phenomenon of *caminada*, the walk, and the pilgrimage used to request land and rights by civil society, Casaldáliga assured his audience that the pilgrimage continued and that thousands continued in hope, walking, singing and clapping. That included the university, not at the service of the system but a university at the service of life, at the service of the dispossessed and not the oligarchy, a university that should be pluricultural, political and militant in the defence of the marginalized of society. He proposed to start a new movement of those outside the university (Movimento dos Sem Universidade –

MSU) because utopias start with a thought and a common consciousness and those thoughts are triggered at the universities. Casaldáliga wanted a utopian university! For him utopia is dream, is stimulus, is service; we are the road and we are the end of history through the fact that all human beings have a divine gene, a divine DNA which points to humanity rather than profit. The fulfilment of that utopia is not the crucifixion but the resurrection because human beings who live in hope are the resurrection and are the human utopia fulfilled in God's actions.

Casaldáliga's utopian dream of a more just society closer to the values of the Kingdom of God and his own aesthetic sociability and literary life does not have a hint of escapism. For his theological narrative of utopianism unveils a certainty that he associates with the resurrection. 'I believe in the Resurrection', he proclaims, but he qualifies such optimism with the following personal assertion: 'Every act of faith in resurrection has to have a corresponding act of justice, of service, of solidarity, of love.'[287] His utopia remained a clear condemnation of capitalism as an economic system and he remained supportive of the Cuban revolution because, in his own words, 'God never left Cuba, he remained there.'[288] Socialism could be outdated as a system vilified by the West but in Casaldáliga's terms socialism with a utopian sharing and a clear human equality remains a close system to gospel values, the values of sharing symbolized by the multiplication of the two loaves and the fish for a multitude. Those actions are not materialistic actions but they constitute expressions of a way of life, of a way of encountering God, they remain expressions of a personal and communal spirituality shared by all Christians. Thus, for a busy bishop and an extrovert disciple of life and poetry, discussions on a Latin American spirituality as a way to God became central to his own pilgrimage as a Christian within the world of Amazonia and the world of the riverside Araguaia.

From the Inside to the Outside

Casaldáliga's common attempt with José María Vigil to frame a spirituality of liberation for the unfinished summa of Latin American theological works represents the inner need of personal testimony and ascension.[289] For many, Latin American theology had nothing to do with the spiritual but with the world of action, and even Gutiérrez' work on a Latin American spirituality was not given the same prominence as his other works.[290] Even in the case of Ernesto Cardenal, poet and contemplative, the emphasis of the literature was always on the minister and the public figure of the Nicaraguan Sandinistas (see Volume 1). However, Casaldáliga's life and theological plan connects directly with the life of the three Jesuits discussed in the first part of this book. For him, it is the inside of the person, the spiritual self that connects with the outside world and through utopian moments of self-awareness challenges the possibility of a non-spiritual world of the material and of matter as the centre of human existence.

Within the history of spirituality, that is, of the different and varied approaches to communication with God and of action within the world, there have been two movements of the human soul signified and represented spatially: from the outside to the inside and vice versa. For the majority of Christians and for the majority of theologians their communication with the God of Life takes places within an active life in which movement and human interaction take most of their daily available hours. Prayer opens and closes the day with conversational spells in which humans try to make sense of life and action around them in relation to a third point of the hermeneutical circle: God. As a result, there is a direct connection and relation between religious practitioners of all faiths and all religions. Others instead, find the sole of their daily life in the inside of themselves and in an ongoing conversation and contemplation of the divine. They do not avoid activities and human interaction but their actions and human interactions come out of a spiritual perspective from the inside. Freer than others from material concerns they relocate God within the spiritual hermeneutical circle to a centre with the human world as a location where they return from time to time during their daily existence.

Casaldáliga remained a contemplative in that he was an active bishop but didn't like to travel, and his whole pastoral perspective came from within. Located within the Amazonia region, he even felt that the visit of all Catholic bishops to Rome in order to report to the Pope (the *ad limina* visit) was not a central point of either his life or, by association, the life of bishops as they tried to serve God.[291] In a sense, Casaldáliga returned to the colonial time of the Jesuits and their reductions and remained within a world that integrated the spiritual and the material by centring all causal explanations on the spiritual world. Casaldáliga felt at home within that reality and, by stressing the importance of the spiritual, didn't avoid the social and the political but, on the contrary, challenged unjust social realities by incorporating a very strong cosmological framework taken from the old tradition of the land (Amazonian life) and the new tradition (Christianity) into his thinking.

In an era in which the majority of people claimed to be spiritual but not necessarily religious, Casaldáliga's contribution to the future of Latin American theology is crucial. His ascent to the mountain of God, a well-known biblical metaphor related to the climbing required for reaching the Jerusalem temple and the metaphor for contemplation used by the Spanish mystic St John of the Cross, outlines his whole life and theological contribution. Action and contemplation came together in his life so that his pastoral work was active, meaningful and intense from a life of contemplation of God's creation and the tranquillity of the mystic that experiences God in the beauty of nature and longs for that emotion to become action and not vice versa. Thus, Casaldáliga, a Spaniard, treasured the poems of St John of the Cross and the Carmelite tradition of ascent towards Mount Carmel in a contextual way so as to write:

If he [John of the Cross] had been a modern Latin American and had lived through the continental councils of Medellín,

Puebla and Santo Domingo, John of the Cross might well –
without betraying either holiness or poetry or orthodoxy –
have written, as one possibility, the 'Ascent of Machu-Pichu':
the ascent and the descent . . .[292]

Within that personal spiritual journey towards God Casaldáliga recognized that there were economic mistakes being
made in Amazonia, particularly the increased cultivation of
cotton and soya bean. It was because of his heightened spiritual
journey into contemplation that he became conscious that the
social conscience of the indigenous populations and of the
Christian communities would make possible an ongoing challenge to the poor fruits of economic globalization. Ever an
optimist, Casaldáliga encouraged people to take part and to
support what he called 'social movements', what in this work I
call 'civil society', thus encouraging the solidarity and action of
Christians within wider organizations and within alliances that
could embrace the majority of Christians of Brazil and civil
organizations concerned with single issues of socio-political
significance such as land and ecological issues. It is for these
reasons that Casaldáliga, without being in an academic setting,
encouraged the ongoing development of a Latin American
theology for the twenty-first century, a theology closely allied
with social actions in the name of the values and attitudes
required by God in order to bring people closer to the values
and ethical attitudes represented in the Gospels through the
Kingdom of God.

In one of his latest pastoral letters, and one of the shortest,
that of August 2006, he narrated the pilgrimage to the martyrs
of the *caminhada* at the shrine of Ribeirão Cascalheira on the
occasion of the thirtieth anniversary of the martyrdom of Fr
João Bosco Penido Burnier. By that time a new bishop had been
appointed to replace him but he was still in Araguaia and he
thanked many people who had written to him wishing him well
and thanking him for years of companionship. Casaldáliga
reminded them that the pilgrimage was not finished and that the
central symbol of such *caminhada* continued to be the presence

of martyrs within the region and within the communities.[293] It is that subversive martyrdom that remains the sign of the Kingdom within a Latin America that faced several presidential elections of some importance in Brazil, Chile and Ecuador.

For Casaldáliga, it was good that there was a vote but he wrote sharply, 'you can vote but you cannot be', meaning that even when finally Latin Americans could vote in the democratic polls their opinion didn't count as much as in the past because of all the economic policies implemented within contemporary globalization.[294] In his writings about the assassinated archbishop of El Salvador, Oscar Romero, Casaldáliga considered him central to the life and to the spiritual life of Latin Americans because of his prophetic vision and because of his life with and for the poor; however, he assessed the recent changes in Latin America as follows: 'from a national security state ordered and controlled by the military to the trans-national security capital, from the military dictatorships to the macro-dictatorship of the neo-liberal empire'.[295]

One of the characteristics shared by the Brazilian bishops such as Casaldáliga and Romero was the possibility of remaining part of the institutional Church and at the same time open to the Spirit, open to learning from the poor, open to the possible dangers of assuming that everything in society was fine and that profit and the markets had to be at the centre of human life and of human existence. The poverty of Romero and of Casaldáliga was the poverty of those who recognize that God is at the centre and the rest is secondary, the poverty of the Spirit to trust in hope that even if society seems to be collapsing all together God is at the centre of the lives of all within a community-oriented pilgrimage towards God. For Casaldáliga the Church needs to confront the different kinds of terrorism, a phenomenon that didn't start with the attacks on New York and Washington DC on 9/11, but a phenomenon that appears everywhere when another human being is attacked by a single thief or by a system that confronts a human being with violence and terror. He proposed three concrete challenges for the Church that could connect the Church with the challenges of a contemporary world: world decentralization, responsible participation, and dialogue in solidarity.[296] For the Church must bring hope to a world that has proclaimed 'the death of God', 'the end of humanity' and 'the end of history' by reminding all that God is still there and that there have been a wide variety of terrorisms throughout the ages.

For Casaldáliga, hope lies within humanity, within human beings and their hopes because God created this world and these human beings.[297] Hope does not lie within war machines or security strategies, for his assessment of the first years of the new millennium communicate a sobering picture of events but a very hopeful human challenge embraced already by many. Thus, Casaldáliga wrote:

> Two years of the new 21st century have already passed and the world continues to be cruel and in solidarity, unjust and hopeful. There is still war and there is still empire, and empire has invented preventative war. The world is still divided into at least three: First, Third, and Fourth. Hunger, poverty, corruption and violence have increased; but conscience, protest, organization, and the explicit will for alternatives have also increased.[298]

Within that mixed picture of insecurity and hope Casaldáliga continued speaking about another kind of terrorism, that spelled out by the United Nations Secretary General Kofi Annan, as systematic and tolerated, the terrorism of poverty created and sustained by the privileged nations unto all citizens of other, less privileged nations.[299] Further, Casaldáliga's hope was very recently expressed through his conviction that the twenty-first century would be a mystical and ecological century and that as many empires have collapsed so the American empire would collapse within this century.[300] That his statement could sound very subversive and problematic is because Casaldáliga embraces the absolute and non-negotiable centrality of the Kingdom of God and the immediate need to go left, to turn crisis into realities and to remain alive within Christianity, alive with challenges, with prayers, within a world that is on the make and needs to be shaped within God's love, solidarity and justice rather than within profit, markets and military security.[301] It is indeed a utopian world, a revolutionary world of mysticism and ideas, that has enough members and enough authority as to confront makers of worlds of poverty, injustice and inequality.

Despite those routinely addressed issues that could relate Christians of Brazil to other world concerns one of Casaldáliga's main aims was always to encourage the participation of lay people within the Catholic Church and particularly the lay ministries of women within the Church. In the following chapter, I examine the work of an academic theologian and a woman who, through her own personal experience and her writings, has challenged the place of theology as solely located within the churches and has expanded feminist narratives into narratives of inclusion for all from the perspective lived by women and by women outside the North Atlantic hegemonic theological axis of exclusion.

8

Marcella Althaus-Reid

During the 1990s, there was a decrease in the numbers of new works on Latin American theology published after the completion of *Mysterium Liberationis*.[302] The different local crises within the Latin American states meant that there was theology done on the ground but that the outside world, that is, the United States and Europe, had fewer works translated from the Spanish and Portuguese, and only theologians from the first generation continued to be read within academic circles of the English-, French- and German-speaking worlds.

However, it was in the mid-1990s that Marcella Althaus-Reid, an Argentinean, started her sustained production of a liberation theology that linked theology with forces that were being unleashed outside the churches, related to theology and sexuality as a critique of an earlier liberation theology and of feminism in its earlier representations. Her book *Indecent Theology* has made her well known in the theological world, and she represents the ongoing possibility of mediating between religion and politics within the central concern of every individual with common human experiences: the need for liberation in issues of gender, personal identity, sexuality and the politics of the control of sexuality within ordered bodies and minds.[303]

Formation of a Theologian

Marcella Althaus-Reid was born in Rosario, Argentina, of parents who did not share the same Christian tradition, one Lutheran, one Catholic, and she was raised in Buenos Aires. She studied at ISEDET (Instituto Superior Evangélico de Estudios Teológicos) in Buenos Aires, where theologians such as J. Severino Croatto and José Míguez Bonino were teaching (on Míguez Bonino, see Volume 1). She trained for the ministry within the Methodist Church and within her first phase of theological engagement she developed expertise in the method of conscientization, a method pioneered by the Brazilian educator and social activist Paulo Freire. She became involved in community projects in deprived areas of Buenos Aires at a time when Argentina had undergone the traumatic experience of a military regime, the Malvinas/Falklands War and a general economic crisis and international isolation.

Twentieth-century Argentinean politics was dominated by the figure of Juan Domingo Perón, and the efforts of his followers, mostly working-class based, to exclude the middle classes from the ongoing running of the nation. However, it is also possible to argue that Argentinean politics were dominated by the Peronist/Anti-Peronist dichotomy with the trade unions forming the social base for the Peronist movement (*sindicalismo peronista*) and the Argentinean Armed Forces pushing for an anti-Peronism narrative for political action.[304] That political and social dichotomy, suppressed for years, came back to the political arena with the return of Perón and his new wife María Estela Martínez de Perón to Argentina (20 June 1973) after 18 years of exile. Subsequently, on 23 September 1973, Perón was elected president of Argentina but he failed to reach an understanding with the trade unions and the business organizations. The situation in Argentina became very violent after a full economic crisis unfolded, inflation rocketed, and, in 1974, the European Common Market closed down meat imports from Argentina.

Moreover, the main political crisis took place within the movement that followed Perón (*peronistas*) in which some revolutionary factions were not happy with his economic practices and the subsequent alliance of Isabel Perón with private businesses that took place after Perón's death in July 1974. In 1975, there was a full economic crisis and the displaced left-wing groups among the followers of Perón, that is, the revolutionary wing of the Peronist Party Montoneros and the Marxist Ejército Revolucionario del Pueblo (ERP), continued the armed struggle with attacks on military barracks, kidnappings of well-to-do people and assassinations. In response to those events the right-wing military groups organized by the Alianza Argentina Anti-Comunista (AAA) targeted opponents, particularly those supporters of the left-wing organizations who because of their positions didn't go into hiding, that is, teachers, lawyers, university professors, medical doctors and middle-class professionals. In previous years, the Minister for Social Welfare, José López Rega, had organized the triple A (AAA) as a neo-fascist group in order to cleanse the Peronist Party of Marxist elements and their supporters and to restore a peaceful state of affairs to Argentina.

As a result of the political chaos and political violence, and encouraged by the experience of the Chilean military, the Argentinean Armed Forces deposed Isabel Perón and took over political power. Argentinean pastoral agents suffered heavy casualties owing to sustained political persecution of 'subversives', while the Argentinean bishops did not speak openly about the gross human rights violations by the military junta led by Jorge Videla, who became President of Argentina in March 1976.[305] Other civil organizations, such as the mothers of the disappeared (Madres de la Plaza de Mayo), took a public stand against human rights violations and every Thursday they paraded in silence at Buenos Aires May Square, requesting information about their loved ones who had been arrested, tortured and made to disappear by the repressive state apparatus.[306] The military regime supported an anti-communist pro-American crusade throughout Latin America and remained in power until the war for the Malvinas/Falklands Islands challenged military authority and their capability of leading the Argentinean nation in the future.[307] On 30 October 1983, the Radical Party won 51.75 per cent of the total vote and, on 10 December 1983, Raúl Alfonsín became the new democratically elected president of Argentina.[308]

Althaus-Reid had the opportunity to connect with some projects within deprived areas of Dundee and Perth (Scotland), and left Argentina, having freshly experienced the trauma of political upheaval. As many of those who left their own country because of political circumstances she started a new life in Scotland with the inherent difficulties of explaining to others that she had a degree in theology rather than a professional qualification or a manual skill. She met Dr Daphne Hampson (later Professor Daphne Hampson), a well-known feminist theologian teaching at St Mary's College, University of St Andrews, however, and with her encouragement Althaus-Reid decided to pursue a doctorate in divinity under Hampson's supervision.[309] She completed her PhD in 1993 with a thesis entitled 'Paul Ricoeur and the methodology of the theology of liberation: The hermeneutics of J. Severino Croatto, Juan Luis Segundo and Clodovis Boff'. Shortly after, she was appointed to a lectureship in theology at New College, University of Edinburgh, and became Director of the Master in Theology programme in theology and development, and has occupied the Chair in Contextual Theology at the same college since 2006.

From Hermeneutics to Indecency

As outlined by Althaus-Reid, her theological development mirrored her movements between universities, in that her doctoral work reflects theologically on the methodology and hermeneutics of Latin American theology as she encountered it in Argentina. She advanced the problem of the 'hermeneutics of suspicion' by challenging the isolation of hermeneutical methodologies and relating Latin America to the influence of Ricoeur and his interpretive principles which treated society as a text and text as social action. Indeed, there has been a close connection at different levels of social interpretation between the work of Ricoeur and the social sciences, including, for example, social anthropology, the history of art and the study of ritual and cosmologies in African societies.[310]

Because of her educational circumstances, Althaus-Reid moved very quickly from a Latin American perspective of theological methodology, a study expected within a doctoral programme, to her ongoing challenges as a woman, as a foreigner and as a scholar, within an academic world, which in Scotland was predominantly male and certainly very closely linked to the churches and to a history of dialogical distrust between the host and immigrant communities. Her initial post-doctoral essays combine her theological preoccupation with Latin America and feminist theology, the role of women within the ministerial office of the churches, and the possibility of establishing a place for the outcasts and marginalized, including women, within the churches.[311] However, instead of following in the steps of Daphne Hampson, namely, locating the cultural and philosophical discourses on women vis-à-vis the patriarchal Church and the patriarchal God, Althaus-Reid created a theological reading that not only relocated the possibility of piety and sexuality but also relocated the possibility of a God at the margins who needed to be unleashed from ecclesiastical control.[312] It must be remembered that Daphne Hampson had decided to challenge intellectually the possibility of the uniqueness of Christianity, a challenge that had isolated her from her male colleagues as well as from the camp of feminist theologians who remained Christians and were looking for a way forward regarding ministerial offices for women within the churches and for an equal role for women within a theological anthropology, and the diverse experiences of Christianity at large in the world. Thus, Hampson wrote:

The argument is that Christians must – by definition, if Christianity is to mean anything – claim that there has been a particularity in history; that is to say that there was a uniqueness present in the Christ event. However, at least since the eighteenth-century Enlightenment it has been known that there can be no such particularity. (I shall argue that modern physics does not make the Christian claim any more possible.) Thus Christian belief becomes a matter of faith.[313]

It is essential to understand that assertion by Hampson in order to appreciate the possibility that, within the context of an over-controlling European systematic theology within the schools of divinity in Scotland, Althaus-Reid's feminist critique was concerned solely with certain theological claims made by Christianity in which there are clearly patriarchal understandings that can change within the overarching vehicle of faith in God and in the *kerygma* of the early Church. Instead, Althaus-Reid does not engage with philosophical arguments but explores the religious experience of Latin America and decides to exchange the symbolic, emotional and human emotions of Latin American popular religiosity for the feelings and emotions of a Latin habitat in which men and women fall in love, loving encounters of different kinds take place, women flirt, men fall in love and in between the two states are many different kinds of emotional involvement that last or that constitute a short enjoyment of life. Thus, Althaus-Reid relates the possibility of a theological methodology that looks at experience and searches for theologians who are in places outside churches, as well as within churches. Her theology of transgression and of transgressive modes of existence is only so because ecclesiastical canons have dictated that feelings and emotions have to be under control and under the control of particular groups of clerics, and within a hetero-sexual world.[314]

Althaus-Reid asks a very interesting question that would have never occurred to me – but after all I am a very traditional Chilean theologian, and a product of those clerical and militaristic societies described by her. At the start of her argument for an indecent theology, she asks about the possibility that a theologian is constrained by decency, by an activity that sometimes has very little to do with real life, with politics and with sexuality. In her example, she contrasts a lemon vendor on the streets of Buenos Aires with an Argentinean theologian. It is possible for the Argentinean lemon vendor to sell lemons without wearing underwear but, she asks, could an Argentinean theologian sit down to write theology without underwear? The metaphor, or social reality, points to the possibility that the writing of theology with or without underwear is constrained or conditioned by a patriarchal system that has imposed a certain decency, an ecclesiastical system that, over centuries, has told women, and women theologians, what to do, and what to write about, a system later reinforced by the military regimes of Latin America.

Althaus-Reid's methodology is outlined very clearly as an exploration of transgression and indecency, as an exploration of human sexuality and the connections between theology and sexuality but always arising out of peoples' experiences and peoples' lives, out of a context in which her narratives, social and individual, resemble human narratives of God's creatures walking, eating, dancing and embracing each other in the streets, the bars and the margins of a lively and human Latin America. Within that theological milieu the poor and the marginalized, including women, have faith but also have pleasure, emotion and feelings: human beings remain sexual beings and human beings at the same time. Referring to that Argentinean theologian of her previous comparison she writes:

> Her task maybe to deconstruct a moral order which is based on a heterosexual construction of reality, which organizes not only categories of approved social and divine interactions but of economic ones too. The Argentinean theologian would like then to remove her underwear to write theology with feminist honesty, not forgetting what it is to be a woman when dealing with theological and political categories. I should call such a theologian, indecent, and her reflection, Indecent Theology.[315]

Her theological reflections come out of the margins of a Latin American theology in which the sole context for doing theology during the first generation was inside the churches and the Christian communities. Therefore, she departs from the feminist critique by women theologians of Latin America and expands her landscape to other unexplored areas of human sentiment and life and to other unexplored landscapes within the urban centres of Latin America, where the margins have their own life and their own spaces. For women theologians of Latin America had focused their efforts within their criticism of a patriarchal society portrayed by the Bible within either a new biblical hermeneutics (see Elsa Tamez in Volume 1) or a general reconstruction of a male/female world more akin to indigenous societies within Latin America and the inclusion of women as equal partners within lay ministries, the struggle for liberation and the Basic Christian Communities.[316]

The change of context for Latin American theology is not a contradictory one as between the coordinates north–south or east–west lies a fuller topographical coverage of social realities associated with different cultural and specific parameters of social, human and sexual existence. For 'sexuality is an unnatural conceptualisation of identities in struggle' so that there is a gap between liberation theology and postcolonial theology to be filled with 'identity and consciousness', and there is a gap between feminist liberation theology and indecent theology to be negotiated through 'sexual honesty'.[317] Within her expansion of an indecent theology, Althaus-Reid develops a sexual political theology by using a multi-disciplinary approach that includes sexual theory, postcolonial criticism, queer studies and queer theology, Marxist studies, continental philosophy and systematic theology.

Her full work provides a re-reading of social realities that seem not to fit within the canonical paradigms of Christianity. As well as a criticism of the narrowness of theology within Latin American *machismo* and patriarchy, however, Althaus-Reid explores the possibility of the use of social stories of an explicit sexual nature in order that the social context might be read theologically. The 'other' as object of study becomes the agent, the writer and the producer of a social reality in which narratives from the margins not only speak of God's realities but also provide textual and social narratives so far ignored by Latin American theologians. Those social narratives are expressed in stories, laughter, teasing, texts read by the poor and by a general sociability that sometimes is sexually explicit and less repressed and conditioned than within the sociability of the economically affluent or well-educated or indeed among the heterosexual majority.[318]

Theology and Latin American theology is described by Althaus-Reid as a passionate affair where those involved want to engage with a God that is alive, a God who has feelings and love for all. In doing so, the love of God comes above the love of families, security and stability, and theologians, academic and otherwise, risk their own security for the ultimate prize: God's embrace. Political commitment is therefore expressed within a human language, the language of lovers, the language so much associated in the past with contemplatives, mystics and particularly female contemplatives who in their own words gave themselves and their lives to God, their love and their spouse. Of course, Althaus-Reid expands the possibility of loving God to all the realms of varied sexualities but writes with the beauty attached to the Spanish poets and to those who have loved and therefore have forgotten any other reality at that time of intensity and passion. She writes:

> We could use a sexual metaphor to describe that passionate commitment which risked so much for the love of a God of Justice: the illicit lovers who risk everything for a furtive embrace, not because they do not value the opinions of co-workers or family and friends, but because their desire is intense, and carries that of life in itself. Moreover, because their passion for a committed theology was driven by the very nature of desire, it carries within itself the duplicity of creation and chaos.[319]

One of the main criticisms made by Althaus-Reid of liberation theology, meaning within this work the first generation, is that the stories of the Bible and their symbolic and salvific contents are always related to a heterosexual world where lesbians and gays are an anomaly. Indeed, the context of the biblical text is that of the centrality of a family, made exclusively by a man and a woman, and their own biological or adopted children.

Liberation theologians of the first generation showed compassion and understanding towards gays and lesbians but didn't include them within their theological adventures because they were, and still are, perceived by a Christian anthropology as anomalies. Indeed, there is a point where not all citizens can be theologians because Christian theologians are heterosexual beings within the parameters of the Church, the Bible and the tradition. Althaus-Reid challenges this view of liberation that excludes some members of society as deviants rather than including them as part of the people of God, as children of God and as journeying with the same God of Life.

The same theological discussion outlined by Althaus-Reid, with a dysfunctional process of differentiation and exclusion, takes place within other contexts in which civil society agrees to the rights of homosexuals to contract civil unions for gay couples and even to adopt children but with the churches exercising a self-exclusion from those civil processes. Without going into other areas of theological discussion one must recognize that Althaus-Reid has in her writings challenged the mere possibility that God would exclude some human beings from life and death because of their sexual orientation. In the end, what is theologically being discussed is not the social or cultural practice of the Church but the characteristics and actions of God within the world. In the words of Althaus-Reid:

> Gender and sexual issues remain conflictive and smoothed over in BCEs [Basic Christian Communities] and in Liberation Theology and where they could have been the issue which provided the challenge to the roots of hierarchical models. Sexual and gender issues are not addenda in the minutes of a meeting, but key epistemological and organisational elements which, if ignored, never allow us to think further and differently.[320]

Her own historical context of an Argentinean dictatorship was full of calls to be straight, to be nationalistic and to be *macho*, so that left-wing guerrillas were publicly associated with gay or feminized men, women leftists had departed from their Christian role of mothers and wives and were deviant within a highly hierarchical Argentinean society commanded by the military and the sexually promiscuous. It is very clear how the Argentinean Church, or at least the majority of the Argentinean bishops, welcomed the possibilities of an established order that the Argentinean military were promising, directly connected to a traditional Christian order and to a traditional sense of father-hood and land given by God to patriots and to their descend-ants, all men of Christianity and order.[321] It is through social texts, through stories and history (the two words have one single word in Spanish *historia*), and the thin boundary between them, that theologizing takes place. The action, the experience comes first within an *orthopraxy* in which the sexuality of all human beings throughout their lives is recognized.

The private sphere of sexual mores, stories and practices becomes for Althaus-Reid the public sphere of common theo-logizing and she challenges the fact that a Latin American feminist theology and the theology by women and for women dealt with such important issues only in the private rather than in the public spheres.[322] The important point made here is that the first place for theologizing human action is the stories and the oral tradition of people that share them daily and that pass them from generation to generation; thus, the theologizing of sexuality and of a sexed Christianity requires a total identifica-tion with people in order to listen to their customs, beliefs and ways of living, all within a general context in which most of these social narrators and their audiences consider themselves Christians and advocate God, the Virgin Mary and the saints at different moments of their social lives. I cannot avoid thinking that the methodology for conscientization of Paulo Freire and the methodology for theologizing sexual existences by Althaus-Reid come very close to the social sciences rather than philo-sophy or philosophical/systematic theology, always understood as bodies of presuppositions and given common understandings that do not allow for the unexpected or for any possible social anomalies that do not fit within textbooks or accepted ideas, mostly European and mostly built up on other peoples' realities and understandings, past and present.

Althaus-Reid's final thoughts about theologians, indecent and systematic, point to a human desire for God, a human desire that for some is mishandled in a desire for food, for money, for lust, but that remains a part of all humans who feel strongly about life and about the divine. Thus, 'Indecent sexual theologies do not need to have teleology, or a system, yet they may be effective as long as they represent the resurrection of the excessive in our contexts, and a passion for organizing the lusty transgressions of political and theological thought.'[323] This is a challenging perspective for Christian theology and significantly new for Latin American theology, unknown and unthinkable for systematic theology, a challenge and a manifesto to postmodernity.

The Relocation of God

Furthermore, the theological challenge by an indecent theology does not end there. May I say that Althaus-Reid's work gets better; it gets frighteningly more interesting by the minute! For if, and only if, there is the possibility of theologizing through the experience of those who have not been considered normative by Christian theology and have even been marginalized by a liberation theology of the first generation, then what has happened to the theology of God as traditionally understood?

Her work on the queerness of God follows her previous theological investigation by asking questions about the nature, location and action of the God of Life within a theological world that resurrects the limits and the excessive as places where to do theology.[324] If the task of liberation theology within the Latin American context was to help workers, church or party workers, to discern God's life within their social struggles and indeed within all areas of life and of oppression, the task of those ordinary theologians included places where the first generation of liberation theologians did not go. At least we know that they didn't go to gay bars or dancing places where gay and lesbians searched for friends and possible relationships as heterosexual people would do maybe in a café, a bar, a dance floor or a discothèque. The fact is that humanly speaking there is no difference between a heterosexual or a gay theologian as a human person in love with God; well, there is a difference in that ecclesiastical understandings do not include gay or lesbian relations among those blessed by the Catholic Church and by part of the Anglican Communion.

It must be remembered that the European colonizers, including Jesuit and Franciscan missionaries, had a difficult encounter with other cosmological ideas of sexuality within society and they were part of a missionary work that suppressed some of those ideas.[325] Thus, the encounter and the problems related to those missionary encounters were not about dogma or the Virgin Mary but the indigenous resistance to the imposition of Christian marriage as part of the incorporation of lands to the Kingdoms of Spain or Portugal. Thus, queer theology in exploring the idea and praxis of God within society does not reject the churches' traditions but asks questions about other possibilities within the love of God and about God himself in order not to discard God but to allow other loving relationships to express the beauty and divine love of God.

Althaus-Reid's open and public analysis of those participating in liturgical rites, mainly of the Catholic Church, reflects the very traditional Catholic Church in Argentina; my experience of being instructed in the experimental liturgical rites that came out of the Second Vatican Council was rather different. Thus, Althaus-Reid explores public demonstrations by devout Catholics in Argentina when there was some encouragement to receive communion standing rather than kneeling. I don't remember ever kneeling for communion in Chile or anywhere else. Nevertheless, the situation from which she is writing is probably more useful for theologizing the socio-religious context in the contemporary climate of the possibility of returning to a celebration of the Eucharist in Latin, and even the frightening possibility of turning the altars back to the Tridentine Rite under the pontificate of Benedict XVI.

One of the important points that she makes in her development of an indecent theology is the issue of the location of the theologian. For it is possible to accept that the theologian is only recording his reflections using particular tools while the rest of the world around him is facing death and destruction. That has not been the case of Jon Sobrino and others, for example; however, there is always a general interest in the theologian's work rather than in the theologian himself or herself. Althaus-Reid writes:

> The point for us to consider is that if we are going to take a position in the small circuit of dualistic and heavily hierarchical understandings of the behaviour of sacramental bodies and souls, then we could start by asking how the theologian should be located, that is, by considering how a theologian is positioned and also, how we can consider the theologian as an event, independently of her doing theology.[326]

One of the interesting ways of analysing theologians is to admit that many of them, and probably all the most brilliant, have searched for God as 'restless nomads', so that 'their search for themselves always draws them on, reaching out for other warm lips, other bodies, like exiles unable to be satisfied with their first country of adoption'.[327] Thus, the queer theologian who searches for further meanings and locates personhood within the ongoing challenges of society and God prepares a response to context that allows for an ever-creative search that consumes and sometimes destroys previous narratives and previous canons. This is not the initial intention; however, it seems to be the road towards an honest search for God within desire and within a further understanding of an ever-developing anthropology, Christian or otherwise; so that 'queer theologies are a refusal to normalisation, to the recycling of old borders and limits of any theological praxis, while resisting current practices of historical formation that make us forget the love which is different'.[328] Difference points to the goodness of God, an all-embracing God of diversified theologies, always loving in context and in the context of the diversified theologian.[329]

The work of Althaus-Reid reiterates the old hermeneutical premises by Dussel and others who, in dealing with the hermeneutical circle and a theological analysis, asked their students to bring a newspaper cutting of their interest in order to search for biblical passages that could be related to that social reality. Thus, popular historians such as Eduardo Galeano have produced social narratives that help us understand the world of those poor youths who, in dealing with magic and magic wands, resemble not the fictional world of Harry Potter but the reality of the socially poor and marginalized who like magic tricks and miracles, and who disappear into other magical worlds by inhaling cheap glue, triggering other theological presuppositions and other concerns for God and those who represent God within their poor neighbourhoods.[330] For Althaus-Reid, Queer Theology has a lot to do with ongoing alternative movements where queer communities have been part of movements for land and for alternative narratives to globalization and economic exclusion. In her assessment:

> The Queer God may then show us God's excluded face, which is the face of a non-docile God, a God who is a stranger at the gates of our existing loving and economic order . . . That alternative can partake neither of capitalism nor of Heterosexual Theology.[331]

Returning to the Sources

To summarize so far, Althaus-Reid has managed to explore social situations of transgression within Christian dicta and Christian practices that remain unresolved in an ongoing dialectic encounter between faith communities and civil society. In doing so, she has not advocated a complete rupture, as some feminist theologians have previously advocated, but consistently she has requested the use of liberation theology's engagement with sociability in order to assess social action from the point of view of a God who loves the poor and the oppressed but wants their liberation here and hereafter.

In other essays she has used practical examples of physical and social anomalies in order to outline the possibility that the oppressed of globalization are using established signs such as the crucifixion to protest against the State.[332] This is an ongoing phenomenon within Latin America that prompted the Paraguayan Bishops' Conference to advise the faithful against this practice. Althaus-Reid comments:

> Popular crucifixions and other bloodletting practices, such as skin cuttings in order to write protest cards with blood or the sewing of lips during hunger strikes, fill us with horror while defying any immediate theological response. As people are crucified with six-inch nails on to their crosses for days, many suffer dangerous infections, which in some cases leave them disabled.[333]

However, it is within those occurrences within people's lives that Althaus-Reid perceives the grace of God at work in the contemporary world. Indeed, she goes further, by arguing that doctrines that were developed within cultural metaphors should be revised because the 'Father', the 'Redeemer' in commercial negotiations with humans to whom he gives freely – and some of them are in debt – reflects a colonial sense of patronage and not a post-colonial discussion on a doctrine that she admits is not negotiable as a Christian doctrine. There is no easy way forward, but she makes her point very clearly when she writes:

> I have a deep distrust (or hermeneutic suspicion) of any theology that, no matter what, always seems to serve the interests of the centre, and to serve them so well, that it even manages to convince the periphery that it is done with the interests of the marginalized at heart.[334]

Althaus-Reid's work returns once and again to the possibility of developing theology from a social praxis and not from a given theological thinking that serves a particular purpose and interest. The fact that there are many diverse theologies, even within liberation theology and within a wider Latin American theology, states clearly that the initial distinction between 'political theology' as a genitive theology and a 'theology of the political', claimed by Clodivis Boff, was a good methodological presupposition.[335] The challenge as outlined by Althaus-Reid is to continue exercising the logic of praxis as a methodology and not summarizing a Latin American theology as already part of a genitive process. However, such a process of reinvention needs to be aware, as it tries to move forward, of the fact that God is located at the margins of society, and therefore, in relation to a centre, may have moved altogether to the margins, thus leaving control by the centre useless and empty. The implications of such a theological assertion could be cataclysmic for the future of Latin American theology. In her own words:

> The future of liberation and popular theologies may depend on this final understanding of the participation of the God at the margins with the projects of the centre. A truly 'marginal God' may have little common ground with the vicarious 'God of the poor' who, although visiting the margins, still lives far away and belongs to a central discourse of theology.[336]

I shall examine that theological presupposition further in Volume 3 of this work because Althaus-Reid has asked the 'one million dollar question' that will decide the future of liberation theology within a particular context, that of the margins, in which theologizing from the margins coincides with the relocation of God from the centre to the margins. In the next and final chapter of this volume, however, I shall explore Iván Petrella's manifesto on liberation theology, his theological position as an agnostic and the possibility that Latin American theology in the shape of liberation theology should discontinue its isolated existence and be integrated into a larger body of praxis called by Petrella a liberation theology for the Americas.

9

Iván Petrella

The work of Althaus-Reid moved the location of women from the churches to civil society and in doing so she moved the person of God, within the hermeneutical circle and into the twenty-first century, a more secularized and less institutionalized mode of divine social existence. As a result, Latin American theology has connected with discourses about God that have moved theology and society together with the reality of women within society, even when women have not been given a full ministerial role within all the faith communities. The Queer God and other manifestations of the God of Life have moved away from a first theological generation fully rooted within the faith communities, in its majority within the Roman Catholic tradition, and further into the challenges of oppressed and marginalized human beings within and without those faith communities. However, those theological movements have also expressed the connections between a social movement from religious centrality in Latin America to larger discussions within the post-dictatorial regimes about the role of religion within society and the challenges to the single perception by the Catholic Church that have arisen in areas such as contraception, abortion, euthanasia, same-sex civil partnerships and the areas of ethics and education.

In this final chapter, I explore a further movement away from the first and second theological generations into the realm of religion and the parameters of the religionists, by examining the cultural and scholarly discourse of the self-exiled Argentinean academic Iván Petrella who was shaped intellectually by some of the best universities in North America and who remains involved in theological and religious thinking within Miami and within a new emerging kind of religious and theological discourse in the United States. It is with trepidation that one encounters a movement to the periphery of God by a scholar who proclaims himself an agnostic and therefore has changed the Latin American context of the Basic Christian Communities for the cultural hybridity of the United States.[337]

Petrella's recent manifesto on liberation theology not only managed to recover the liberationist imagination on the one hand but also managed to remind us that the cultural discourse of Latin Americans or *latinos* working within the United States has a slightly different flair from the materialistic theology of the first or second generation of Latin American theologians, on the other hand.[338] Among those few Latin American theologians who have managed to remain engaged with a North American and more academic discourse on theology and religion one can include Enrique Dussel because of his wide-ranging symbolic model founded on economics, philosophy and history.[339] Petrella's critique shows a new direction and, as with any new venture, it will need years, and maybe another generation, for a post-writing evaluation. Nevertheless, it marks the appearance of something new and something different within the discourse of liberation theology as a world phenomenon; previously, liberation theology seemed to have been left in the past of the Berlin Wall and of the military regimes in Latin America. If Juan Luis Segundo and his two types of liberation theology alerted liberationists of the 1980s to the difference between the action of the Christian communities and the discourse of the academic theologians, Petrella's middle-way alerts us to the fact that socio-cultural presuppositions and theological distrust remain divided between the theory about God and practices springing from belief in God.[340]

Iván Petrella

Liberation within the North

Iván Petrella was born in Buenos Aires, where he was a supporter of the River Plate football club; and he is still under 40
years of age.[341] His writings and engagement with religion and
with religious discourse as a theological narrative of liberation
are firmly grounded within an analytical world of ideas and
they follow the academic mode that outlines the study of religion as an academic discipline of diversity, in which an agnostic
such as Petrella finds a home and a social marker. He studied at
Georgetown University within the area of International Relations (School of Foreign Service) and completed his doctorate
on religion and law at Harvard University in 2002 after studying for a masters in theological studies at the same university.[342]
At the same time that Petrella was completing his doctorate,
Argentina was facing a full economic crisis that not only created
social violence but also proclaimed the end of the twentieth-
century Argentinean State; the twenty-first-century Argentinean State was unable to cope with globalization and did not
even have money to look after its citizens any longer. The citizens, temporarily, took over the streets and took matters into
their own hands.

Even when his initial intention was to return to Argentina
after his doctoral studies, Petrella moved to the United States
because he realized that there was no place for him within a
failing Argentinean State that had had five presidents in a short
period of time and that economically was in complete collapse
and anarchy.[343] It is possible, and I share that experience with
him, that already his love for books and ideas had made him into
a person who could not find a place within Argentinean society,
battered over the years by a decrease in the number of publishing houses, lack of university funding for research and the lack
of a social climate conducive to a critical discussion about a
project of nation rather than solely focused on the possible
choice of economic systems of governance.

If for Petrella this period represented a frustrating transition
from graduate student to employed body, that period of the

history of Argentina was an interesting one for the production of theological narratives on social action because new movements outside the Church arose out of the economic disasters triggered by international economic policies. For example, during the 2001–2 economic crises the *piqueteros* – a group protesting against the Argentinean economic collapse – took control of areas of Buenos Aires, while the solidarity of many kept feeding starving middle-class Argentineans who had lost all their savings and their investments as a result of the collapse of the banking structures.[344] Some of those groups, particularly the relatives of the disappeared, strengthened their international networks and became part of international efforts to apply international law in order to capture and to bring to trial torturers and assassins who had led the military regimes and their systematic violations of human rights.[345] Those groups became the future of civil society among a self-destructive Argentinean market economy and a silenced Catholic Church with little moral authority left after the period of the 'dirty war'.

At this stage, Petrella's return to Argentina and his move back to the United States resembled previous movements by Enrique Dussel, Marcella Althaus-Reid and other Argentineans who left under unforeseen circumstances in order to continue their reflection from the outside and their lives within an international periphery. Petrella's appointment to the University of Miami, where he has been teaching within the area of religion, gave him the opportunity to consolidate his scholarly work and the reflections that had started during his time at Harvard. His academic position puts him into an interesting contextual position in that he is in a religious studies department and not in a seminary but operating within the divisions of academia and scholarship in the United States, divisions that are much more prominent than in Europe, where academic departments have both ordained ministers and lay lecturers rather than one or the other. Thus, for an Argentinean newspaper, he is a theologian while for others in the United States he is a scholar of religion, two hats in one: a scholar of religion who studied with Francis Schüssler Fiorenza (Charles Chauncey Stillman Chair of Roman

Catholic Theological Studies at Harvard Divinity School) and
Roberto Mangabeira Unger (Roscoe Pound Chair of Law) at
Harvard University.

Intellectual Manifesto

Petrella's *The Future of Liberation Theology* comes out of a
post-socialist period in which he reflects on the past, the present
and the future of liberation theology and tries to understand the
crisis in liberation theology on the one hand and its possible
future on the other. It is a scholarly discussion, presented in an
orderly manner that for the most part assumes theology as an
intellectual endeavour and a programmatic sense for the future.
Petrella's general critique of liberation theology relates to the
fact that, according to him, liberation theology had the tools to
provide a critique of society but failed to provide a concrete
alternative to the project it criticized. In a changing context,
the lack of a concrete historical project with which liberation
theology can engage does not seem to be the main source of a
possible crisis, while Petrella assumes that it is one of the
reasons for a crisis; instead, according to Petrella, 'the main
obstacles towards such development do not come from the shift
in context but rather are internal to liberation theology itself'.[346]
Within the conclusion to his work, Petrella summarizes his very
thorough analysis of written theologies of liberation with the
centrality of a possible reconstruction of a historical project
that has been lost, using a single sentence, a sentence spoken
from the heart that seemed to have been forgotten throughout
his philosophical analysis:

> Throughout this book I stress the indissoluble link between
> the theological and the political in liberation theology. While
> I focus on the implications of this link for recovering the
> notion of a historical project in an attempt to reconstruct
> liberation theology for the 21st century, I also believe that
> liberation theology is a spiritual exercise, a call to both social

and personal conversion, as well as a hope for ultimate redemption.[347]

His manifesto expands a self-critical reflection that embraces most of the questions asked about liberation theologies in general and Latin American theologies in particular after the collapse of the Soviet Union and of political systems associated with socialism within the 1990s. Petrella's manifesto makes eight particular points,[348] a fact that makes his ongoing discussions plausible, accessible and clear to others' discussions and critiques:

1 Liberation theology operates in two ways: one directed towards the Christian tradition, the other towards society. It maintains three fundamental paradigms, namely (i) God is recognized in bodily form, (ii) there is a unified anthropology that makes the body a vehicle for salvation, and (iii) the history of salvation is located within human history.
2 Liberation theology lacks a historical project wherein to develop 'liberation' and 'the preferential option for the poor', thus becoming a domesticated theology not different from the North Atlantic theology.
3 There are three factors that have influenced the domestication of liberation theology: (i) the fall of the Berlin Wall, (ii) the overemphasis of liberation theology on scripture and tradition rather than on context, and (iii) its monolithic over-simplification of capitalism.
4 North American theologies share the same kind of domestication in that Black and Latino theologies have become monolithic entities that have avoided the issue of material liberation, thus stressing ethnicity over the use of law and the social sciences. They have a middle-class flavour in that they want to be established but do not represent the liberation processes required by the poor.
5 Liberation theology challenges the maturity of European philosophy and theology as understood after the Enlightenment and within democratic systems such as those of the

United States and Europe. Liberation theology tries to find an alternative way to that hegemonic position not only on politics but also on philosophical and theological issues.

6 There is a division between theologians and communities that needs to be overcome. It is a mistake to think that communities engage in historical projects and that the theologian comes later and systematizes a theology for the project. Both, theologian and community, work together as part of the community and, while the community acts within a context, that action can also be influenced by the ideas of a theologian.

7 Liberation theology is sometimes not helped by the fact that Christian theologians rely solely on the Christian tradition. Liberation theologians need further tools and need to be conversant with the social sciences and law. However, they then face the possibility of being ignored by theologians if they use the social sciences within their analysis.

8 Liberation theology must be disconnected from Church or academia, it must engage with identity politics and it must 'theorize political and economic systems as partial, incomplete and open to piece-by-piece change'. Petrella concludes that: 'These are the building blocks for a 21st century liberation theology. Let us start now. There is no better time to work for the future than the present.'[349]

Petrella's contribution to discussions on the diversity of a Latin American theology is crucial: he has asked all the central, hermeneutical questions about a project that, for those who perceived it as a cohesive intellectual project associated with Marxist social theory and with socialism, seemed to be obsolete, that is, dead. For international relations, for example, liberation theology was part of an emerging discussion of power relations and a challenge to the United States' foreign policy, a political alternative that never made a real impact. As a professor of international relations commented to me recently, when hearing that I was writing on liberation theology: 'I thought that liberation theology was dead.' However, Petrella's tools are the hermeneutics of the study of international relations and the study of religion, and here it is that his discussion and critique remains outside the two central places of liberation theologians. I return to the seminal essay by Juan Luis Segundo on 'two types of liberation theology'.[350] Theology, for Segundo, has been a reflection of the educated arising out of universities, those who have acquired the tools of the history of doctrine and biblical scholarship in order to tease once and again 'liberation' as a 'trope' within God's history of salvation and God's contemporary plan for Latin America. Segundo's idea of a theology of liberation complements that of his friend and companion of adventures in France, Gustavo Gutiérrez, who systematized a reflection on the realities of the poor, locating the poor and the marginalized at the centre of a theological reflection for liberation.[351] Their context was that of the oppressed masses of Latin America in the twentieth century: for Segundo, the oppressed middle-class reflection groups that suffered suppression under the military, for Gutiérrez, the hungry and economically deprived inhabitants of the slums of Lima.

Petrella's manifesto argues that liberation theology needs to find a historical project and adopt it. This is challenging and enriching; however, I would be bold enough to argue that it constitutes a different project from that of Segundo, Gutiérrez, Althaus-Reid or me. It reflects a trend of philosophical and academic engagement that has its location within the United States and that requires the predicaments of cultural and philosophical reflection embraced by Eduardo Mendieta; this is a new and different type of theology from that of the first or second generation of Latin American theologians who understood Latin America as different from the United States and in an ongoing dialectical relationship.[352] In fact, when reading Petrella's manifesto, I became more and more aware that his context for theologizing was missing but that a rich critique was forthcoming. By the time that I started asking myself questions about Petrella's search for a social context, he had made me aware that a second monograph was in preparation in which he was going to consider a new challenge/context including material liberation in the study of North American theologies or liberation theologies in the United States. Thus, *The Future of Liberation Theology* and *Beyond Liberation Theology* need to be read together, as a body of scholarship that makes sense and that provides a challenge to all liberation theologians.

New Contexts

Petrella's *Beyond Liberation Theology* explores a particular context for his ideas and that context is that of liberation theology of a globalized kind, from the point of view of poverty, heavily influenced by Latin America but located in the United States, a topic that Petrella considers central for the development of a context in liberation theology.[353] Within that work, he articulates the possibility of using the social sciences, particularly economics, in order to reassess the context for a historical project of liberation within communities that are still marginalized. If the economically poor are the target of liberation, Petrella argues, it must be recognized that the world divide does not cut only through a rich–poor nations divide but that there are 'zones of social abandonment', zones that are spreading in the First World and particularly within the United States. An example of that 'zone of social abandonment' in the United States is the fact that 12.1 per cent of its population (34.6 million) falls below the poverty line.[354] Petrella's contribution suggests that diverse forms of liberation theology have not confronted the spread of zones of social abandonment because they are not prepared to depart from other issues, such as race, ethnicity, gender, sexuality and ecology. His critique of Latino and Black theologies is direct: they have failed to provide a theological system that can challenge the ongoing processes of poverty creation across the economic success of the United States economy because they have not found commonalities within their theologies. For, Petrella argues, one is not necessarily poor because one is ethnically Hispanic or racially Black.

Society is not divided any longer between whites and blacks but between those who have enough and those who do not.

His outside perspective could eventually backfire on him, as I can imagine riots by Blacks and Hispanics attending the annual meeting of the American Academy of Religion. However, his perspective continues to be orderly, well argued and rich in challenges for further theological explorations. If within his previous manifesto he successfully summarized eight presuppositions to be discussed, in this second work, work on poverty and economics within liberation theology, he outlines the following central points that he discusses throughout his work with examples and by providing economic figures:

1 The Americas as a whole must be taken as the context for liberation theologies; Black, Womanist and Latino theologies of liberation must locate their claims within a transcontinental perspective, a liberation theology for the Americas.
2 That transcontinental perspective requires that liberation theologies within the United States overcome their obsession with legitimizing themselves through racial and ethnic categories.
3 A liberation theology for the Americas needs to address the lack of neutrality of theological concepts so that the political, economic and social have a particular grounding.
4 A liberation theology for the Americas must incorporate the social sciences and social theory as intrinsic elements of the theological enterprise. Petrella argues for the centrality of critical legal theory that allows examining in detail the existing capitalisms that affect the distribution of resources in society.
5 The development of a diversity of liberation theology allows a healthy academic development but nevertheless it is a hindrance to struggles for liberation, and to support such unity Petrella cites the Boff brothers who wrote: 'There is one and only one theology of liberation. There is only one point of departure – a reality of social misery – and one goal – the liberation of the oppressed.'[355]

176

Iván Petrella

The Centrality of Materialism

In my view, what unites the different discourses on liberation is the centrality of a materialistic discourse, that is, that of Marxism, socialism or empiricism. That materialistic discourse connects those who do not believe in God, for example, Petrella, and those who do believe in the God of Life and the scriptural actions of the God of History, for example, Gutiérrez, Segundo, Casaldáliga or me. What separates all these material theologians are the location or context in which they move and their own location within the hermeneutical circle. That unity in diversity, so central to contextual theologies, already provided a dynamic tension for the first generation of Latin American theologians so that for some of them theology was in practice 'a second act' (Gutiérrez, Casaldáliga), while for others it was 'a first act' (Segundo, Dussel).

The conversion metaphor of Petrella is a contextual one, located within a philosophical discourse of personhood and scholarship in the United States. His argument is clear, candid and direct in relation to the contextual realities of a country that dominates the world economy and the world political order but that fails to deal with its own socio-economic problems, health service and just international relations. This failure is ever more surprising when an ongoing administration that adheres to Christian principles and Christian ethics in a very public manner fails to connect with the values of the Kingdom as spelled out within the Gospels. Petrella's work has managed to bridge an artificial division between North and South by reminding us that 'liberation' as a process and as a utopia needs to take place within North America as well as in Latin America. Theologically, that discourse of a common liberation unites all liberation theologies; however, contextually it has less resonance within Latin Americans such as myself because the context of the Southern hemisphere is somehow different. The scholarly and experiential hybridism of a new theological generation becomes difficult and problematic as a heuristic device because it provides for an ongoing fragmentation that makes its dialogue more difficult but also more meaningful within a contextual difference, within a contextual isolation. In that respect I am in agreement with those who argue that 'liberation theology' is dead if liberation theology is still perceived as a unified discourse and social project related to a socialist political option. If liberation theology is a hermeneutical interpretation of God's work in the world through diachronically actualized actions and narratives, however, liberation theologies are still alive and well.

The historical project for liberation theology is present there and everywhere where communities and individuals have to be conscientized about their role and their utopian aim to build a better world.[356] This utopian conversion in the work of Petrella takes place in the name of a personal conversion and a humanist one; in my faith context, it takes place because the God of History has entered human history, and the poor and marginalized have understood their central role within God's plan for the Kingdom of God, now and not yet. It is clear that theology (and therefore liberation theology as one kind of theology) can be understood in two different manners: as reason seeking understanding and/or faith seeking understanding about metaphysical realities. Here I return to my advocacy for an ongoing mediation between the study of religion (religious studies) and the study of theology and I point to the possibility that Petrella as writer, theologian, speaker and activist can locate himself within the social text and within the social arena in order to outline clearly every human being's own context.[357] The context is not to be created but it is already around us where the poor and the materially or otherwise marginalized exist.

If Petrella tells us that there are academics who mourn because their subject of study is not central to the academic curriculum or because fewer books on that subject are being sold, that is a poor reflection of the understanding of what Gutiérrez and Segundo outlined as utopia for a Latin American world in their own spatial and historical contexts. Nevertheless, Petrella's work has outlined the challenges of that ongoing project within a contemporary world embraced by a search for

personal liberation and fulfilment that sometimes is disconnected from the world of others. His main contribution is to
remind all involved in theological work or in the study of religion that without a historical project, without a materialistic
project that involves human beings with names and with locations in a particular situation, such a project would remain an
intellectual challenge but it would never become a liberation
theology, for a liberation theology is as much about God as it is
about human beings and the human beings are the ones that
different scholars can relate to within a wide variety of social
contexts.

I remain sceptical about the possibility that ideas about
liberation or writings about liberation would actually liberate
but I recognize that in the context of a literary society ideas
could trigger the possibility of progress and a move towards
liberation. It is here that the challenge arises once and again out
of Petrella's rich reflection: how do we mediate our literary
societies and their liberation with the less literary world of the
poor and marginalized here, in Latin America or in the United
States? It is my opinion that it is the study of the historical and
of the social that remains crucial within this process of conversion or conscientization. For if we do not know about people's
sufferings or if we do not speak about our own sufferings the
forces of oppression could certainly take over our bodies, our
minds and our communities, as happened when social silence
filled disastrous moments of human history. Filled with goods,
media and quick-fixes, we could face the danger of forgetting
others as mirrors of ourselves, of our own existence and of
God's existence in us. Eric Hobsbawm has summarized this
dangerous possibility as follows:

> The past is another country, but it has left its mark on those
> who once lived there. But it has also left its mark on those too
> young to have known it, except by hearsay, or even, in an
> a-historically structured civilization, to treat it, in the words
> of a game briefly popular towards the end of the twentieth
> century, as a 'Trivial Pursuit'.[358]

Within that past and indeed in the present, the United States has developed a mentality of empire by which the previously known 'backyard of the United States', be it Central America or South America, faces the dilemmas of the poor and the marginalized in a different way. As a result of that past, as outlined by Hobsbawm, I am more sceptical than Petrella about the possibilities of developing a liberation theology that embraces the Americas. However, I am open to seeing that possibility realized once the divisions between ethnicity, race and aspirations for different identities are resolved theologically within the United States. I perceive Latin American theology as a liberation theology and liberation theology as a contextual political theology that cannot embrace all the possibilities within a wider umbrella classified as a liberation theology for the Americas. The history of the Americas has shown that, until there is a full exchange and understanding between the English-speaking and the Spanish/Portuguese-speaking parts of the Americas, the English-speaking parts would expect the Spanish speakers to make the effort for commonality in terms given by the peoples of the empire and not vice versa.

I leave the common project to Petrella and others, while I locate myself very strongly within the boundaries, geographical and theological, of Central and South America and within two large groups of Portuguese- and Spanish-speaking peoples who, 500 years ago, were colonized by the kingdoms of Spain and Portugal, and where significant eruptions by the poor as agents of their history have taken place. Petrella's significant contribution makes possible further avenues of investigation on the transcultural, the transnational, and the transreligious aspects of the politics of the Americas.

Postscript

Already in 1974, while teaching at Harvard University, Juan Luis Segundo had anticipated that the methodology and hermeneutics of liberation theology would influence many developments within a more autonomous and more just Latin America. Segundo wrote,

> It is my opinion that the 'theology of liberation', however well or poorly the name fits, represents a point of no return in Latin America. It is an irreversible trust in the Christian process of creating a new consciousness and maturity in our faith. Countless Christians have committed themselves to a fresh and radical interpretation of their faith, to a new re-experiencing of it in their lives. And they have done this not only as isolated individuals but also as influential and sizeable groups within the Church.[359]

Thirty years later, and after examining several theologians, older and younger, of the first, second and third generations, it is possible to suggest that Segundo was correct: the context has changed but the hermeneutics of suspicion and the position of Latin American theologians side by side with the concerns of civil society manifest an ongoing and still unstoppable way of doing theology, of being Christian, of being citizens and of an ongoing reflection upon praxis. Latin American theologians brought new insights to the life of the Church and of civil society in Latin America through their involvement in the life of the Christian communities and through a systematic reflection on the poor and the marginalized between the Second Vatican Council and the advent of the new millennium. Christian communities and their theologians became involved within civil society to the point where it became difficult to differentiate between civil society groups and Christian groups. The new 'trope' expressed as a discourse for human rights united the aims of the Latin American theologians and the humanists within civil society.

With those developments in mind, Latin American theologians of a new generation can move into the twenty-first century, with new social contexts, new challenges and new hopes. At this stage, new questions need to be asked leaving behind the post-mortem examination of the Berlin Wall or the transition to democratic regimes within a post-dictatorial Latin America, the central question being: in which way are we to understand the possibilities of liberation theology, or indeed of Latin American theologies, for the twenty-first century?

The construction of local and contextual theologies depends on a particular context, and therefore no theologizing in any circumstance can be discarded. However, it is difficult to suggest that the writing of theology and by theologians could take place outside the Church or academia; indeed most liberation theologians have been so far either connected with the churches where theology occupies a central place or they have operated within educated circles of academia where theology is taught and researched, and where they have, as in the case of Enrique Dussel, the possibility of exploring multidisciplinary dimensions for their theologizing without excluding their involvement with social communities and within Christian communities and their concerns for the poor and the marginalized.[360] The 'doing' of theology remains central within the actions by social actors and within the social context in which they are located.

It is interesting that Petrella outlines a multidisciplinary existence for liberation theologians that speaks of their peripheral intellectual existence:

> The professional practice of the theologian also discourages interdisciplinary work. This is so because theology suffers from lack of self-confidence. Within the academia, theology is often seen as not truly 'academic', as not truly rigorous. This attack has forced the theologian to retrench and focus more minutely on traditional theological concerns. As long as the concerns are traditionally theological, the theologian feels safe from outside criticism, master of his or her territory.[361]

The theologian is at the periphery of academia, I would say; however, the theologian carries out multidisciplinary work because disciplines such as history, languages, classics, archaeology, literary criticism and philosophy are needed in order to write theology.[362] I agree with Petrella in his pointing to the fact that the social sciences are traditionally less used in European theology (particularly Protestant theology) and that European philosophy occupies a central place. The theologian moves intellectually within the periphery of academia, a pronounced experience of theologians working within seminaries in the United States, places that are not perceived as central to the life and thought of scholars within top US universities. However, is that a bad paradigm? Is it a situation that really affects the development of liberation theology for the twenty-first century? After all, all scholars are discipline specialists and could feel throughout their lives that their disciplines are not as centrally considered as they would like them to be. I would not think that a theological positioning within the periphery is a bad thing after all because too many social (and theological) disasters have occurred when there has been only a single way or manner to understand life, humanity, death and the intellectual under-standing of an afterlife.

Following that sobering note, let me conclude these post-script remarks with a reminder of the dialectics between liber-ating action and liberating thought, between 'the first step' and 'the second step' within liberation theology. For the first gener-ation of liberation theologians, the life of the Christian commu-nities was at the centre (Volume 1), for a later generation the actions and concerns of civil society were at the centre with the churches fulfilling the social role of ancillary bodies (Volume 2), for the current orphans of a previous generation like myself the churches have become ever more part of the periphery of society. However, I am prepared to say that there, at the periph-ery, is where they belong and it is very appropriate that they remain at the periphery.

The experience of the first disciples, whom I shall call 'the Galilean 12' in Volume 3, was the Jesus-experience of a gang of disciples from Galilee who made their way to the big city of Jerusalem with a message of solidarity with the poor, the marginalized and those in need, a message that according to their master, Jesus of Nazareth, came from God and was already present in the writings of the prophets of the Old Testament. Jesus was arrested, tortured and killed and his Father decided to raise him from the dead. That reality became the first confession of a group of followers and that proclamation – the *kerygma* – made a bunch of disciples who had lived through the Jesus-experience into leaders of self-made communities on the fringes of the Roman Empire. All those disciples and communities were part of a social, religious and political periphery. Are we then to be afraid of undergoing the same experience as theologians? My answer is an unequivocal 'no'.

Theologians, trained and given the tools that allow them to think and to write on that experience, live the experience of Christian communities and they live the experience of involvement in social issues, taxation, life and death, they raise families, some of them remain celibate, some others operate within social communities but outside the institutional churches, but they all return to a reflection on liberation, a reflection helped by that trope that help them to act and reflect and act again while writing and teaching because they have received education and they have been part of a particular social experience. However, I would argue that their model is the periphery of society, not the centre, because the Jesus-experience is not central to the majority of people's lives; otherwise we would live in a theocracy or a Jesus-theocracy.

A Latin American theology for the twenty-first century does not come out of a reinvention of the ongoing diversity of narratives, social experiences and discourses but it comes out of a cyclical experience of the periphery by asking the question: who are the marginalized around me? Once those changing realities are outlined and expressed, the solidarity by action, word and written word follows within a utopian return to that gang in the Galilee of the Gentiles. Liberation theology is not a utilitarian system of political analysis but an extension of the action of people and Christian communities which, in their turn, are the extension of the God of Jesus, a God who prefers the poor, a God who loves justice and a God who offers to be part of human history now and in the future. If theologies of liberation throughout the Americas and within Latin America have diversified, it would be tricky to operate in landscape metaphors of linear movement; rather, cyclical metaphors of centre–periphery in a contextual setting would help us not only to outline the principles of a theology of the periphery but to live those peripheral moments of redemption with joy and hope. For, as Casaldáliga has pointed out, the poor and the Brazilians are joyful people of carnival, and even through their difficulties they dance and sing in community; thus, he writes in his dialogue with Brazil: 'Your religious expression is joyful by nature: you celebrate life, dance life; you know how to fill liturgy with light, music and colour.'[363] Therefore, it is the utopia of the periphery that needs to be re-assessed by liberation theologians rather than systematic points of reflection and action; it is, after all, the periphery that lives in poverty and destitution and it is the periphery that theologians must embrace in order to remain part of a cyclical encounter with the God of Life and the God of History, himself at the periphery of globalization and the contemporary markets of death. God is not only located at the periphery, God lives at the periphery of society, God is the peripheral One! – 'I am who I am', in the periphery!

Inhabitants of peripheries do not perceive themselves as outcasts all the time; they fail to feed their children, to buy medicines needed for the sick and to send their children always to school because of lack of fees. However, their daily lives are filled with a sense of dependency on community, on solidarity in the midst of aggression, greed and domestic violence. It is not the world of poverty that Latin American theology perceives as utopian but the attitudes of those who, because of their need for solidarity, wait in hope for a better world and therefore wait for the values of the Kingdom of God to be realized; they wait while acting; they are wise assessors of possibilities and they dislike oppressors because they have themselves the experience of oppression. In the words of the Indian Jesuit Samuel Rayan sj:

> The poor who form the bulk of the world's population, are breaking out of the dark holes, the ghettoes, slums, Reservations and Bantustans, and the silence and self-contempt in which dominant classes have for centuries tried to consign us.

We are breaking into the thick of history, into the halls of the Powerful, into elite fortresses where decisions are made which (mis)shape history and affect us, the poor, fatally.[364]

If we middle-class academics can empathize with the previous statement, it means that we have moved emotionally and theologically to the periphery and therefore to the utopian unrealized world of the losers in globalization but the winners at the end; the marginalized now but the central players in a different stage, not only of the future, but also of the now, the privileged of God, the main actors in the history of salvation.

It is possible to argue that the history and politics of Latin American theology is full of moments of rupture, not philosophical or even existentialist moments, but utopian moments. Individual men and women, communities as well as members of social groups relocate their geographical bearings searching for a different way of life, a different dream, a different way of looking at things. Those characters within the history of Latin America are not happy with what they see, but they are more unhappy about not making a difference in their lives, sharing the youthful spirit of a new community, of a new world, of a new Kingdom. Most of those utopian individuals chose to move to the periphery of society and chose to share the lives of ordinary people who are either suffering or are marginalized.[365] It is this particular phenomenon, social, human and divine, that marks theological narratives of service, prophetic announcement and political commitment, that makes the periphery and that brings out the periphery as a creative space, a creative moment, a creative possibility in which human beings searching for the Kingdom of God become makers of worlds, makers of utopia and makers of a Kingdom here now and still and always within the diachronic 'not yet'. It is to that periphery that theologians must turn in order to find the living God who after all chose to live among the poor and the marginalized. Thus, liberation theologies as an umbrella for theological diversity encounter a further complexity, the theology of the periphery or a strong peripheral theology for the twenty-first century.

Notes

Introduction

1 Mario I. Aguilar, *The History and Politics of Latin American Theology*, Volume I, London: SCM Press, 2007. For the history of the Catholic Church and developments within Catholic theology in the nineteenth and twentieth centuries, see, Adrian Hastings, 'Catholic History from Vatican I to John Paul II', and Enrique Dussel, 'Latin America', in Adrian Hastings (ed.), *Modern Catholicism: Vatican II and After*, London: SPCK and New York: Oxford University Press, 1991, pp. 1–13, 319–25. For a general historical narrative on the developments of a Latin American liberation theology, see David Tombs, *Latin American Liberation Theology*, Leiden: Brill, 2002. For documentation related to the development of Latin American theology after Vatican II see Alfred T. Hennelly (ed.), *Liberation Theology: A Documentary History*, Maryknoll, NY: Orbis, 1990.

2 Marcella Althaus-Reid, 'Who Framed Clodovis Boff? Revisiting the Controversy of "Theologies of the Genitive" in the Twenty-First Century', in Erik Borgman and Felix Wilfred (eds), *Theology in a World of Specialization*, *Concilium*, 2, 2006, London: SCM Press, pp. 99–107, 101.

3 Karl Mannheim, 'The Problem of Generations', in Paul Kecskemeti (ed.), *Essays on the Sociology of Knowledge*, London: Routledge and Kegan Paul, 1952, pp. 276–320, 301.

4 Jon Sobrino SJ and Ignacio Ellacuría SJ (eds), *Mysterium liberationis: Fundamental Concepts of Liberation Theology*, Maryknoll, NY: Orbis, 1993; abridged edition published as Jon Sobrino and Ignacio Ellacuría (eds), *Systematic Theology: Perspectives from Liberation Theology*, Maryknoll, NY: Orbis, 1996. Spanish original published as *Mysterium liberationis: Conceptos fundamentales de la teología de la liberación*, 2 vols, Madrid: Editorial Trotta, 1990.

5 I refer to the Liberation and Theology Series, Tunbridge Wells: Burns & Oates, originally published in Spanish by Ediciones Paulinas of Madrid.

6 Jon Sobrino, 'The Resurrection of One Crucified: Hope and a Way of Living', in Andrés Torres Queiruga, Luiz Carlos Susin and Jon Sobrino (eds), *The Resurrection of the Dead*, *Concilium*, 5, 2006, London: SCM Press, pp. 100–9, 107.

7 See David Tombs, *Latin American Liberation Theology*, Boston and Leiden: Brill, 2002, pp. 256–70.

8 Franz Hinkelammert, 'Globalization as Cover-Up: An Ideology to Disguise and Justify Current Wrongs', in Jon Sobrino sj and Felix Wilfred (eds), *Globalization and Its Victims*, *Concilium*, 5, 2001, London: SCM Press, pp. 25–34; cf. Germán Gutiérrez, 'Latin America: Economics, Ethics and Alternatives' in the same volume, pp. 75–80.

9 Jon Sobrino sj, 'Redeeming Globalization through Its Victims', in Jon Sobrino and Felix Wilfred (eds), *Globalization and Its Victims*, pp. 105–14.

10 Leonardo Boff elaborated on 'theologies of the periphery' referring to the centrality given to European theologies and therefore calling those European theologies 'theologies of the centre' in his sharp summary of theological developments within the Ecumenical Association of Third World Theologians (EATWOT), from 1974 to 1983: see Leonardo Boff, 'Theologies of the "Periphery" and the "Centre": Encounter or Confrontation?', in Claude Geffré, Gustavo Gutiérrez and Virgil Elizondo (eds), *Different Theologies, Common Responsibility: Babel or Pentecost?*, *Concilium*, 1, 1984, pp. 87–97.

11 Leonardo Boff, *Ecology and Liberation: A New Paradigm*, Maryknoll, NY: Orbis, 1995, and *Cry of the Earth, Cry of the Poor*, Maryknoll, NY: Orbis, 1997.

12 Francis McDonagh, 'The Santo Domingo Conference', in Gustavo Gutiérrez, Francis McDonagh, Cândido Padin osb and Jon Sobrino sj, *Santo Domingo and After: The Challenges for the Latin American Church*, London: Catholic Institute for International Relations (CIIR), 1993, pp. 5–27, 7.

13 There were also problems with the election of episcopal representatives from the different national episcopal conferences with a certain tendency by the Roman Curia to interfere in those local choices for the appointment of delegates to the Santo Domingo meeting, pointing to a more canonical and bureaucratic understanding of 'collegiality', a change disliked by some Latin American bishops who had been previously active at the conferences of Medellín and Puebla: see, for example, Cândido Padin osb, 'Reflections on Collegiality: A Letter to My Brother Bishops', in Gustavo Gutiérrez, Francis McDonagh, Cândido Padin osb and Jon Sobrino sj, *Santo Domingo and After*, pp. 60–7.

14 Jon Sobrino sj, 'The Winds of Santo Domingo and the Evangelization of Culture', in Gustavo Gutiérrez, Francis McDonagh, Cândido

Notes

Padin OSB and Jon Sobrino SJ, *Santo Domingo and After*, pp. 28–49, 40. Sobrino's essay was originally published in *Revista Latinoamericana de Teología*, 27, 1992, pp. 273–93.

15 After complaints by some Latin American bishops that their input had not been taken seriously by the redactors of the 'Working Document' at the headquarters of the Latin American Episcopal Conference (CELAM), a new working document was issued, late, for all standards of possible discussion and with the Vatican's additions to the text made by Jorge Medina Estévez, a Chilean conservative bishop and second general secretary to the Santo Domingo conference: see Francis McDonagh, 'The Santo Domingo Conference', in Gustavo Gutiérrez, Francis McDonagh, Cândido Padin OSB and Jon Sobrino SJ, *Santo Domingo and After*, p. 11.

16 In his contribution to the Latin American *Summa Theologica*, Volume 11, Ronaldo Muñoz had correctly argued that 'our knowledge of the God of Jesus Christ – as the distinct and central "object" of the Christian faith and of any consistent, Christian theological undertaking – does not reach us separately from our own reality and human hopes, those we share in history here and now': Ronaldo Muñoz, *The God of Christians*, Liberation and Theology 11, Tunbridge Wells: Burns & Oates, 1991, p. 3.

17 Jon Sobrino SJ, 'The Winds of Santo Domingo and the Evangelisation of Culture', in Gustavo Gutiérrez, Francis McDonagh, Cândido Padin OSB and Jon Sobrino SJ, *Santo Domingo and After*, pp. 42–4.

18 Gustavo Gutiérrez, 'An agenda', in Gustavo Gutiérrez, Francis McDonagh, Cândido Padin OSB and Jon Sobrino SJ, *Santo Domingo and After*, pp. 50–9. For a historical analysis of the option for the poor within Catholic social teaching, see Donal Dorr, *Option for the Poor: A Hundred Years of Catholic Social Teaching*, Maryknoll, NY: Orbis, revised edition 1992.

19 On the alliance between religion and politics vis-à-vis neo-liberalism and capitalism in Latin America, see John Gledhill, 'Resisting the Global Slums: Politics, Religion and Consumption in the Remaking of Life Worlds in the Twenty-First Century', *Bulletin of Latin American Research*, 25, 3, 2006, pp. 322–39.

20 See, for example: Nicholas Deakin, *In Search of Civil Society*, Basingstoke and New York: Palgrave, 2001; John Hall and Frank Trentmann (eds), *Civil Society: A Reader in History, Theory and Global Politics*, Basingstoke and New York: Palgrave Macmillan, 2005; Mary Kaldor, *Global Civil Society: An Answer to War*, Cambridge: Polity, 2003; John Keane, *Global Civil Society?*, Cambridge: Cambridge University Press, 2003; Nicanor Perlas, *Shaping Globalization: Civil Society, Cultural Power and Threefolding*, Quezon City: Center for

Alternative Development Initiatives – CADI, and Saratoga Springs, NY: Global Network for Social Threefolding – GlobeNet3, 2000; and Fran Tonkins, Andrew Passey, Natalie Fenton and Leslie C. Hems (eds), *Trust and Civil Society*, Basingstoke and London: Macmillan, and New York: St. Martin's Press, 2000.

21 John Keane, *Global Civil Society?*, p. 8.

22 Mary Kaldor, *Global Civil Society*, pp. 7–12.

23 See, for example, David Strand, 'Civil Society and Public Sphere in China', Jeffrey N. Wasserstrom and Liu Xinyong, 'Hegemonic Ideas and Class in Chinese Associations', Nancy N. Chen, 'The Inner and Public Practices of Qigong', Ernest Gellner, 'The Vitality of Islam', and Augustus Richard Norton, 'Pockets and Deficits of Civility in the Middle East', in John Hall and Frank Trentmann (eds), *Civil Society*, pp. 255–61, 261–5, 265–8, 268–71, 275–9. However, note that the Madres de la Plaza de Mayo of Argentina are mentioned and described in *Civil Society*, pp. 212–15.

24 The association organizes meetings periodically and publishes an academic journal with the title *Voices from the Third World*, currently edited and printed in India.

25 IV Conferencia General del Episcopado Latinoamericano, Santo Domingo, Dominican Republic, 12–28 October 1992, 'Nueva Evangelización, Promoción Humana, Cultura Cristiana', *Santo Domingo: Conclusiones*, Santafé de Bogotá, Colombia and Santiago: Conferencia Episcopal de Chile, 1993, §§ 292, 296 and 299.

26 'Al servicio de un nuevo trato con el pueblo Mapuche', 21 January 2003, document for reflection privately circulated to the Christian communities of the diocese of Temuco.

27 Jon Sobrino, 'Preface' to Jon Sobrino and Ignacio Ellacuría (eds), *Systematic Theology*, pp. ix–x.

28 In this work, I concern myself solely with Latin America: however, it must be remembered that African and Asian theologies have been for years recognized as academic disciplines within those two continents and elsewhere.

29 K. C. Abraham, 'EATWOT looks ahead', *Voices from the Third World*, 27, 2, 2004, pp. 74–85.

30 Nigel Rapport, 'The "Contrarieties" of Israel: An Essay on the Cognitive Importance and the Creative Promise of Both/And', *Journal of the Royal Anthropological Institute* (N.S.) 3, December 1997, pp. 653–72.

31 Sheila Cassidy, *Made for Laughter*, London: Darton, Longman and Todd, 2006, p. 211.

Notes

Chapter 1

32 For the life and theology of Archbishop Oscar Romero, see Mario I. Aguilar, *The History and Politics of Latin American Theology*, Volume I, London: SCM Press, 2007, Chapter 6. A moving tribute to the murdered Jesuits, their biographies and some of their writings is available in Jon Sobrino SJ, Ignacio Ellacuría and others, *Companions of Jesus: The Jesuit Martyrs of El Salvador*, Maryknoll, NY: Orbis, 1990.

33 Since Ellacuría's assassination and after a slow time of transition the UCA continued its social projects and its involvement with progressive ideas under the leadership of new rectors: Francisco Javier Ibizate SJ and José María Tojeira SJ.

34 Jon Sobrino SJ, *Cristología desde América Latina* (esbozo a partir del seguimiento del Jesús histórico), Mexico, DF: Centro de Reflección Teológica, 1976, English translation *Christology at the Crossroads: A Latin American Approach*, Maryknoll, NY: Orbis, 1978; *Resurrección de la verdadera Iglesia: Los pobres, lugar teológico de la eclesiología*, Santander: Sal Terrae, 1981, English translation *The True Church of the Poor*, London: SCM Press, 1985; *Jesús en América Latina: Su significado para la fe y la cristología*, San Salvador: Universidad Centroamericana, and Santander: Sal Térrea, 1982, English translation *Jesus in Latin America*, Maryknoll, NY: Orbis, 1987; *Jesucristo liberador: Lectura histórica-teológica de Jesús de Nazaret*, Madrid: Trotta, 1991, English translation *Jesus the Liberator: A Historical-Theological Reading of Jesus of Nazareth*, Maryknoll, NY: Orbis and Tunbridge Wells: Burns & Oates, 1993; and *Fe en Jesucristo: Ensayo desde las víctimas*, Madrid: Trotta, 1999.

35 Jon Sobrino SJ, 'Preface', in Jon Sobrino SJ, Ignacio Ellacuría and others, *Companions of Jesus*, p. x.

36 *Departamentos* in El Salvador: Ahuachapán, Cabañas, Chalatenango, Cuscatlan, La Libertad, La Paz, La Unión, Morazán, San Miguel, San Salvador, Santa Ana, San Vicente, Sonsonate and Usulután.

37 Thomas P. Anderson, *Matanza: El Salvador's Communist Revolt of 1932*, Lincoln, Nebraska: University of Nebraska Press, 1971.

38 For a fuller history of the Church in El Salvador, see 'The Emergence of the Poor and the Shifting of Context in El Salvador', in Mario I. Aguilar, *Current Issues on Theology and Religion in Latin America and Africa*, Lewiston, Queenston and Lampeter: Edwin Mellen Press, 2002, pp. 59–85. For a political history, see Thomas P. Anderson, *The War of the Dispossessed: Honduras and El Salvador 1969*, Lincoln, Nebraska: University of Nebraska Press, 1981; and *Politics in Central America*, New York: Praeger, 1988.

39 Alain de Janvry, *The Agrarian Question and Reformism in Latin America*, Baltimore: Johns Hopkins University Press, 1986.

40 Tricia Juhn, *Negotiating Peace in El Salvador: Civil–Military Relations and the Conspiracy to End the War*, London: Macmillan, 1998, p. 1. See also Victor Bulmer-Thomas, *The Political Economy of Central America Since 1920*, New York: Cambridge University Press, 1987; and Jeffrey Paige, 'Coffee and Power in El Salvador', *Latin American Research Review*, 28, 1993, pp. 7–40.

41 There is an enormous amount of literature related to this period: see Hugh Byrne, *El Salvador's Civil War: A Study of Revolution*, Boulder, Colorado, and London: Lynne Rienner, 1996; James Dunkerley, *The Long War: Dictatorship and Revolution in El Salvador*, London: Junction Books, 1982, *Power in the Isthmus*, London: Verso, 1988 and *The Pacification of Central America*, London: Verso, 1994; Tommie Sue Montgomery, *Revolution in El Salvador: From Civil Strife to Civil Peace*, Boulder, Colorado, and Oxford: Westview Press, 1995; and William Stanley, *The Protection Racket State: Elite Politics, Military Extortion and Civil War in El Salvador*, Philadelphia: Temple University Press, 1996.

42 The Truth Commission for El Salvador presented its final report in New York on 15 March 1993 under the title *From Madness to Hope: The 12-Year War in El Salvador*. For a general chronology and interpretation of the truth commissions of El Salvador and Guatemala, see the helpful paper by David Tombs, 'Unspeakable Violence: The UN Truth Commissions in El Salvador and Guatemala', in Iain S. Maclean (ed.), *Reconciliation, Nations and Churches in Latin America*, Aldershot and Burlington, Vermont: Ashgate, 2006.

43 In 1999, Jon Sobrino was awarded the prize for Basque of the year, Premio Vasco Universal 1999, together with Juan Oiarzábal. The prize is awarded annually by the Basque Government and when he accepted the prize in person Sobrino sent a clear message to the Basque separatist movement ETA, stating that no socio-ethnic, class or political demand was worth a human life.

44 The Jesuits emphasized a process of religious discernment before priestly ordination by making the Ignatian *Exercises*, a set of meditations and themes written by the Jesuit Founder, St Ignatius of Loyola, in the sixteenth century. Within those spiritual exercises that last for a calendar month the candidate with the help of a spiritual director asks question of himself and of God about God's will and decides to join the Jesuits for life, becoming for the rest of his life a Jesuit first, a priest second. The bonding of the *Exercises* can be compared to the bonding of a military group, after all most of the first Jesuits were soldiers, a bonding that explains the enormous sense of loss experienced by Sobrino when his whole community of Jesuit companions was assassinated. Sobrino wrote about the role of the *Exercises* and the religious life with-

in the realities of the poor and the marginalized of Latin America: see 'The Christ of the Ignatian Exercises', in Jon Sobrino SJ, *Christology at the Crossroads*, pp. 396–424, and 'Religious Life in the Third World' in Jon Sobrino SJ, *The True Church and the Poor*, pp. 302–37.

45 Reflections by Sobrino on Nairobi at the World Social Forum, January 2007, reproduced by Tina Beattie, 'Has liberation theology had its day', *The Tablet*, 10 February 2007, pp. 4–5.

46 Radio Televisión Española (RTE), 'El jesuita Jon Sobrino en *De Cerca*', 15 September 2006.

47 The Jesuit Provincials of all Latin America met in Rio de Janeiro, Brazil, from the 6 to 14 May 1968, and sent a letter to all Jesuits outlining their own need for conversion and their particular proposed involvement with those who suffered oppression. Fr Pedro Arrupe, Superior General of the Jesuits, was present at the meeting and he encouraged them to look at and re-examine their apostolate within Latin America. In the letter, the Jesuit Provincials asserted that: 'In all our activities, our goal should be the liberation of humankind from every sort of servitude that oppresses it: the lack of life's necessities, illiteracy, the weight of sociological structures which deprive it of personal responsibility over life itself, the materialistic conception of history': see Provincials of the Society of Jesus, 'The Jesuits in Latin America', May 1968, § 3. The document is available in Alfred T. Hennelly (ed.), *Liberation Theology: A Documentary History*, Maryknoll, NY: Orbis, 1990, pp. 77–83.

48 José Simeón Cañas was a priest and a member of the Constitutional Assembly who advocated and obtained in 1824 the abolition of slavery in Central America. The University of Central America (UCA) has today 8,700 students and 340 staff members.

49 Ignacio Ellacuría SJ, 'The Task of a Christian University', in Jon Sobrino SJ, Ignacio Ellacuría SJ and others, *Companions of Jesus*, p. 150.

50 Jon Sobrino SJ, 'The University's Christian Inspiration', in Jon Sobrino, Ignacio Ellacuría and Others, *Companions of Jesus*, pp. 170–1.

51 Jon Sobrino SJ, *Jesucristo liberador* and *Fe en Jesucristo*. Previous Christological work by other Latin American writers, including Leonardo Boff, can be found in José Miguez Bonino (ed.), *Faces of Jesus: Latin American Christologies*, Maryknoll, NY: Orbis, 1984, reprinted Eugene, Oregon: Wipf and Stock Publishers, 1998.

52 Some of this analysis of Sobrino's more recent Christology comes from Jorge Costadoat SJ, 'La liberación en la teología de Jon Sobrino', *Teología y Vida*, 45, 2004, pp. 62–84.

53 Jon Sobrino SJ, *Jesucristo liberador*, pp. 47–8.

54 Jon Sobrino SJ, *Christology at the Crossroads*, pp. 2–10.

55 Ignacio Ellacuría SJ, *Freedom Made Flesh: The Mission of Christ and His Church*, Maryknoll, NY: Orbis, 1976, pp. 15–27.

56 In the European context, rational arguments and speculative reasoning dominated theology after the scientific revolution of the sixteenth and seventeenth centuries, whereby theology was perceived as a science rather than as an art of divine writings. Today, systematic theology as a science related to philosophy reproduces a European self which pretends through rational arguments to understand God. This rational approach has not only created a centrality to rational theology through systematics but has also denied the role of experience in the understanding of the divine self and his action in the world, a phenomenon much more appreciated within the other Abrahamic faiths, namely, Judaism and Islam; see the interesting parallels between rationalism and mysticism in the study of world religions by Karen Armstrong, *The Spiral Staircase: A Memoir*, London: Harper Perennial, 2005, pp. 327–9.

57 At times, and following Sobrino, Latin American theologians and particularly expatriate missionaries have had difficulties with the large phenomenon of popular religiosity where favours and petitions to the Virgin Mary or to the saints imply a physical sacrifice and a personal commitment but do not challenge social structures that create poverty, illness or malnutrition. The Latin American bishops have always embraced popular religiosity as a Latin American contextualization of the gospel and lately the work by Diego Irarrázaval has incorporated aspects of popular religiosity within a theology of inculturation for Latin America; see Diego Irarrázaval, *Inculturation: New Dawn of the Church in Latin America*, Maryknoll, NY: Orbis, 2000, and 'Dying and Rising Again in a Popular Tradition', in Andrés Torres Queiruga, Luiz Carlos Susin and Jon Sobrino (eds), *The Resurrection of the Dead*, Concilium, 5, 2006, London: SCM Press, pp. 25–34.

58 Jon Sobrino sj, *Jesus the Liberator*, p. 13.

59 *Fe en Jesucristo*, p. 136.

60 Sobrino's words regarding the crucifiers are the following: 'Si en la cruz Dios parece estar a merced de ellos, en la resurrección se muestra triunfando sobre ellos' (If on the cross God seems to be at their mercy, in the resurrection he shows himself triumphant over them), *Fe en Jesucristo*, p. 131.

61 Jon Sobrino sj, *Jesus the Liberator*, pp. 264–5.

62 Jorge Costadoat sj, 'La liberación en la teología de Jon Sobrino', p. 83.

63 'Special Column: A Declaration of the Journal *Concilium* on the events in Washington DC and New York in September of This Year', in Jon Sobrino sj and Felix Wilfred (eds), *Globalization and Its Victims*, Concilium, 5, 2001, London: SCM Press, pp. 7–9, 9.

64 Juan Arias, *Paulo Coelho: Confessions of a Pilgrim*, London: HarperCollins, 2001, p. 11.

65 The general literature on globalization is vast and useful works that sometimes relate to religion include Ian Clark, *Globalization and Fragmentation: International Relations in the Twentieth Century*, Oxford: Oxford University Press, 1998; John Gray, *False Dawn: The Delusions of Global Capitalism*, London: Granta, 1998; Wayne Hankey and Douglas Hedley, *Deconstructing Radical Orthodoxy: Post-modern Theology, Rhetoric and Truth*, Aldershot: Ashgate, 2005; David Held, Anthony McGrew and others, *Global Transformations: Politics, Economics and Culture*, London: Polity Press, 2000; James H. Mittelman, *Wither Globalization? The Vortex of Knowledge and Ideology*, London: Routledge, 2004; Chamsy el-Ojeili and Patrick Hayden, *Critical Theories of Globalization*, Basingstoke: Palgrave Macmillan, 2006; Ronald Robertson, *Globalization, Social Theory and Global Culture*, London: Sage, 1993; Jan Aart Scholte, *Globalization: A Critical Introduction*, New York: St. Martin's Press, 2000.

66 Theodore H. von Laue, *The World Revolution of Westernization: The Twentieth Century in Global Perspective*, Oxford: Oxford University Press, 1987.

67 Jon Sobrino SJ, 'Redeeming Globalization through Its Victims', in Jon Sobrino SJ and Felix Wilfred (eds), *Globalization and Its Victims*, pp. 105–14, 105.

68 Jon Sobrino SJ, 'Reflexiones a propósito del terremoto', San Salvador, 16 January 2001, <http://ciberiglesia.net/documents/>.

69 Jon Sobrino SJ, 'Redeeming Globalization through Its Victims', p. 108.

70 Sobrino borrows this theoretical idea from Ignacio Ellacuría, 'The Kingdom of God and Unemployment in the World', *Concilium*, 160, 1982, p. 95: see Jon Sobrino SJ, 'Redeeming Globalization through Its Victims', pp. 112–13.

71 Jon Sobrino SJ, 'Carta a Ellacuría: fineza y santidad', El Salvador, 18 November 2003, available at <http://www.adital.org.br/site/>.

72 Jon Sobrino, 'Carta a Jesús en Navidad', 10 December 2006, available at <http:blogs.periodistadigital.com/contracorriente.php/2006/12/10/jon_sobrino_carta_a_jesus_en_navidad>.

73 Robert Mickens, 'Iron fist, but velvet glove', *The Tablet*, 17 March 2007.

Chapter 2

74 El Salvador had a civil war from 1979 to 1992 in which the military committed atrocities against peasants in order to exterminate the guerrilla movement (Farabundo Martí National Liberation Front – FMNL) that had been active since the halting of the agrarian reform

programme in 1976; a military coup took place in 1979, carried out by reformist army officers led by Colonel Adolfo Majano and by a conservative group of officers led by Colonels Jaime Abdul Gutiérrez and José Guillermo García, with links and support from the American Embassy and with the recognition of the military governments of Chile, Argentina, Brazil and Panama: see Hugh Byrne, *El Salvador's Civil War: A Study of Revolution*, Boulder, Colorado, and London: Lynne Rienner, 1996, pp. 53–4.

75 Martha Doggett, *Death Foretold: The Jesuit Murders in El Salvador*, Washington DC: Georgetown University Press, 1993;, Jon Sobrino SJ, Ignacio Ellacuría SJ and others, *Companions of Jesus: The Jesuit Martyrs of El Salvador*, Maryknoll, NY: Orbis, 1990; and Teresa Whitfield, *Paying the Price: Ignacio Ellacuría and the Murdered Jesuits of El Salvador*, Philadelphia, Pennsylvania: Temple University Press, 1995.

76 Joseph O'Hare SJ, 'Six Slain Jesuits', in Jon Sobrino SJ, Ignacio Ellacuría SJ and others, *Companions of Jesus*, pp. 174–80, 177.

77 See, for example, selected works by Ignacio Ellacuría SJ, *Veinte años de historia en El Salvador 1969–1989: Escritos Políticos*, Volume I, San Salvador: UCA Editores, 1991; A. González Fernández (ed.), *Filosofía de la realidad histórica*, Madrid: Trotta and Fundación Xavier Zubiri, 1991, *El compromiso político de la filosofía en América Latina*, Santafé de Bogotá, Colombia: Editorial El Búho, 1994, *Escritos Filosóficos Tomo I: Escritos de juventud 1956–1968*, San Salvador: UCA Editores, 1996; and Juan José Tamayo (ed.), *Ignacio Ellacuría, teólogo mártir por la liberación del pueblo*, Madrid: Nueva Utopía, 1990. Works by others on the life and thought of Ignacio Ellacuría include those by Kevin F. Burke, *The Ground beneath the Cross: The Theology of Ignacio Ellacuría*, Washington DC: Georgetown University Press, 2004, Kevin F. Burke and Robert Lasalle-Klein (eds), *Love that Produces Hope: The Thought of Ignacio Ellacuría*, Collegeville, Minnesota: Liturgical Press, 2006; Juan Antonio Senent de Frutos, *Ellacuría y los derechos humanos*, Bilbao: Desclée de Brouwer, 1998; and Lucía Sols, 'El legado de Ignacio Ellacuría', *Cristianisme i Justícia*, Barcelona, 86, 1998, pp. 3–32.

78 One of his brothers became a Jesuit and worked in Taiwan and translated Ellacuría's *Teología política* (San Salvador: Arzobispado de San Salvador, 1973) into the Chinese language.

79 For a fuller biographical entry see Mario I. Aguilar, 'Ignacio Ellacuría', in Gary Anderson and Kathryn G. Herr (eds), *Encyclopedia of Activism and Social Justice*, London: SAGE, 2007.

80 José Ortega y Gasset (1883–1955), Spanish philosopher, professor of metaphysics at the University of Madrid and founder of the jour-

Notes

nal *Revista de Occidente*. Ortega y Gasset wrote on history, politics, aesthetics and art criticism, history of philosophy, metaphysics, epistemology and ethics. One of his best-known works, *The Revolt of the Masses* (1929) criticized twentieth-century society as dominated by masses of mediocre and indistinguishable individuals, an idea that connected with other 'mass' theoreticians such as Karl Mannheim, Eric Fromm and Hannah Arendt.

81 Karl Rahner SJ (1904–84), a German systematic theologian and a Jesuit, appropriated and rearranged diverse theological and philosophical sources and retrieved the neo-scholastic theology of a previous generation, becoming one of the most influential theologians of the Second Vatican Council. His theological work was prolific: 1,651 publications, 4,744 including reprints and translations. His main contribution to theology was the systematic construction of a coherent vision of the world as a mysterious arena where God's self-communication takes place in Jesus and the Spirit. His doctoral work, later reshaped and rejected by his thesis director, was on a metaphysical reflection on the possibility of knowing God, an investigation that was of interest to Ignacio Ellacuría. Rahner taught at Innsbruck from 1948 to 1964, in Munich from 1964 to 1967, and in Munster from 1967 to 1971.

82 This facet of Ellacuría's personality has been misinterpreted. In fact, he was at the centre of political life in El Salvador but he was not trusted by either government or opposition and certainly was also misunderstood by some of his fellow Jesuits. Later commentators have also missed this point; for example, Tricia Juhn who, writing in her monograph concerning El Salvador's peace negotiations, suggests the following: 'For his part, Cristiani [Alfredo Cristiani was a politician who represented the most democratic part of the Alianza Republicana Nacionalista (ARENA) of El Salvador] began, through intermediaries, conversations with the Jesuit Ignacio Ellacuría, an intellectual leader of the left, regarding the possibility of renewing a serious dialogue', in Tricia Juhn, *Negotiating Peace in El Salvador: Civil–Military Relations and the Conspiracy to End the War*, London: Macmillan, 1998, p. 47.

83 Pontifical universities have rectors, known as university principals within British universities and university presidents within universities in the United States.

84 For the reflections by Ellacuría on the Church and Oscar Romero see 'El verdadero Pueblo de Dios según Mons. Romero', in Ignacio Ellacuría SJ, *Conversión de la Iglesia al Reino de Dios: Para anunciarlo y realizarlo en la historia*, Santander: Editorial Sal Terrae, 1984; the conclusion of this essay, translated by Phillip Berryman, has been published as 'Persecution for the Sake of the Reign of God', in Jon Sobrino SJ, Ignacio Ellacuría SJ and others, *Companions of Jesus*, pp. 64–75.

85 José Napoleón Duarte, with Diana Page, *Duarte: My Story*, New York: Putnam, 1986.

86 Ellacuría wrote about the 'historical effectiveness' of utopia and prophecy understood as two movements of the Spirit that went hand in hand: see Ignacio Ellacuría SJ, 'Utopia and Prophecy in Latin America', in Ignacio Ellacuría SJ and Jon Sobrino SJ (eds), *Mysterium liberationis: Fundamental Concepts of Liberation Theology*, Maryknoll, NY: Orbis, and North Blackburn, Victoria, Australia: CollinsDove, 1993, pp. 289–328.

87 Some of those ideas had been expressed already in his intellectual change regarding ecclesiology and the realities of the Church of the poor in relation to the sacramental life of the Catholic Church; see Ignacio Ellacuría SJ, 'The Church of the Poor, Historical Sacrament of Liberation', in Ignacio Ellacuría SJ and Jon Sobrino SJ (eds), *Mysterium liberationis*, pp. 543–64. Earlier reflections had focused on issues of popular religiosity rather than on a Church of the poor; see Ignacio Ellacuría SJ, 'Notas teológicas sobre religiosidad popular', *Fomento Social*, July–September 1977, pp. 253–60.

88 Alfredo Cristiani governed El Salvador from 1989 to 1994 and while the start of his administration saw continuous repression and violence Cristiani managed, to his own advantage, to bring a difficult process to an end so that the final peace treaty was signed at Chapultepec Castle in Mexico City on 16 January 1992 and the Army as well as the guerrillas (FMNL) ordered their troops to stand down on 31 January 1992; see Tricia Juhn, *Negotiating Peace in El Salvador*, p. 121.

89 See general policies of the ARENA party in *Manual del dirigente*, San Salvador: ARENA, 1990.

90 D'Aubuisson founded the ARENA Party and was head of the Salvadoran military's special intelligence unit (ANSESAL – Agencia Nacional de Servicios Especiales de El Salvador).

91 Hugh Byrne, *El Salvador's Civil War*, p. 145.

92 Ellacuría spoke about the purification of the Church and its re-conversion to the Third World: see Ignacio Ellacuría SJ, *Freedom Made Flesh: The Mission of Christ and His Church*, Maryknoll, NY: Orbis, 1976, p. 145.

93 Ignacio Ellacuría SJ, 'The Crucified People', in Ignacio Ellacuría SJ and Jon Sobrino SJ (eds), *Mysterium liberationis*, pp. 580–603, 589.

94 Ignacio Ellacuría SJ, 'The Historicity of Christian Salvation', in Ignacio Ellacuría SJ and Jon Sobrino SJ (eds), *Mysterium liberationis*, pp. 251–89, 253.

95 *Gaudium et Spes* 1.

96 Ignacio Ellacuría SJ, *Freedom Made Flesh*, p. 235.

97 Ignacio Ellacuría SJ, 'Posibilidad y modo de aproximación entre

filosofía escolástica y la filosofía vitalista moderna (Reflexiones ante el libro de Ramírez: *La filosofía de Ortega y Gasset*, 1958)', Escritos Filosóficos I, San Salvador: UCA, 1958, pp. 223–50, and 'Técnica y vida humana en Ortega y Gasset: Estudio de *Meditación de la técnica*', manuscript written by Ellacuría while at Innsbruck, March to May 1961.

98 Ellacuría develops a triad of conceptual tensions through 'principialidad intelectiva', 'principialidad de la realidad' and 'principialidad de la esencia'.

99 It has been suggested by J. M. Ashley that Ellacuría's attempts at a philosophy and a theology related to the historical Jesus were structured by the *Exercises* of St Ignatius of Loyola, founder of the Jesuits, a theme that still remains unexplored within Ellacuría's own writings and letters: see J. Matthew Ashley, 'Ignacio Ellacuría and the Spiritual Exercises of Ignatius of Loyola', *Theological Studies*, 61, 2000, pp. 16–39.

100 Thesis title: 'Ensayo de una teoría fenomenológica del juicio'.

101 From the first period his best-known work is *Naturaleza, historia, Dios*, Madrid: Editorial Nacional, 1944. His major work in metaphysics is *Sobre la esencia*, Madrid: Editorial Alianza, 1962.

102 Xavier Zubiri, *Inteligencia sentiente: Inteligencia y realidad*, Madrid: Editorial Alianza, 1980, *Inteligencia y Logos*, Madrid: Editorial Alianza, 1982, and *Inteligencia y Razón*, Madrid: Editorial Alianza, 1983. Other works by Zubiri include: *Cinco lecciones de filosofía*, Madrid: Editorial Alianza, 1985; *Reflecciones teológicas sobre la Eucaristía*, Bilbao: P. U. Deusto, 1980; *El hombre y Dios*, Madrid: Editorial Alianza, 1984; *Sobre el hombre*, Madrid: Editorial Alianza, 1986; *Estructura dinámica de la realidad*, Madrid: Editorial Alianza, 1989; *Sobre el sentimiento y la volición*, Madrid: Editorial Alianza, 1992; *El problema filosófico de la historia de las religiones*, Madrid: Editorial Alianza, 1993; *Los problemas fundamentales de la metafísica occidental*, Madrid: Editorial Alianza, 1994; *Espacio, tiempo y materia*, Madrid: Editorial Alianza, 1996; and *El problema teologal del hombre: cristianismo*, Madrid: Editorial Alianza, 1997.

103 See, as an example of his theological depth, the last paper he wrote before his assassination: Ignacio Ellacuría SJ, 'Utopía y profetismo en América Latina', *Revista Latinoamericana de Teología*, 17, 1989, later published as 'Utopia and Prophecy in Latin America'.

104 Ignacio Ellacuría SJ, 'Filosofía, para qué?', *Abra* – San Salvador, 2, 1976, pp. 42–8, and the university course 'Filosofía de la realidad histórica'.

105 Ignacio Ellacuría SJ, 'Aporte de la Teología de la Liberación a las religiones abrahámicas en la superación del individualismo y del positivismo', *Revista Latinoamericana de Teología*, 10, 1987, pp. 3–28.

106 Ignacio Ellacuría SJ, 'The Task of a Christian University', talk

delivered at the University of Santa Clara graduation ceremony on 12 June 1982, available in Jon Sobrino SJ, Ignacio Ellacuría SJ and others, *Companions of Jesus*, pp. 147–51.

107 Ignacio Ellacuría SJ, 'The Task of a Christian University', in Jon Sobrino SJ, Ignacio Ellacuría SJ and others, *Companions of Jesus*, pp. 147–51, 150.

108 Ignacio Ellacuría SJ, 'La teología de la liberación frente al cambio socio-histórico de América Latina' and 'En torno al concepto y a la idea de la liberación', *Implicaciones sociales y políticas de la Teología de la Liberación*, Seville: Escuela de Estudios Hispanoamericanos, 1989, pp. 69–89, 91–101.

Chapter 3

109 Josep-Ignasi Saranyana and Carmen-José Alejos Grau (eds), *Teología en América Latina III: El siglo de las teologías latinoamericanistas 1899–2001*, Madrid: Iberoamericana and Frankfurt am Main: Vervuert, 2002, p. 313.

110 See, for example, Juan Luis Segundo SJ, *Teología para el laico adulto*, 5 volumes, Buenos Aires: Carlos Lohlé, 1968–71; English translation published as *A Theology for Artisans of a New Humanity*, Maryknoll, NY: Orbis, 1973–74.

111 Alfred T. Hennelly, *Liberation Theologies: The Global Pursuit of Justice*, Mystic, Connecticut: Twenty-Third Publications, 1997, p. 26.

112 Juan Luis Segundo SJ, *Une réflexion chrétienne sur la personne*, Paris: Aubier, 1963.

113 Gustavo Gutiérrez, 'Juan Luis Segundo: una amistad para toda la vida', *Signos*, January 1996, p. 8, reprinted in *Misión de Fe y Solidaridad* 62–3, June/July 1996, pp. 51–2.

114 Juan Luis Segundo SJ, *Theology and the Church: A Response to Cardinal Ratzinger and a Warning to the Whole Church*, London: Geoffrey Chapman, and Minneapolis, Minnesota: Winston Press, 1985, p. 75.

115 Thesis on Berdyaev published as *Berdiaeff, une réflexion chrétienne sur la personne*, Paris: Aubier, 1963.

116 Kenneth Leech, 'Liberating Theology: The Thought of Juan Luis Segundo', *Theology*, 84, 1981, pp. 258–66.

117 The ideology of the Tupamaros was nationalistic in so far as they perceived an independent Uruguay within the Latin American context and opposed American interests; it was socialist in that their inspiration was the socialist revolution in Cuba and they wanted a total social change and economic redistribution within Uruguay. Briefly, the Tupamaros wanted to create many Vietnams in Latin America, armed

Notes

against American imperialism. See Benjamín Nahum, *Manuel de historia del Uruguay* II: 1903–2000, Montevideo: Ediciones de la Banda Oriental, 2005, pp. 272–5; see also Gonzalo Varela, *De la república liberal al estado militar: Crisis política en Uruguay 1968–1973*, Montevideo: Ediciones del Nuevo Mundo, 1988.

118 Alavaro Rico, Carlos Demasi, Rosario Radakovich, Isabel Wschebor and Vanesa Sanguinetti, *15 días que estremecieron al Uruguay: Golpe de estado y huelga general 27 de junio–11 de julio de 1973*, Montevideo: Editorial Sudamericana Uruguaya and Editorial Fin de Siglo, 2006.

119 On 15 March 1974, the military rulers of the Southern Cone, Generals Ernesto Geisel (Brazil), Hugo Banzer (Bolivia), Augusto Pinochet (Chile) and the Uruguayan president Bordaberry met in Brazilia to discuss the Marxist aggression within their countries. See Virginia Martínez, *Tiempos de dictadura 1973/1985: Hechos, voces, documentos – La represión y la resistencia día a día*, Montevideo: Ediciones de la Banda Oriental, 2005, p. 35.

120 Juan Luis Segundo sj, *Liberation of Theology*, Maryknoll, NY: Orbis, 1976.

121 Virginia Martínez, *Tiempos de dictadura* 1973/1985, p. 128.

122 Juan Luis Segundo sj, 'Clemencia para los vencidos', *La Plaza*, February 1982; Segundo wrote: 'En nombre, pues, de la eficacia y realismo de una apertura y de una institucionalización que inspiren confianza y susciten consenso, quiero sumar mi voz a las que no se dejan oír dentro del país, reclamando una vez más, clemencia para los vencidos, es decir la libertad de los presos políticos' (Thus, in the name of political expediency, openness and a political process that could inspire trust and consensus, I want to add my voice to those unable to be heard within this country, requesting once again clemency for the fallen, that is, freedom for all political prisoners), in Virginia Martínez, *Tiempos de dictadura* 1973/1985, p. 169.

123 Fr Luis Pérez Aguirre died in January 2001.

124 'Amnistía general o generosa?', in Virginia Martínez, *Tiempos de dictadura* 1973/1985, p. 187.

125 For a historical overview of this period and the ambiguous role played by the Catholic Church in Uruguay, see Jeffrey Klaiber sj, *The Church, Dictatorships, and Democracy in Latin America*, Maryknoll, NY: Orbis, 1998, pp. 110–20; Gonzalo Varela, *De la república liberal al estado militar: Uruguay 1968–1973*, Montevideo: Ediciones del Nuevo Mundo, 1988; and Juan Villegas, María Luisa Coolighan and Juan José Arteaga, *La Iglesia en el Uruguay*, Montevideo: Instituto Teológico del Uruguay, 1978.

126 Servicio Paz y Justicia de Uruguay, *Nunca más: Informe sobre la*

violación a los derechos humanos 1972–1985, Montevideo: SERPAJ, 1989, English translation published as The Peace and Justice Service of Uruguay, *Uruguay Nunca Más: Human Rights Violations 1972–1985*, Philadelphia: Temple University Press, 1992.

127 The Frente Amplio had been founded in 1971 and, after Uruguay's return to democracy, became quite central to the ongoing democratic alliances that followed Sanguinetti's government. For a political history of the Frente Amplio, see Adolfo Garcé and Jaime Yaffé, *La era progresista: El gobierno de izquierda en Uruguay: de las ideas a las políticas*, Montevideo: Editorial Fin de Siglo, 2005.

128 After his death, a full bibliographical compilation of his work was published as 'Una teología con sabor a vida', *Misión de Fe y Solidaridad* [Uruguayan Jesuit magazine], 62/63, June/July 1996, also published in Portuguese by the Jesuits in Brazil.

129 *ENLACE* (news from the Uruguayan Province of the Jesuits) 27, January/February 1996, pp. 13–14 and *CIAS* (magazine of the Centro de Investigación y Acción Social of the Argentinean Province of the Jesuits) 457, October 1996, pp. 487–8.

130 Agustín Canessa, 'Humanista que salva la historia', Montevideo, 24 October 2005.

131 See, for example: Juan Luis Segundo SJ, *Liberation of Theology*; *Faith and Ideologies*, Maryknoll, NY: Orbis, 1984; *Theology and the Church*, Minneapolis: Winston, 1985; *The Liberation of Dogma*, Maryknoll, NY: Orbis, 1992; and *Signs of the Times: Theological Reflections*, Maryknoll, NY: Orbis, 1993.

132 Less-known works that outline this change in his pastoral and theological preoccupations include Juan Luis Segundo SJ, *De la sociedad a la teología*, Buenos Aires: Editorial Carlos Lohlé, 1970; *Qué es un cristiano: Etapas pre-cristianas de la fe, concepción cristiana del hombre*, Montevideo: Editorial Mosca Hermanos, 1971; *Acción pastoral latinoamericana: Sus motivos ocultos*, Buenos Aires: Editorial Búsqueda, 1972; *El dogma que libera: Fe, revelación y magisterio dogmático*, Santander: Ediciones Sal Terrae, 1989; *Qué mundo? Qué hombre? Qué Dios?*, Santander: Ediciones Sal Terrae, 1993; *El caso Mateo: Los comienzos de una ética judeo-cristiana*, Santander: Ediciones Sal Terrae, 1994; and *Infierno: Un diálogo con Karl Rahner*, Montevideo: Editorial Trilce and Buenos Aires: Editorial Lohlé-Lumen, 1998.

133 Segundo refers to Jon Sobrino SJ, 'Appendix: The Christ of the Ignatian Exercises', in *Christology at the Crossroads: A Latin American Approach*, London: SCM Press, 1978, pp. 396–424. See Juan Luis Segundo SJ, 'Una primera semana sin cristología?', *Manresa*, 68, 1996, pp. 233–47. Many of those discussions related to the content, context

Notes

and contemporary applications of the Ignatian *Exercises* can be found in David L. Fleming SJ, *Notes on the Spiritual Exercises of St. Ignatius of Loyola*, St. Louis, Missouri: Review for Religious, 1983.

134 A first and larger part of the *Exercises* was written by Ignatius in relation to his personal conversion at the city of Manresa while the second and shorter part, and probably some revisions of the first part of the book, were written while Ignatius was a student at the Sorbonne in Paris. See Juan Luis Segundo SJ, *The Christ of the Ignatian Exercises*, Jesus of Nazareth Yesterday and Today 4, Maryknoll, NY: Orbis, 1987, p. 9. There are different annotated versions of the Ignatian Exercises, however all English texts are translations from the Spanish original; see, among others, W. H. Longridge [translator], *The Spiritual Exercises of Saint Ignatius of Loyola*, with a commentary and a translation of the *Directorium in Exercitia*, London: Robert Scott, 1919.

135 Segundo refers to Pierre Teilhard de Chardin SJ, *The Divine Milieu*, New York: Harper & Row, 1960.

136 Juan Luis Segundo SJ, *The Christ of the Ignatian Exercises*, p. 63.

137 See for example, Juan Luis Segundo SJ, 'La opción por los pobres como clave para entender el Evangelio', *Sal Terrae*, 74, 1986, pp. 473–82.

138 Among his systematic works see, for example, Juan Luis Segundo SJ, *Our Idea of God*, Maryknoll, NY: Orbis, 1973; *An Evolutionary Approach to Jesus of Nazareth*, Maryknoll, NY: Orbis, 1985; *The Historical Jesus of the Synoptics*, Maryknoll, NY: Orbis, 1986; *The Humanist Christology of Paul*, Maryknoll, NY: Orbis, 1986; and *The Christ of the Ignatian Exercises*.

139 Juan Luis Segundo SJ, *Función de la Iglesia en la realidad rioplatense*, Montevideo: Barreiro y Ramos, 1962.

140 Juan Luis Segundo SJ, 'The Future of Christianity in Latin America', in Alfred T. Hennelly (ed.), *Liberation Theology: A Documentary History*, Maryknoll, NY: Orbis, 1990, pp. 29–37. The original French text was published in *Lettres*, Paris, November 1962, and an English translation appeared in *Cross Currents*, 13, Summer 1963, pp. 273–81.

141 Juan Luis Segundo SJ, 'The Future of Christianity in Latin America', p. 37.

142 Juan Luis Segundo SJ, 'Revelation, Faith, Signs of the Times', in Ignacio Ellacuría SJ and Jon Sobrino SJ (eds), *Mysterium liberationis: Fundamental Concepts of Liberation Theology*, Maryknoll, NY: Orbis, 1993, pp. 328–49; see his previous work, 'Revelación, fe, signos de los tiempos', *Revista Latinoamericana de Teología*, 5, 1988, pp. 123–44.

143 Juan Luis Segundo SJ, 'Revelation, Faith, Signs of the Times', p. 329.

144 Karl Rahner SJ, *Foundations of Christian Faith*, New York: Crossroad, 1978.

145 Andrés Torres Queiruga, *La revelación de Dios en la realización del hombre*, Madrid: Cristiandad, 1987.

146 Juan Luis Segundo SJ, 'Revelation, Faith, Signs of the Times', p. 345.

147 Juan Luis Segundo SJ, 'Revelation, Faith, Signs of the Times', p. 346.

148 Juan Luis Segundo SJ, *Liberation of Theology*, p. 209.

149 Segundo in his *Liberation of Theology*, p. 228, is commenting on and cites from Joseph Ratzinger, *Le nouveau peuple de Dieu*, Paris: Aubier, 1971, p. 140; see Segundo's later work, *Masas y minorías en la dialéctica divina de la liberación*, Buenos Aires: Editorial La Aurora, 1973.

150 Congregation for the Doctrine of the Faith, 'Ten Observations on the Theology of Gustavo Gutiérrez', in Alfred T. Hennelly (ed.), *Liberation Theology*, pp. 348–50, §2.

151 Congregation for the Doctrine of the Faith, 'Ten Observations on the Theology of Gustavo Gutiérrez', § 7.

152 Karl Rahner SJ, 'Letter to Cardinal Juan Landázuri Ricketts of Lima, Peru', Innsbruck, 16 March 1984, in Alfred T. Hennelly (ed.), *Liberation Theology*, pp. 351–2; German text available in Norbert Greinacher, *Konflikt um die Theologie der Befreiung: Diskussion und Dokumentation*, Cologne: Benziger Verlag, 1985, pp. 184–6.

153 Cardinal Joseph Ratzinger, 'Liberation Theology', March 1984, in Alfred T. Hennelly (ed.), *Liberation Theology*, pp. 367–74; also available in *The Ratzinger Report: An Exclusive Interview on the State of the Church*, San Francisco: Ignatius Press, 1985, pp. 174–86.

154 Cardinal Joseph Ratzinger, 'Liberation Theology', p. 373.

155 Cardinal Joseph Ratzinger, 'Liberation Theology', p. 374.

156 Editorial Board of Concilium, 'Statement of Solidarity with Liberation Theologians', 24 June 1984, in Alfred T. Hennelly (ed.), *Liberation Theology*, pp. 390–2; published in *Origins*, 14, 26 July 1984, pp. 134–5.

157 Congregation for the Doctrine of the Faith, 'Instruction on Certain Aspects of the "Theology of Liberation"', Vatican City, 6 August 1984, in Alfred T. Hennelly (ed.), *Liberation Theology*, pp. 393–414, 394. The full text is also available in Juan Luis Segundo SJ, *Theology and the Church*, pp. 169–88.

158 Leonardo Boff, 'Vatican Instruction Reflects European Mind-Set', *Folha de São Paulo*, 31 August 1984, text available in Alfred T. Hennelly (ed.), *Liberation Theology*, pp. 415–18; Gustavo Gutiérrez, 'Criticism Will Deepen, Clarify Liberation Theology', 14 September

1984, text available in Alfred T. Hennelly (ed.), *Liberation Theology*, pp. 419–24.

159 The following attack on liberation theology took place in March 1985 when Leonardo Boff came under the doctrinal scrutiny of the CDF: see Congregation for the Doctrine of the Faith, 'Notification Sent to Fr. Leonardo Boff Regarding Errors in His Book *Church, Charism and Power*', 11 March 1985, text available in Alfred T. Hennelly (ed.), *Liberation Theology*, pp. 425–30. Leonardo Boff appeared in front of Ratzinger at the Vatican on 7 September 1984 and defended his theological position; see Leonardo Boff, 'Defense of His Book, *Church, Charism and Power*', 7 September 1984, in Alfred T. Hennelly (ed.), *Liberation Theology*, pp. 431–4. See also Harvey Cox, *The Silencing of Leonardo Boff: The Vatican and the Future of World Christianity*, Oak Park, Illinois: Meyer Stone Books, 1988.

160 Juan Luis Segundo SJ, *Theology and the Church*, p. 154.

161 Juan Luis Segundo SJ, *The Liberation of Dogma*.

162 One of his most active contemporary critics is the Jesuit Horacio Bojorge in his work *Teologías deicidas: El pensamiento de Juan Luis Segundo en su contexto*, Madrid: Editorial Encuentro, 2000, and available through the web at Catholic.net [<http://es.catholic.net>]. Bojorge is a Uruguayan Jesuit, professor of theology at the San Miguel Seminary (Buenos Aires) where Segundo studied. Bojorge's writings are close to spiritualistic movements such as the Neo-Catecumenado and the Catholic Charismatic Renewal and his theology is founded in the traditional sources of Catholic theology. His main criticism of Segundo is that his sources, including Western philosophical paradigms such as Marxism, contradict the theological methodologies approved by the magisterium and that his heterodoxy makes his theological method full of mistaken assumptions, with a lack of adherence to theological doctrines. Bojorge's book is interesting because it contains all the usual criticisms of theologies of liberation but, at the end of the day, cannot challenge the possibility of existence for emerging new theologies within a wider theological world.

163 Juan Luis Segundo SJ, *Signs of the Times*.

164 His critical stance within theology has been applied within other theological contexts; see, for example, John Wilcken, 'Juan Luis Segundo and Australian Theology', *Pacifica*, 15, 3, 2002, pp. 324–36.

165 Thomas C. Fox, 'Liberation Theology Founder Dead at 70: Father Juan Luis Segundo Obituary', *National Catholic Reporter*, 2 February 1996.

Chapter 4

166 The Latin term *Jesuita* appeared in northern European texts of the fifteenth century, meaning a good Christian and a follower of Jesus; see John W. O'Malley, *The First Jesuits*, Cambridge, Massachusetts, and London: Harvard University Press, 1993, p. 69.

167 Juan Luis Segundo sj, 'Two Theologies of Liberation', Toronto, 22 March 1983, in Alfred T. Hennelly (ed.), *Liberation Theology: A Documentary History*, Maryknoll, NY: Orbis, 1990, pp. 353–66.

168 Important dates in the history of the Jesuits include the following: 27 September 1540, when Pope Paul III issued the papal bull *Regimini militantis Ecclesiae* that authorized the existence of the Society of Jesus, a few years before the Council of Trent (1545–63); 21 July 1550, when Pope Julius III issued the bull *Exposcit debitum* that approved the Constitutions of the Society of Jesus, a document that had been drafted by Ignatius; and 1622, when Pope Gregory XV canonized Ignatius of Loyola and his companion Francis Xavier, missionary to Asia.

169 Provincials of the Society of Jesus, 'The Jesuits in Latin America', May 1968, in Alfred T. Hennelly (ed.), *Liberation Theology*, pp. 77–83.

170 Provincials of the Society of Jesus, 'The Jesuits in Latin America', § 3.

171 Provincials of the Society of Jesus, 'The Jesuits in Latin America', § 7.

172 Provincials of the Society of Jesus, 'The Jesuits in Latin America', § 10.

173 The incident at the Malloco farm is narrated in Mario I. Aguilar, *A Social History of the Catholic Church in Chile I: The First Period of the Pinochet Government 1973–1980*, Lewiston, Queenston and Lampeter: Edwin Mellen Press, 2006, pp. 96–9.

174 Cardinal Raúl Silva Henríquez, *Memorias* III, Santiago: Editorial Copygraph, 1991, p. 82, in Mario I. Aguilar, *A Social History of the Catholic Church in Chile II: The Pinochet Government and Cardinal Silva Henríquez*, Lewiston, Queenston and Lampeter: Edwin Mellen Press, 2006, p. 265.

175 See Sheila Cassidy, *Audacity to Believe*, London: Darton, Longman and Todd, 1992, pp. 156–333, and *Made for Laughter*, London: Darton, Longman and Todd, 2006, pp. 82–99.

176 *The Mission*, produced by Warner Bros in 1986 starring Robert De Niro and Jeremy Irons, music by Ennio Morricone, written by Robert Bolt, produced by Fernando Ghia and David Puttnam, directed by Roland Joffé. Among those who acted in the film was the rebel American Jesuit Dan Berrigan sj, anti-Vietnam and anti-nuclear campaigner; see Dan Berrigan sj, *The Mission: A Film Journal*, New York:

Notes

Harper and Row, 1986. Berrigan appears in one of the opening scenes among the Jesuits who sent a Jesuit missionary (Jeremy Irons) to climb the hills and to make contact with the indigenous peoples that lived there.

177 Robert Bontine Cunninghame Graham, *A Vanished Arcadia: Being Some Account of the Jesuits in Paraguay 1607–1767*, London: Century, 1988 [1901], pp. 47–8.

178 The Spanish word *reducción* (sometimes translated in English as reduction) was the name for a missionary establishment where indigenous populations lived and were under the protection of the Jesuits.

179 Robert Bontine Cunninghame Graham, *A Vanished Arcadia*, pp. 51–2.

180 T. Frank Kennedy SJ, 'An Integrated Perspective: Music and Art in the Jesuit Reductions of Paraguay', in Christopher Chapple (ed.), *The Jesuit Tradition in Education and Missions: A 450–Year Perspective*, Scranton: University of Scranton Press; London and Toronto: Associated University Presses, 1993, pp. 215–25, 215.

181 T. Frank Kennedy SJ, 'An Integrated Perspective', p. 216.

182 Charles III signed the Royal Decree at Prado, Madrid, on 5 April 1767, with the title 'Real cédula para que en los reinos de las Indias se cumpla y observe el Decreto relativo al extrañamiento y ocupación de temporalidades de los Religiosos de la Compañía de Jesús' (Royal decree to the effect that orders the expulsion and the confiscation of temporal goods of the religious members of the Society of Jesus be obeyed). The Royal Decree was sent by the Count of Aranda to the Governor of Buenos Aires, General Bucareli y Ursúa, who ordered the arrest of the Jesuits, the confiscation of their lands and personnel and their repatriation to Spain, all Jesuits being immediately replaced by other clergy: see Silvio Palacios and Ena Zoffoli, *Gloria y tragedia de las misiones guaraníes: Historia de las Reducciones Jesuíticas durante los siglos XVII y XVIII en el Río de la Plata*, Bilbao: Ediciones Mensajero, 1991, p. 165.

183 Edwin Williamson, *The Penguin History of Latin America*, London: Penguin, 1992, pp. 162–4. Among them the Mexican Jesuit scholar Francisco Javier Alegre and the Jesuit Francisco Javier Clavijero, historian and anthropologist of ancient Mexico and of California: see Miguel Batlori, *La cultura hispano-italiana de los jesuitas expulsos*, Madrid: Editorial Gredos, 1966; Allan Figueroa Deck, *Francisco Javier Alegre: A Study in Mexican Literary Criticism*, Rome: Historical Institute of the Society of Jesus, 1976, and 'Jesuit Contributions to the Culture of Modernity in Latin America: An Essay toward a Critical Understanding', in Christopher Chapple (ed.), *The Jesuit Tradition in Education and Missions*, pp. 169–81; and Bernabé Navarro, *Cultura mexicana moderna*, Mexico, DF: UNAM, 1964.

184 John W. O'Malley, *The First Jesuits*, p. 16.

185 John W. O'Malley, *The First Jesuits*, p. 372.

186 Paul G. Crowley sj, 'Theology in the Jesuit University: Reassessing the Ignatian Vision', in Christopher Chapple (ed.), *The Jesuit Tradition in Education and Missions*, pp. 155–68.

187 David L. Fleming sj, 'The Ignatian Spiritual Exercises: Understanding a Dynamic', in David L. Fleming sj, *Notes on the Spiritual Exercises of St. Ignatius of Loyola*, St. Louis, Missouri: Review for Religious, 1983, pp. 2–18, 3.

188 Michael Floss, *The Founding of the Jesuits 1540*, London: Hamish Hamilton, 1969, pp. 61–7.

189 John W. O'Malley, *The First Jesuits*, p. 25.

190 These norms and practices were revised by the 34th General Congregation of the Jesuits in 1995; Gero McLoughlin sj writes: 'The requirement that novices make the *Exercises* appears in the General Examen that is shown to candidates. The General Examen is part of the Constitutions (almost a preamble). The reference is cited like this Examen, c.4, § 9–10. The requirement also appears in the Complementary Norms and is cited CN 46 § 2. As regards the tertianship, making the Spiritual Exercises is not specifically required either by the Constitutions or by the Complementary Norms . . . The Complementary Norms also speak of the Spiritual Exercises as the "source and centre of our vocation"' (Gero McLoughlin sj to Mario I. Aguilar, Edinburgh, 13 March 2007).

191 Herbert F. Smith sj, 'The Nature and Value of a Directed Retreat', and William A. Barry sj, 'Silence and the Directed Retreat', in David L. Fleming sj, *Notes on the Spiritual Exercises of St. Ignatius of Loyola*, pp. 20–6, 68–71.

192 Paul J. Bernadicou sj, 'The Retreat Director in the Spiritual Exercises', in David L. Fleming sj, *Notes on the Spiritual Exercises of St. Ignatius of Loyola*, pp. 27–38.

193 George P. Leach sj, 'Growing Freedom in the Spiritual Director', and William J. Connolly sj, 'Appealing to Strength in Spiritual Direction', in David L. Fleming sj, *Notes on the Spiritual Exercises of St. Ignatius of Loyola*, pp. 39–47, 48–51.

194 William A. Barry sj, 'The Contemplative Attitude in Spiritual Direction', in David L. Fleming sj, *Notes on the Spiritual Exercises of St. Ignatius of Loyola*, pp. 52–60, 57.

195 Judith Roemer osf, 'Discernment in the Director', in David L. Fleming sj, *Notes on the Spiritual Exercises of St. Ignatius of Loyola*, pp. 249–56.

196 William J. Connolly sj, 'Freedom and Prayer in Directed Retreats', in David L. Fleming sj, *Notes on the Spiritual Exercises of St. Ignatius of Loyola*, pp. 61–7, p. 63.

Notes

197 William A. Barry SJ, 'On Asking God to Reveal Himself in Retreat', in David L. Fleming SJ, *Notes on the Spiritual Exercises of St. Ignatius of Loyola*, pp. 72–7.

198 Prayer within the *Exercises* is understood as listening, seeing, responding and acting; see John R. Sheets SJ, 'The Four Moments of Prayer', in David L. Fleming SJ, *Notes on the Spiritual Exercises of St. Ignatius of Loyola*, pp. 163–74.

199 David L. Fleming SJ, 'The Ignatian Spiritual Exercises: Understanding a Dynamic', p. 5.

200 W. H. Longridge, *The Spiritual Exercises of Saint Ignatius of Loyola*, translated from the Spanish with a commentary and a translation of the *Directorium in Exercitia*, London: Robert Scott, 1919, p. 26.

201 Charles J. Healey SJ, 'Prayer: The Context of Discernment', David T. Asselin SJ, 'Christian Maturity and Spiritual Discernment', John R. Sheets SJ, 'Profile of the Spirit: A Theology of Discernment of Spirits', and Herbert F. Smith SJ, 'Discernment of Spirits', in David L. Fleming SJ, *Notes on the Spiritual Exercises of St. Ignatius of Loyola*, pp. 195–200, 201–13, 214–25, 226–48.

202 See, as an example of the possible texts and reflections generated by the topic and experience of conversion, Carolyn Osiek RSCJ, 'The First Week of the *Spiritual Exercises* and the Conversion of St. Paul', and William A. Barry SJ, 'The Experience of the First and Second Weeks of the *Spiritual Exercises*', in David L. Fleming SJ, *Notes on the Spiritual Exercises of St. Ignatius of Loyola*, pp. 86–94, 95–102.

203 William Connolly SJ, 'Story of the Pilgrim King and the Dynamics of Prayer', in David L. Fleming SJ, *Notes on the Spiritual Exercises of St. Ignatius of Loyola*, pp. 103–7.

204 William J. Connolly SJ, 'Experiences of Darkness in Directed Retreats', in David L. Fleming SJ, *Notes on the Spiritual Exercises of St. Ignatius of Loyola*, pp. 108–14.

205 Dominic Maruca SJ, 'The Graces of the Third and Fourth Week', in David L. Fleming SJ, *Notes on the Spiritual Exercises of St. Ignatius of Loyola*, pp. 134–43.

206 Charles C. Murphy SJ, 'On Leaving Retreat: To Go Out Can Be To Go In', in David L. Fleming SJ, *Notes on the Spiritual Exercises of St. Ignatius of Loyola*, pp. 144–55; and William O'Malley SJ, *The Fifth Week*, Chicago: Loyola University Press, 1976.

207 William J. Connolly SJ, 'Social Action and the Directed Retreat', in David L. Fleming SJ, *Notes on the Spiritual Exercises of St. Ignatius of Loyola*, pp. 286–90.

208 William J. Byron SJ, 'Social Consciousness in the Ignatian Exercises', in David L. Fleming SJ, *Notes on the Spiritual Exercises of St. Ignatius of Loyola*, pp. 272–85, 279.

209 Fr Kolvenbach reminded participants that the Jesuits had decided to encourage every member of the Society of Jesus to use two main languages for all meetings: English and Spanish, the contemporary languages of the majority of Catholics in the world.

210 Peter-Hans Kolvenbach sj, 'Opening Remarks to the Joint Meeting of the JC USA and CPAL Conferences', Miami, Florida, 23 May 2004.

211 'Migration in the Americas', available through the US-based Jesuit webpage at <http://www.jesuit.org>.

Chapter 5

212 In writing and referring to 'the Church' I use the terminology of the Second Vatican Council. Thus I understand this term as 'the people of God', not the hierarchical structure of Bishops' Conferences: see *Lumen Gentium* § 9–17. It is common within the literature to assert, for example, that the Argentinean Church did not support the search for the disappeared. Yes, most of the bishops didn't speak out; however, some who tried to speak out had attempts made on their lives; and the Christian communities of the poor neighbourhoods supported the cause of the persecuted and the push for a restoration of democracy in Argentina.

213 Samuel Blixen, *El vientre del cóndor: Del archivo del terror al caso Berríos*, Montevideo: Brecha, 1994; Alfredo Boccia Paz, Miguel H. López, Antonio V. Pecci and Gloria Giménez Guanes, *En los sótanos de los generales: Los documentos ocultos del Operativo Cóndor*, Asunción: Expolibro/Servilibro, 2002; Stella Calloni, *Los años del lobo: Operación Cóndor*, Buenos Aires: Ediciones Continente, 1999; John Dinges, *Operación Cóndor: Una década de terrorismo internacional en el Cono Sur*, Santiago: Ediciones B, 2004; Nilson Cézar Mariano, *Operación Cóndor: Terrorismo de estado en el Cono Sur*, Buenos Aires: Lohlé-Lumen, 1998; and Francisco Martorell, *Operación Cóndor: El vuelo de la muerte –La coordinación represiva en el Cono Sur*, Santiago: LOM, 1999.

214 Since the beginning of the Cold War, more than 50,000 Latin American officers had been trained by the Pentagon: see Patricio Manns, *Chile: Una dictadura militar permanente 1811–1999*, Santiago: Editorial Sudamericana, 1999, p. 43. According to the brochure published by the SOA, nearly 59,000 Latin American military, policemen and civilians were trained at the SOA: see Jack Nelson-Pallmeyer, *School of Assassins: The Case for Closing the School of the Americas and for Fundamentally Changing U.S. Policy*, Maryknoll, NY: Orbis, 1997, p. 2.

Notes

215 Elías Padilla Ballesteros, *La memoria y el olvido: Detenidos desaparecidos en Chile*, Santiago: Ediciones Orígenes, 1995.

216 In Chile, for example, there were large numbers of foreign migrants from other Latin American countries who had arrived seeking shelter from other authoritarian regimes. They were a prime target for the military after the 1973 military coup; many of them were killed and their bodies buried without the knowledge of their families who lost touch with them but never suspected that they had been arrested, killed and buried somewhere within Chilean territory.

217 Cardinal Aloísio Lorscheider, 'Fifty Years of the CNBB: A Bishops' Conference Based on the Council: Evangelization Projects; Political and Ecclesiastical Tensions and Challenges', and Faustino Teixeira, 'Stories of Faith and Life in the Base Communities', in José Oscar Beozzo and Luiz Carlos Susin (eds), *Brazil: People and Church[es]*, *Concilium*, 3, 2002, London: SCM Press, pp. 25–30, 38–46. For a general sociopolitical analysis see Scott Mainwaring, *The Catholic Church and Politics in Brazil 1916–1985*, Stanford: Stanford University Press, 1986.

218 W. E. Hewitt, *Base Christian Communities and Social Change in Brazil*, Lincoln and London: University of Nebraska Press, 1991.

219 This legal case was researched at the archives of the Fundación Documentación y Archivo de la Vicaría de la Solidaridad in Santiago and is one of the cases examined in Mario I. Aguilar, *A Social History of the Catholic Church in Chile IV: Torture and Forced Disappearance 1973–1974*, Lewiston, Queenston, and Lampeter: Edwin Mellen Press, 2007.

220 The Movimiento de Izquierda Revolucionario (MIR) was a left-wing paramilitary organization that started at the University of Concepción in the late 1960s. The MIR challenged the social policies of Presidents Eduardo Frei and Salvador Allende and after the military coup, fought the military through an urbanized guerrilla association. The destruction of the MIR was the central task of the Chilean security services after the military coup.

221 The DINA (Nacional Intelligence Directorate) was created by Decree Law 521 of 14 June 1974 as a 'military body of a technical and professional nature, under the direct command of the junta. Its mission is to be that of gathering all information from around the nation and from different fields of activity in order to produce the intelligence needed for policy formulation and planning and for the adoption of those measures required for the protection of national security and the development of the country' (*Report of the Chilean National Commission on Truth and Reconciliation*, Volume I, Notre Dame, Indiana: University of Notre Dame Press and Center for Civil and Human Rights of Notre Dame Law School, 1993, p. 82).

222 RUT [Rol Unico Tributario] 6.364.277–0, born 13 December 1953, domicile Cirujano Videla 1504, Ñuñoa, Santiago: see 'Ficha' [folder of legal documents] of Bárbara Gabriela Uribe Tamblay, Fundación Documentación y Archivo de la Vicaría de la Solidaridad, Arzobispado de Santiago.

223 That communal experience changed Bárbara's vision of society and of her own personal plans for the future. After returning to Santiago, she became involved in community work in shanty towns and, together with Edwin shared a commitment to the MIR. Bárbara's sister wrote: 'All llegar a Santiago, se incorporó al trabajo poblacional, especialmente en La Bandera y Nuevo Amanecer. Se vinculó al MIR y fue una activa militante de esa organización. Nunca estuvo de acuerdo con la forma-ción teórica de izquierda, decía que se aburría leyendo libros de Marx y Lenín, estaba convencida que la injusticia no era una cuestión de libros, del pasado, sino que era una acción permanente, un acto de servicio, un acto de amor. No la comprendieron mucho, sin embargo, ella hizo durante su militancia este ejercicio: dar hasta que le doliese. Es así como de la casa se fueron desapareciendo las comidas, los útiles escolares, la ropa, para dárselos a las familias más necesitadas. La casa se llenó de jóvenes, de pobladores a quienes ella traía para acogerlos. Y también la casa se llenó de música, su voz clara, diáfana y con un timbre mara-villoso, transformada los días en cantos, en nuevos cantos que nos con-tagiaban a todos soñando con un nuevo amanecer' (When she moved to Santiago, she joined the political activities of the shanty towns, particu-larly those at La Bandera and Nuevo Amanecer. She adhered to the polit-ical ideas of the MIR and became an active militant of that political organization. She never agreed with the theoretical ideas of the left; indeed, she mentioned that she got bored reading works by Marx and Lenin. She was convinced that social injustice was not a matter of books or the past but required an ongoing action, an act of service, an act of love. Many didn't understand her; however, she made her political activity a service: to give until it hurt. Thus, food started disappearing, and school purchases and clothing were given by her to the poor. Our home was filled with youth and with the poor she invited in, to fill it with other more needy people. At the same time, our home was filled with music. She had a beautiful voice that transformed every day with a song, a new song that invited us to dream of a new dawn), see 'Bárbara y Edwin' at <http://memoriaviva.com>.

224 Bárbara told another prisoner at the Cuatro Alamos detention centre: 'Yo sé que se llevan al Flaco [Edwin] y lo van a matar, yo soy su compañera y quiero seguir su mismo camino, no soportaría la vida sin él' (I know that they are bringing the Flaco [Edwin] to another place and that they will kill him. I am his compañera [partner] and I would like to

Notes

follow him. I could not stand life without him), Agrupación de Familiares de Detenidos Desaparecidos, *Dónde están? – Mujeres chilenas detenidas desaparecidas*, Santiago: Agrupación de Familiares de Detenidos Desaparecidos, 1986, p. 20.

225 Cristián Van Yurick was older than Edwin, married to Eugenia Yulis; they had a daughter by the name of Francisca. Osvaldo Romo was a member of the MIR that after the military coup became part of the security services and a person who enjoyed torturing and raping prisoners. Romo has been in jail since 1992 and has given interviews to the Chilean journalist Nancy Guzmán, later broadcasted through several American television networks, including CNN: see Nancy Guzmán, *Romo: Confesiones de un torturador*, Santiago: Editorial Planeta, 2000.

226 RUT 6.426.158–4 Santiago, born 30 November 1953, domicile Cirujano Videla 1504, Ñuñoa, Santiago, see 'Ficha' of Edwin Francisco Van Yurick Altamirano, Fundación Documentación y Archivo de la Vicaría de la Solidaridad, Arzobispado de Santiago.

227 One of the key aims of legal investigations by special judges appointed to work on cases of forced disappearance by former Justice Minister Soledad Alvear was to try to determine who decided the prisoners' fate and who was responsible for the killings and forced disappearances. While most DINA agents accused of illegal association, kidnapping and torture have admitted to those crimes, it has not been possible to determine who selected the prisoners to be killed, who killed them and where their bodies are. Most of the discoveries of human remains related to this period have occurred through confidential information provided to priests and bishops or simply by the fact that members of the public have reported findings or they have known of the presence of human remains in a particular locality.

228 Through an examination of the historical archives of this period it is possible to suggest that the unexpected visitor was Bishop Enrique Alvear, looking for a female detainee taken by the DINA from his northern pastoral area of Santiago: see Maximiliano Salinas C., *Don Enrique Alvear: El obispo de los pobres*, Santiago: Ediciones Paulinas, 1991, p. 238.

229 Because of his British ancestry, Edwin Van Yurick and his wife were considered by the British Embassy as entitled to dual nationality and therefore entitled to diplomatic help by the British Government through the British Embassy in Santiago.

230 *Report of the Chilean National Commission on Truth and Reconciliation*, Volume 2, p. 528. The legal case in which the DINA agent Osvaldo Romo was accused of kidnapping and murder was closed several times by the application of the 1978 Amnesty Law (DL 2.191):

see 'Este año, 14 casos de desaparecidos fueron amnistiados', *El Mercurio*, 20 November 2004.

231 William T. Cavanaugh, *Torture and Eucharist: Theology, Politics, and the Body of Christ*, Oxford and Malden, Massachusetts: Blackwell, 1998, p. 279. For Cavanaugh's further analysis on the Eucharist and social desire, see his essay 'Consumption, the Market, and the Eucharist', in Christophe Boureux, Janet Martin Soskice and Luiz Carlos Susin (eds), *Hunger, Bread and Eucharist*, Concilium, 2, 2005, London: SCM Press, pp. 88–95.

232 Thomas C. Wright and Rody Oñate, *Flight from Chile: Voices from Exile*, Albuquerque, New Mexico: University of New Mexico Press, 1998; and E. Weinstein, E. Lira and others, *Trauma, duelo y reparación: Una experiencia de trabajo psicosocial en Chile*, Santiago: FASIC/Interamericana, 1987. Years later, the trial of General Augusto Pinochet in London helped to dissipate some of the social fears and helped some victims to reconstitute themselves by articulating their own historical narratives: see the analysis by Ariel Dorfman, *Exorcising Terror: The Incredible Unending Trial of General Augusto Pinochet*, London: Pluto Press, 2003.

233 Movements that acted as social bodies and took to the public landscapes protesting against torture arose out of that healing process: see, for example, Hernán Vidal, *El Movimiento contra la Tortura Sebastián Acevedo: Derechos humanos y la producción de símbolos nacionales bajo el fascismo chileno*, Santiago: Mosquito Editores, 2002.

234 Sheila Cassidy, *Audacity to Believe*, London: Darton, Longman and Todd, 1992, pp. 267–72, and *Made for Laughter*, London: Darton, Longman and Todd, 2006, pp. 94–9.

235 William T. Cavanaugh, *Torture and Eucharist*, p. 281.

236 Horacio Verbitsky, *The Flight: Confessions of an Argentine Dirty Warrior*, New York: The New Press, 1996.

237 Elsa Esquivel Rojo, 'To Disappear Is Not to Die', in Patricia Politzer (ed.), *Fear in Chile: Lives under Pinochet*, New York: The New Press, 2001, pp. 140–53.

238 José Comblin, 'The Theme of Reconciliation and Theology in Latin America', in Iain S. Maclean (ed.), *Reconciliation, Nations and Churches in Latin America*, Aldershot and Burlington, Vermont: Ashgate, 2006, pp. 135–70, 169.

239 See, for example, Franz Hinkelammert, 'Globalization as Cover-Up: An Ideology to Disguise and Justify Current Wrongs', in Jon Sobrino SJ and Felix Wilfred (eds), *Globalization and Its Victims*, Concilium, 5, 2001, London: SCM Press, pp. 25–34.

240 John Paul II, 'Towards a Common Ethical Code for Humankind: Address to the Pontifical Academy of Social Sciences 2001', in Karl-Josef

Kuschel and Dietmar Mieth (eds), *In Search of Universal Values*, *Concilium*, 4, 2001, London: SCM Press, pp. 11–14, 12.

241 Konrad Raiser, 'Global Order and Global Ethic', in Karl-Josef Kuschel and Dietmar Mieth (eds), *In Search of Universal Values*, pp. 19–25 at p. 20.

242 For a summary of the theological developments in Jewish theology see Rosemary Radford Ruether, 'The Holocaust: Theological and Ethical Reflections', in Gregory Baum (ed.), *The Twentieth Century: A Theological Overview*, London: Geoffrey Chapman; Maryknoll, NY: Orbis, and Ottawa: Novalis, 1999, pp. 76–90.

243 See Diego Irarrázaval, 'Dying and Rising again in a Popular Tradition', in Andrés Torres Queiruga, Luiz Carlos Susin and Jon Sobrino SJ (eds), *The Resurrection of the Dead*, *Concilum*, 5, 2006, London: SCM Press, pp. 25–34.

244 Gustavo Gutiérrez, 'Speaking about God', in Claude Geffré, Gustavo Gutiérrez and Virgil Elizondo (eds), *Different Theologies, Common Responsibility: Babel or Pentecost?*, *Concilium*, 1, 1984, Edinburgh: T&T Clark, pp. 27–31.

Chapter 6

245 On issues of cultural and symbolic continuation within the Zapatista movement, see June C. Nash, *Mayan Visions: The Quest for Autonomy in an Age of Globalization*, London and New York: Routledge, 2001.

246 For an assessment of the religious process of colonial conversion within sixteenth-century Mexico, see Amos Megged, *Exporting the Catholic Reformation: Local Religion in Early-Colonial Mexico*, Leiden, New York and Cologne: Brill, 1996.

247 For a full diachronic history of Chiapas from colonial times to the 1970s, see Robert Wasserstrom, *Class and Society in Central Chiapas*, Berkeley, Los Angeles, and London: University of California Press, 1983.

248 For a sociocultural understanding of the growth and social efficacy of the Zapatista movement, see June C. Nash, 'The Power of the Powerless: Update from Chiapas', *Cultural Survival*, 19, 1, 1995, pp. 14–18, 'The Fiesta of the World: The Zapatista Uprising and Radical Democracy in Mexico', *American Anthropologist*, 99, 2, 1997, pp. 261–74, and 'Press Reports on the Chiapas Uprising: Towards a Transnationalized Communication', *Journal of Latin American Anthropology*, 2, 2, 1997, pp. 42–75.

249 The total population of Mexico is 89.5 million people.

250 Data taken from 'Facts and Figures about Chiapas', in Guiomar

Rovia, *Women of Maize: Indigenous Women and the Zapatista Rebellion*, London: Latin American Bureau, 2000, p. 182.

251 See Samuel Ruiz García, Sixth Annual University of Alberta Visiting Lectureship in Human Rights, 26 February 2004, at <http://www.uofaweb.ualberta.ca/humanrightslecture/>.

252 Sheila M. Dabu, 'Bishop Ruiz speaks out for Chiapas', *Catholic New Times*, 3 July 2005.

253 Bishop Samuel Ruiz, Address to the 'Food for Chiapas campaign', McMaster University, Toronto, 2 June 2005.

254 Subcomandante Marcos is not a member of an indigenous group himself but a university lecturer who was deeply moved by the social injustices towards the indigenous populations of Mexico and decided to be an instrument of social organization in Chiapas.

255 *Zapatistas!* 62, 71.

256 Nicholas P. Higgins, *Understanding the Chiapas Rebellion: Modernist Visions & The Invisible Indian*, Austin: University of Texas Press, 2004.

257 The newly created 'autonomous municipalities' were San Pedro Michoacán, Tierra y Libertad, San Juan de la Libertad, San Juan Cancuc, Zona Autónoma de Tenejapa, Moisés Ghandi, Nuevo Bochil, Santa Catarina, Magdalena de la Paz, Ernesto Ché Guevara, San Andrés Sac'amché de los Pobres, Tzol Choj, Sitalá, Ixtapa, Amatenango de Valle, Nuevo Venustiano Carranza, Nicolás Ruiz, Socoltenago and Pohló: see Anna María Garza Caligaris and Rosalda Aída Hernández Castillo, 'Encounters and Conflicts of the Tzotzil People with the Mexican State: A Historical-anthropological Perspective for Understanding Violence in San Pedro Chenalhó, Chiapas', in Rosalda Aída Hernández Castillo (ed.), *The Other Word: Women and Violence in Chiapas before and after Acteal*, Copenhagen: International Work Group for Indigenous Affairs, 2001, pp. 39–55, 50.

258 For the history and ethnography of these developments within the EZLN and within Mexican society, see Neil Harvey, *The Chiapas Rebellion: The Struggle for Land and Democracy*, Durham, North Carolina, and London: Duke University Press, 1998, Chapter 8.

259 See, for example, Chiapaslink, *The Zapatistas: A Rough Guide*, Bristol: Chiapaslink, 2000.

260 Rosalda Aída Hernández Castillo, 'Prologue to the English Edition', in Rosalda Aída Hernández Castillo (ed.), *The Other Word*, pp. 11–15, 14.

261 Julia Preston, 'In Chiapas some towns are at odds with Catholic bishop', *New York Times*, 16 June 1998.

262 Aída Hernández Castillo has provided a very clear description of what paramilitary groups are: 'armed groups with direct or indirect links

to the state, and which perform specific actions to debilitate dissidents who oppose the current regime. Their actions always take place at key political moments and have clear objectives and perpetrators': see, 'Prologue to the English Edition', in Rosalda Aída Hernández Castillo (ed.), *The Other Word*, p. 15.

263 The testimonies of this massacre were taken at the Fray Bartolomé de Las Casas Human Rights Centre. As an example, I cite the testimony of an 11-year-old girl who escaped the massacre by hiding, and provided a chilling testimony: 'When the men left, Micaela went to hide on the bank of the stream. From there she saw how they came back with machetes in their hands; the same ones and others with them; they were whooping and laughing and talking among themselves, "we have to get rid of the seed," they were saying. They stripped the dead women and cut off their breasts. They put a stick between the legs of one woman and opened the bellies of the pregnant women and took out their babies and played ball with them tossing them from machete to machete. After that they left', in 'Before and after Acteal: Voices, remembrances and experiences from the women of San Pedro Chenaló', in Rosalda Aída Hernández Castillo (ed.), *The Other Word*, pp. 21–38, 33.

264 For a description of the nature and actions of those paramilitary groups, see the bulletin *Chiapas al Día* published by the Centro de Investigaciones Económicas y Políticas de Acción Comunitaria A.C. (CIEPAC – Centre for Economic and Political Research for Community Action), issues §§ 139, 140, 144, 154.

Chapter 7

265 Diego Irarrázaval, *Inculturation: New Dawn of the Church in Latin America*, Maryknoll, NY: Orbis, 2000.

266 For a historical overview see Luis Alberto Gómez de Souza, 'The Origins of Medellín: From Catholic Action to the Base Church Communities and Social Pastoral Strategy (1950–68)', in José Oscar Beozzo and Luiz Carlos Susin (eds), *Brazil: People and Church(es)*, *Concilium*, 3, 2002, London: SCM Press, pp. 31–7.

267 Peter Flynn, *Brazil: A Political Analysis*, London and Boulder, Colorado: Ernest Benn and Westview Press, 1978, pp. 308–65; and Alfred Stepan, *Rethinking Military Politics: Brazil and the Southern Cone*, Princeton: Princeton University Press, 1988.

268 Thomas E. Skidmore, 'Brazil's Slow Road to Democratization: 1974–1985', in Alfred Stepan (ed.), *Democratizing Brazil: Problems of Transition and Consolidation*, New York and Oxford: Oxford University Press, 1989, pp. 5–42.

269 The Operación Cóndor comprised a network of intelligence

services from the Southern Cone, most of them associated with the military regimes of the 1970s, which started after a meeting of delegates in Santiago in 1974. The general coordinator of the whole operation was General (R) Manuel Contreras, head of the Chilean state intelligence services – DINA, known as Cóndor number 1: see Samuel Blixen, *El vientre del cóndor: Del archivo del terror al caso Berríos*, Montevideo: Brecha, 1994; Alfredo Boccia Paz, Miguel H. López, Antonio V. Pecci and Gloria Giménez Guanes, *En los sótanos de los generales: Los documentos ocultos del Operativo Cóndor*, Asunción: Expolibro/Servilibro, 2002, Stella Calloni, *Los años del lobo: Operación Cóndor*, Buenos Aires: Ediciones Continente, 1999; John Dinges, *Operación Cóndor: Una década de terrorismo internacional en el Cono Sur*, Santiago: Ediciones B, 2004; Nilson Cézar Mariano, *Operación Cóndor: Terrorismo de estado en el Cono Sur*, Buenos Aires: Lohlé-Lumen, 1998; and Francisco Martorell, *Operación Cóndor: El vuelo de la muerte –La coordinación represiva en el Cono Sur*, Santiago: LOM, 1999.

270 Scott Mainwaring, *The Catholic Church and Politics in Brazil 1916–1985*, Stanford: Stanford University Press, 1986.

271 Ralph Della Cava, 'The "People's Church", the Vatican and Abertura', in Alfred Stepan (ed.), *Democratizing Brazil: Problems of Transition and Consolidation*, New York and Oxford: Oxford University Press, 1989, pp. 143–67, 152–3.

272 W. E. Hewitt, *Base Christian Communities and Social Change in Brazil*, Lincoln, Nebraska, and London: University of Nebraska Press, 1991; and Maria Helena Moreira Alves, *Estado e oposição no Brasil 1964–1984*, Petrópolis: Editora Vozes, 1984.

273 Thomas C. Bruneau, T*he Political Transformation of the Brazilian Catholic Church*, New York: Cambridge University Press, 1974, and *The Church in Brazil*, Austin: University of Texas Press, 1982; Cardinal Aloísio Lorscheider, 'Fifty Years of the CNBB: A Bishop's Conference Based on the Council – Evangelization Projects, Political and Ecclesiastical Tensions and Challenges', in José Oscar Beozzo and Luiz Carlos Susin (eds), *Brazil: People and Church(es)*, pp. 25–30.

274 Pedro Casaldáliga, '2000 Years of Jesús, 20 Years of Romero: A Fraternal Circular Letter', São Félix do Araguaia, In the year 2000.

275 The Claretian missionaries were founded in Vic, Spain, on 16 July 1849, by a group of young priests led by Antonio Claret, later to become Archbishop of Cuba, 20 days after the foundation of this new missionary congregation. The official name of the Claretian missionaries is the Congregation of Missionary Sons of the Immaculate Heart of Mary. Anthony Mary Claret was canonized by the Vatican on 7 May 1950, and today Claretian missionaries have 2,000 members working in 61 countries.

Notes

276 Pedro Casaldáliga, *Yo creo en la justicia y en la esperanza: El credo que ha dado sentido a mi vida*, Bilbao: Desclée de Brower, 1976, English translation published as *I Believe in Justice and Hope*, Notre Dame, Indiana: FIDES-Claretian, 1978.

277 Teófilo Cabestrero, *Diálogos en Mato Grosso con Pedro Casaldáliga*, Salamanca: Sígueme, 1978, English translation published as *Mystic of Liberation: A Portrait of Bishop Pedro Casaldáliga of Brazil*, Maryknoll, NY: Orbis, 1981.

278 Pedro Casaldáliga, 'Open Letter to the Soul of Brazil', in José Oscar Beozzo and Luiz Carlos Susin (eds), *Brazil: People and Church(es)*, pp. 123–8, 123.

279 Pedro Casaldáliga, 'Una Igleja de Amazonia em conflito com o latifundio e marginalização social', 23 October 1971; see also Pedro Casaldáliga, *Tierra nuestra, libertad*, Buenos Aires: Editorial Guadalupe, 1974.

280 For the twenty-fifth anniversary of the priest's assassination Casaldáliga organized a one-day pilgrimage that started with a common lunch on 14 July and ended with a common lunch on the following day, 15 July 2001: see Pedro Casaldáliga, 'Vidas por la causa: Romería de los mártires de la caminada', 14–15 July 2001, Ribeirão Cascalheira, Prelatura de São Féliz do Araguaia, MT, Brazil.

281 Vasconcelos Quadros, 'El Obispo de los excluídos', *Familia Cristiana*, October 2002.

282 Domingo Oriol, 'Entrevista a Pedro Casaldáliga', *La Vanguardia* (Barcelona), Thursday, 13 January 2005.

283 Pedro Casaldáliga, 'But the Wind Continues', Circular Letter February 2005, São Félix do Araguaia.

284 On that occasion the Portuguese translation of his biography, originally written in Catalan, was launched and Casaldáliga asserted that he liked to remain on the red soil, the distinctive colour of the Amazonian soil: see Francesc Escribano, *Descalç sobre la terra vermella: Vida del bisbe Pere Casaldáliga*, Barcelona: Edicions 62, 1999, Portuguese translation published as *Descalço sobre a terra vermelha*, São Paulo, 2000, Spanish translation published as *Descalzo sobre la tierra roja: Vida del Obispo Pedro Casaldáliga*, Barcelona: Ediciones Península, 2000.

285 Casaldáliga played with the term *honoris causa* and insisted that his doctorate was *passionis causa* because of his passion for utopia.

286 The theme of the Kingdom of God connects all of his works: see Pedro Casaldáliga, *Al acecho del Reino: Antología de textos 1968–1988*, Madrid: Nueva Utopía and Ediciones Endymión, 1989, and Mexico City: Claves Latinoamericanas, 1990, English translation *In Pursuit of the Kingdom: Writings 1968–1988*, Maryknoll, NY: Orbis, 1990.

287 Pedro Casaldáliga, 'I believe in Resurrection', in Andrés Torres

Queiruja, Luiz Carlos Susin and Jon Sobrino SJ (eds), *The Resurrection of the Dead, Concilium*, 5, 2006, London: SCM Press, pp. 121–3, 123.

288 Pedro Casaldáliga, 'Declaración de amor a la revolución total de Cuba', Vitral [Cuba], 5, 29, January–February 1999, <http:///www. vitral.org/vitral/vitral.html>.

289 Pedro Casaldáliga and José María Vigil, *Espiritualidad de la liberación*, São Paulo: CESEP – São Paulo and Ediciones Paulinas, 1993, English translation published as *The Spirituality of Liberation*, Liberation and Theology 12, Tunbridge Wells: Burns & Oates, and Maryknoll, NY: Orbis, 1994.

290 Gustavo Gutiérrez, *Beber en su propio pozo*, Lima: CEP, 1983, English translation published as *We Drink from Our Own Wells: The Spiritual Journey of a People*, London: SCM Press, and Maryknoll, NY: Orbis, 1984. Other Latin Americans working on a more traditional vein of spirituality include Segundo Galilea and his works *Aspectos críticos en la espiritualidad actual*, Bogotá: Indo-American Press Service, 1975; *El camino de la espiritualidad*, Bogotá: Ediciones Paulinas, 1983; *El futuro de nuestro pasado: Ensayo sobre los místicos españoles desde América Latina*, Bogotá: CLAR, 1983; and *Espiritualidad de la liberación*, Santiago: ISPAJ, 1973, and Bogotá: CLAR, 1979.

291 Pedro Casaldáliga, *En rebelde fidelidad, Diario 1977–1983*, Bilbao: Desclée de Broker, 1983.

292 Pedro Casaldáliga and José María Vigil, *The Spirituality of Liberation*, pp. xv–xvi.

293 Pedro Casaldáliga, *Orações da caminhada*, Campinas, SP: Editora Verus, 2005.

294 Pedro Casaldáliga, 'La romería continúa', São Félix do Araguaia, MT, Brazil, August 2006.

295 Pedro Casaldáliga, 'Carta abierta al hermano Romero', 24 March 2005.

296 Pedro Casaldáliga, 'El mundo vuelve a empezar', Carta Circular 2002.

297 Pedro Casaldáliga, *Cartas marcadas*, São Paulo: Paulus, 2005.

298 Pedro Casaldáliga, 'In the Dark Hour of the Dawn', Circular Letter 2003.

299 Pedro Casaldáliga, 'Pasar haciendo caminos', Circular Fraterna April 2004.

300 Pedro Casaldáliga, 'Utopía necesaria como el pan de cada día', Circular Fraterna January 2006.

301 Pedro Casaldáliga, *Cuando los días dan que pensar: Memoria: ideario, compromiso*, Madrid: PPC, 2005.

Notes

Chapter 8

302 Ignacio Ellacuría SJ and Jon Sobrino SJ (eds), *Mysterium libera-tionis: Fundamental Concepts of Liberation Theology*, Maryknoll, NY: Orbis, and North Blackburn, Victoria, Australia: CollinsDove, 1993.

303 Marcella Althaus-Reid, *Indecent Theology: Theological Perver-sions in Sex, Gender and Politics*, London: Routledge, 2000.

304 This dichotomy is elegantly explained by Laura Tedesco, *Dem-ocracy in Argentina: Hope and Disillusion*, London: Frank Cass, 1999, pp. xix–xx. See also D. James, *Resistance and Integration: Peronism and the Argentine Working Class 1946–1976*, Cambridge: Cambridge University Press, 1988.

305 The Military Junta was made up of the Commanders-In-Chief of the Argentinean Armed Forces: Lt. General Jorge R. Videla, Brigadier Orlando E. Agosti and Admiral Emilio E. Massera. Following a previous agreement, Videla took over as president.

306 Jo Fisher, *Mothers of the Disappeared*, London: Zed, and Boston: South End, 1989.

307 Ariel C. Armony, *Argentina, the United States, and the Anti-Communist Crusade in Central America 1977–1984*, Athens, Ohio: Ohio University Center for International Studies, 1997.

308 The Peronist Party got only 40.16 per cent of the total vote.

309 Daphne Hampson, *Theology and Feminism*, London: Blackwell, 1990; *After Christianity*, London: SCM Press, 1996; and (ed.), *Swallow-ing a Fishbone? Feminist Theologians Debate Christianity*, London: SPCK, 1996.

310 Laurel Birch Aguilar, *Inscribing the Mask: Interpretation of Nyau Masks and Ritual Performance among the Chewa of Central Malawi*, Fribourg: University of Fribourg Press, 1996.

311 Marcella Althaus-Reid, 'Walking with Women Serpents', *Minis-terial Formation*, 62, 1993, pp. 31–41; 'When God Is a Rich White Woman Who Does Not Walk: The Hermeneutical Circle of Mariology in Latin America', *Theology and Sexuality*, 1, September 1994, pp. 55–72; and 'Do Not Stop the Flood of My Blood: A Critical Christology of Hope amongst Latin American Women', *Studies in World Christian-ity*, 1, 2, 1995, pp. 143–59.

312 Marcella Althaus-Reid, 'Sexual Strategies in Practical Theology: Indecent Theology and the Plotting of Desire with Some Degree of Success', *Theology and Sexuality*, 7, September 1997, pp. 45–52; and 'On Using Skirts without Using Underwear: Indecent Theology Contesting the Liberation of the Pueblo, Poor Women Contesting Christ', *Feminist Theology*, 20, January 1999, pp. 39–51.

313 Daphne Hampson, *After Christianity*, p. 12.

314 In the introduction to a volume of her collected essays, Althaus-

Reid narrates how she was challenged by another feminist theologian when she decided to change the context of her theological questioning. It was clear to her that once liberation theology as the theology of political acts had been assimilated into the theological world other questions relating to the politics of Christian theology had to be asked: see Marcella Althaus-Reid, 'Introduction – From Feminist Theology to Indecent Theology: On Going Beyond', in *From Feminist Theology to Indecent Theology*, London: SCM Press, 2004, pp. 1–9.

315 Marcella Althaus-Reid, *Indecent Theology*, p. 2.

316 See, for example, Virginia Fabella and Mercy Oduyoye (eds), *With Passion and Compassion: Women Doing Theology*, Maryknoll, NY: Orbis, 1988; Elsa Tamez (ed.), *Through Her Eyes*, Maryknoll, NY: Orbis, 1989; and Ana María Tepedino and Margarida L. Ribeiro Brandáo, 'Women and the Theology of Liberation', in Ignacio Ellacuría SJ and Jon Sobrino SJ (eds), *Mysterium liberationis*, pp. 221–31.

317 Marcella Althaus-Reid, *Indecent Theology*, pp. 6–7.

318 I cannot avoid the fact that indecent theology reminds me of the centrality of 'joking relationships' within social anthropology where those relations that produce laughter within a particular community are so important to understand social groups and kinship relations. Those 'joking relationships' are usually of a sexual nature and they provide an ongoing social mechanism for learning sociability and the social roles assigned to different members of a social group.

319 Marcella Althaus-Reid, *Indecent Theology*, p. 125.

320 Marcella Althaus-Reid, *Indecent Theology*, p. 132.

321 It is more difficult to explain why, in the same circumstances of Chile, there was less support by the Catholic Church to the ruling military; however, this is not a theme developed by Althaus-Reid within her work or that one would expect to be central to her development of a contextual theologizing of sexuality within Argentina.

322 For a Roman Catholic like me this is understandable as the central power of Episcopal authority and the teaching office within the Catholic Church is located within a celibate male group.

323 Marcella Althaus-Reid, *Indecent Theology*, p. 200.

324 Marcella Althaus-Reid, *The Queer God*, London and New York: Routledge, 2003.

325 Marcella Althaus-Reid, *The Queer God*, p. 9.

326 Marcella Althaus-Reid, *The Queer God*, p. 12.

327 Marcella Althaus-Reid, *The Queer God*, p. 49.

328 Marcella Althaus-Reid, *The Queer God*, p. 50.

329 See, for example, Luiz Carlos Susin, 'Introduction: Emergence and Urgency of the New Pluralist Paradigm', in Andrés Torres Queiruga, Luiz Carlos Susin and José María Vigil (eds), *Pluralist Theology: The*

Notes

Emerging Paradigm, *Concilium*, 1, 2007, London: SCM Press, pp. 7–12.

330 Althaus-Reid points here to the interesting socio-historical work of Eduardo Galeano, *Patas arriba: La escuela del mundo al revés*, Madrid: Siglo Veintiuno, 2000.

331 Marcella Althaus-Reid, *The Queer God*, p. 153.

332 She also used this theological interpretation of the social when she delivered the 2007 Archbishop Oscar Romero Lecture at the Centre for the Study of Religion and Politics (CSRP) of the University of St Andrews, Scotland, 21 March 2007.

333 Marcella Althaus-Reid, 'On Dying Hard: Lessons from Popular Crucifixions and Undisciplined Resurrections in Latin America', in Andrés Torres Queiruga, Luiz Carlos Susin and Jon Sobrino SJ (eds), *The Resurrection of the Dead*, *Concilium*, 5, 2006, London: SCM Press, pp. 35–43, 37.

334 Marcella Althaus-Reid, 'Grace and the Other: A Postcolonial Reflection on Ideology and Doctrinal Systems', in Elen van Wolde (ed.), *The Bright Side of Life*, *Concilium*, 4, 2000, London: SCM Press, pp. 63–9, 64.

335 Marcella Althaus-Reid, 'Who Framed Clodovis Boff? Revisiting the Controversy of "Theologies of the Genitive" in the Twenty-First Century', in Erik Borgman and Felix Wilfred (eds), *Theology in a World of Specialization*, *Concilium*, 2, 2006, London: SCM Press, pp. 99–107.

336 Marcella Althaus-Reid, 'The Divine Exodus of God: Involuntarily Marginalized, Taking an Option for the Margins, or Truly Marginal?', in Werner Jeanrond and Christoph Theobald (eds), *God: Experience and Mystery*, *Concilium*, 1, 2001, London: SCM Press, pp. 27–33, 33.

Chapter 9

337 It is worth mentioning once again that theologians do not need to have faith and they do not need to belong to a faith community in order to do theology. Nevertheless, the majority of theologians do belong to a faith community or have an ecclesiastical affiliation. In practice though, the boundary between the work of theologians and religionists within academia 'maybe more akin to a geological fault than a secure boundary': see Ellen T. Armour, 'Theology in Modernity's Wake', *Journal of the American Academy of Religion*, 74, 1, 2006, pp. 7–15, 9. I have remarked on this thin line between the two and the need to mediate good scholarship by religionists and theologians: see 'Introduction: Objectivity in the Study of Religion and the Archaeology of Academia', in Mario I. Aguilar, *Current Issues on Theology and Religion in Latin America and Africa*, Lewiston, Queenston, and Lampeter: Edwin Mellen Press, 2002, pp. 1–22.

338 Iván Petrella, *The Future of Liberation Theology: An Argument and Manifesto*, Aldershot and Burlington, Vermont: Ashgate, 2004; later edition London: SCM Press, 2006; I cite from the 2004 original edition throughout this chapter. For some cultural and philosophical essays on Latin America from those working within North America, see D. Batstone, E. Mendieta, L. A. Lorentzen and D. Hopkins (eds), *Liberation Theologies, Postmodernity and the Americas*, New York: Routledge, 1997.

339 See, for example, Enrique Dussel, *History and the Theology of Liberation: A Latin American Perspective*, Maryknoll, NY: Orbis, 1976; *Philosophy of Liberation*, Maryknoll, NY: Orbis, 1985; *The Invention of the Americas: Eclipse of 'the Other' and the Myth of Modernity*, New York: Continuum, 1995; and *The Underside of Modernity: Ricoeur, Apel, Taylor and the Philosophy of Liberation*, New York: Humanities Press, 1996.

340 Juan Luis Segundo SJ, 'The Future of Christianity in Latin America', November 1962, in Alfred T. Hennelly (ed.), *Liberation Theology: A Documentary History*, Maryknoll, NY: Orbis, 1990, pp. 29–37.

341 To be of a younger generation is not a problem; Cardinal Silva Henríquez of Chile used to say that one could come out of such a condition. In terms of academic criticism, however, it means that the assessment of Petrella's ideas and their influence in social movements and academia, and within liberation theology, will have to wait for their potential to be identified.

342 Petrella's father, Fernando Petrella, is an Argentinean member of the Ministry of Foreign Affairs and a career diplomat, a historical fact that gave Iván Petrella the opportunity to live in the United States and to have an international outlook. In fact, he has lived half of his life outside Argentina with the following residential pattern: Buenos Aires, New York, Buenos Aires, Rome, Buenos Aires, Washington DC, Buenos Aires, Boston and Miami (Iván Petrella to Mario I. Aguilar, 23 March 2007).

343 Marina Artusa, 'Iván Petrella: Solo le pido a Dios', *Viva: La revista de Clarín*, 2 April 2006.

344 Marcela López Levy, *We Are Millions: Neo-Liberalism and New Forms of Political Action in Argentina*, London: Latin America Bureau, 2004.

345 The mothers of the Argentinean disappeared, known as the Madres de la Plaza de Mayo, kept a weekly silent walk around that square in Buenos Aires in order to direct public opinion towards the lack of effort by subsequent Argentinean administrations to provide information on the 25,000 people who disappeared during the military

Notes

regime: '30 years on, mothers continue to march for missing children', *The Times*, 10 December 2005, p. 54; and Jo Fisher, *Mothers of the Disappeared*, London: Zed, and Boston: South End Press, 1989.

346 Iván Petrella, *The Future of Liberation Theology*, p. 17.

347 Iván Petrella, *The Future of Liberation Theology*, p. 137.

348 Iván Petrella. *The Future of Liberation Theology*, pp. 146–9.

349 Iván Petrella, *The Future of Liberation Theology*, p. 149.

350 Juan Luis Segundo SJ, 'The Future of Christianity in Latin America', November 1962, in Alfred T. Hennelly (ed.), *Liberation Theology*.

351 Gustavo Gutiérrez, 'The Task of Theology and Ecclesial Experience', in Leonardo Boff and Virgil Elizondo (eds), *La Iglesia Popular: Between Fear and Hope*, *Concilium*, 6, 1984, Edinburgh: T&T Clark, pp. 61–4.

352 See, for example, Eduardo Mendieta, 'From Christendom to Polycentric Oikonumé: Modernity, Postmodernity, and Liberation Theology', in David Batstone, Eduardo Mendieta, Lois Ann Lorentzen and Dwight N. Hopkins (eds), *Liberation Theologies, Postmodernity, and the Americas*, pp. 253–72.

353 Iván Petrella, *Beyond Liberation Theology: A Polemic*, London: SCM Press, forthcoming. I am grateful to Iván Petrella for letting me read the introduction and some chapters of his forthcoming book.

354 Iván Petrella, *Beyond Liberation Theology*, 'Introduction'.

355 Clodovis Boff and Leonardo Boff, *Salvation and Liberation: In Search of a Balance between Faith and Politics*, Maryknoll, NY: Orbis, 1984, p. 24.

356 See Paulo Freire, 'Conscientizing as a Way of Liberating', in Alfred T. Hennelly (ed.), *Liberation Theology*, pp. 5–13.

357 Mario I. Aguilar, 'Introduction: Objectivity in the Study of Religion and the Archaeology of Academia', in *Current Issues on Theology and Religion in Latin America and Africa*, Lewiston, Queenston, and Lampeter: Edwin Mellen Press, 2002, pp. 1–22.

358 Eric Hobsbawm, *Interesting Times: A Twentieth-Century Life*, London: Abacus, 2003, p. 7.

359 Juan Luis Segundo SJ, *Liberation of Theology*, Maryknoll, NY: Orbis, 1976, p. 3.

360 See, for example, the academic complexity achieved by Enrique Dussel in the 1990s in his essay 'The Architectonic of the Ethics of Liberation: On Material Ethics and Formal Moralities', in David Batstone, Eduardo Mendieta, Lois Ann Lorentzen and Dwight N. Hopkins (eds), *Liberation Theologies, Postmodernity, and the Americas*, pp. 273–304.

361 Iván Petrella, *The Future of Liberation Theology*, p. 149.

362 My multidisciplinary position is completely different from that of other theologians who distrust the use of the social sciences: see, for example, John Milbank, *Theology & Social Theory: Beyond Secular Reason*, Oxford: Blackwell, 1993.

363 Pedro Casaldáliga, 'Open Letter to the Soul of Brazil', in José Oscar Beozzo and Luiz Carlos Susin (eds), *Brazil: People and Church(es)*, *Concilium*, 3, 2002, London: SCM Press, pp. 123–8, 125.

364 Samuel Rayan SJ, 'Irruption of the Poor: Challenges to Theology', in Leonardo Boff and Virgil Elizondo (eds), *Option for the Poor: Challenge to the Rich Countries*, *Concilium*, 5, 1986, Edinburgh: T&T Clark, pp. 101–12. 101.

365 See, for example, Francis M. McDonagh (trans.), 'Religious Life among the Poor: Two Accounts from Brazil', in Leonardo Boff and Virgil Elizondo (eds), *La Iglesia Popular: Between Fear and Hope*, pp. 56–60.

Index

Americas
 as context for liberation
  theologies 176, 177–8
 interrelationships between their
  peoples 94–5
 liberation theologies in 176,
  177–9
Annan, Kofi (UN Secretary
 General) 148
ANSESAL (Agencia Nacional de
 Servicios Especiales de El
 Salvador) 198n. 90
Aranda, Count of (Pedro Pablo
 Abarca de Bolea) 207n. 182
Araucanía Region (southern
 Chile), indigenous protests in
 14
ARENA (Alianza Republicana
 Nacionalista) 50, 197n. 82,
 198n. 90
Argentina
 the disappeared 99
 economic crises, twenty-first
  century 169–70
 Military Junta 105, 152, 210n.
  212, 221n. 305
 Peronist period 151–2
 Roman Catholic Church's
  cooperation with the Military
  Junta 105, 210n. 212
Arns, Evaristo, Cardinal 137
Arns, Paulo Evaristo, Mgr 140
Arrupe, Pedro (Superior General
 of the Jesuits) 193n. 47
Ashley, J. M. 199n. 99
Atlacatl Regiment (Salvadorian
 Army) 43, 51
Augustine of Hippo, St, on grace
 52
Auschwitz, God's presence 111
autonomous municipalities 123,
 216n. 257

Bachelet, Michele (Chilean

president) 8, 14
Banco Interamericano del
 Desarrollo (BID)(Inter-
 American Development Bank),
 funding of the UCA 29
Banzer, Hugo 201n. 119
Barry, William A, on the work of
 spiritual directors 90
Basic Christian Communities 99,
 105, 125, 136, 137
Benedict XVI (Pope) 74
 Christology similar to that of
  Segundo 75
 criticisms of liberation theology
  67, 71–2, 201n. 159
 criticisms of Ruiz García 199
 criticisms of Sobrino's
  Christology 41
 Segundo criticizes 64, 70
Berdyaev, Nicolai, influence on
 Segundo 60
Berrigan, Dan 206n. 176
Bianchi, Andrea 86
Bible reading 136
Bible stories, Althaus-Reid's
 views 158
BID (Banco Interamericano del
 Desarrollo)(Inter-American
 Development Bank), funding of
 the UCA 29
the body, as a vehicle for
 salvation 172
Boff, Clodis 166
Boff, Clodovis 176
Boff, Leonardo 18, 114, 176
 influenced by Brazilian military
  dictatorship 136
 involvement with the periphery
  5, 188n. 10
 resigns his priesthood 7
 response to Vatican criticisms of
  liberation theology 73, 205n.
  159
 theology of the periphery 130

Index

Bojorge, Horacio 205n. 162
Bolt, Robert 206n. 176
Bonino, José Míguez 2, 151
Bordaberry, Juan María
(president, Uruguay) 61–2,
201n. 119
Bosco Penido Burnier, João
139–40, 146, 219n. 280
bourgeois society (*Bürgerliche
Gesellschaft*) 10
Brazil
  Casaldáliga's love for 139
  military dictatorship, influence
  on Leonardo Boff 136
Brazilian Episcopal Conference,
  support for the disappeared 99
Brazilians, as people of carnival
  185
British Embassy (Chile), concern
  for cases of the disappeared
  102, 213n. 229
Broglie, Luis de 55
Bucareli y Ursúa (General) 207n.
  182
Bürgerliche Gesellschaft
  (*bourgeois society*) 10
Bush, George W. (president, USA)
  95
Byron, William J., on the Jesuit
  option for Jesus Christ and the
  poor 93–4

Camara, Helder 125, 137
caminhada, martyrs 142, 146–7
Las Cañadas (Chiapas) 125
Cañas, José Simeón 193n. 48
Canessa, Agustín 63
canon, formation 68–9
Cardenal, Ernesto 125, 144
Cariola, Patricio, work with the
  Pro Paz Committee 82
Casaldáliga, Pedro 125, 135–6,
  138–41
  commemoration of assassination

of Bosco Burnier 219n. 280
  concerns with destruction of the
  Amazonian forest 137–8
  on globalization 147
  God's centrality to society
  147–8
  passion for the utopia of the
  Kingdom of God 141–3,
  148–9
  spirituality of liberation 144–6
  theology 20, 130, 185
Cassidy, Sheila 21, 83, 104
Castro, Carmen 55
Cataldino, José 84
Catherine II 'the Great' (Empress
  of Russia) 87
Catholic bishops of southern
  Chile, support for indigenous
  peoples 14–15
Cavanaugh, William T.,
  theological link between
  torture and the Eucharist
  103–4
CDF (Congregation for the
  Doctrine of the Faith) 41,
  70–1
  see also Vatican
CELAM (Latin American
  Episcopal Conference) 117,
  189n. 15
Centre for Human Rights Fray
  Bartolomé de las Casas 117
Centre of Theological and Social
  Studies (Montevideo) 59
Centro de Investigación Acción
  Social (Pedro Fabro Centre for
  Theological and Social Studies)
  60–1
Chapultepec Castle (Mexico City)
  198n. 88
Charles III (king of Spain),
  expulsion of the Jesuits from
  Latin America 86, 207n. 182
Chase Manhattan Bank 122

Chávez, Hugo 8
Chiapas (Mexico) 115–16
 army numbers and brutality
  128, 129
 Chiapas uprising (1994) 19,
  115, 120–4, 128–32
Chile
 churches' concerns with human
  rights (1970s) 6
 churches' work with the
  relatives of the disappeared
  105
 the disappeared 99–102, 211n.
  216, 213n. 227
 indigenous rights in 14–16
 Jesuit activities under the
  military dictatorship 82–3
Chilean Intelligence Services
  (DINA) 98
Christian communities
 centrality to liberation
  theologies 183
 involvement in civil society
  181
 responses to the Chiapas
  uprising 129–30
Christian liberation, Ellacuría's
  views 53
Christian values, identified with
  human rights under the Latin
  American democratic regimes
  105–6
Christianity
 dogmatism in, Segundo's views
  65–6
 uniqueness challenged by
  Daphne Hampson 154–5
Christology
 Ellacuría's views 33
 Knitter's views 130
 Santo Domingo conference 7
 Sobrino's views 26, 31–7,
  39–40, 41–2
 see also Jesus Christ

Church 210n. 212
 Casaldáliga's challenges to
  147–8
 as the context for theology 182
 Ellacuría's relationship with
  51–3
 functioning in the area of the
  Rio de la Plata, Segundo's
  views 65
 God's activity in 34
 liberation theologies' need for
  divorce from 173
 role in reconciliation, Comblin's
  views 107
 as servant 114, 117
 Sobrino sees as the location for
  the teaching of the Kingdom of
  God 32
 see also Roman Catholic Church
churches
 involvement in human rights
  109–10
 involvement in society and a
  post-Cold War situation
  criticized 4–5
 peripheral role in liberation
  theologies 183
 responses to the problem of the
  disappeared 99, 105
 women's role in 154
CIMI (Conselho Indigenista
  Missionário) 138
Cinco Días (magazine), Segundo's
  contributions to 62
Ciudad Real (Paraguay) 84
civil society 9–12
 as basis of Latin American
  theologies 114
 Casaldáliga's views 146
 centrality to liberation
  theologies 183
 Christian involvement in 181
 God's support for in Chiapas
  132

Index

Index

theology 19, 44
Zubiri's influence on 55–7
Emmaus road, disciples'
experience 104
English language 210n. 209
environmental concerns, and
liberation theologies 135
Episcopal Commission for
Indigenous Peoples of the
Mexican Bishops 117
episcopal representatives, election
for the Santo Domingo
conference 188n. 13
ERP (Ejército Revolucionario del
Pueblo) 152
Espinoza Pólit, Aurelio, influence
on Ellacuría 45, 46
essence, concept of, in Zubiri's
philosophical work 54
Estudios Centroamericanos
(journal), Ellacuría's
contributions to 46, 48–9
ETA 192n. 43
Eucharist, theological link with
torture 103–4
Europe, treatment of indigenous
peoples 131
European Common Market 151
European philosophy
challenged by liberation
theologies 172–3
in theology 182–3
Exodus (book of), translated into
the Tzeltal language 125
Exposcit debitum 206n. 168
EZLN
involvement in Chiapas uprising
115, 116, 119, 120–3
women's membership 129

faith
paradigms challenged by Latin
American theologians 4
Segundo's views 67–8

in theologies 178
Falklands war 152
Farabundo Martí National
Liberation Front (FMNL) 51,
195n. 74
Ferdinand VI (king of Spain) 86
Ferguson, Adam 10
feudal systems, Chiapas (Mexico)
116
Fields, Father, work with the
Guaraní people 84
Fiorenza, Francis Schüssler 170
Fleming, David L., on the
Spiritual Exercises 88
FMNL (Farabundo Martí
National Liberation Front) 51,
195n. 74, 198n. 88
forced disappearances 97–9
condemnation sought by
relatives of the disappeared
108
and human rights 19
see also the disappeared
foreign debt cancellation 127
foreign migrants, human rights
abused in Chile 211n. 216
Fox, Thomas 76
Fox, Vincente (president, Mexico)
126
Frankfurt University, Sobrino
studies at 28
Fray Bartolomé de Las Casas
Human Rights Centre 217n.
263
Frei, Eduardo (president, Chile)
211n. 220
Freire, Paulo 94, 151
Frente Amplio 63, 202n. 127
From Madness to Hope
(Salvadorian Truth
Commission) 192n. 42
Fuenzalida Devia, Samuel (DINA
agent) 102
Fundación Documentación y

Archivo de la Vicaría de la
Solidaridad (Santiago) 211n.
219

'Galilean 12!', Jesus-experience
183–4
García, José Guillermo (Colonel)
196n. 74
gay sexuality, Church's rejection
of 162
Geisel, Ernesto 201n. 119
gender 11–12
Ghia, Fernando 206n. 176
globalization 4
adverse effects on national
identity 16–17
Argentina's inability to cope
with causes economic crises
169–70
Casaldáliga's views 147
challenged by democratic South
American governments 8
effects on civil society in Latin
America 11, 12
preoccupation with religion
39–40
Sobrino's views 38–40
globalized ethics 109–11
God
actions, in Chiapas 128
Althaus-Reid's views of 161–5,
166
centrality to society 147–8
does not rejoice in suffering 75
as God of the periphery 1, 20,
154, 185
historical involvement 108
justice of, and the resurrection of
Jesus 35, 37
Kingdom of *see* Kingdom of
God
knowledge about 189n. 16
love of 158
nature, in the centre and the

periphery 131–2
presence 98, 111–12
relationship with humanity 76,
144, 172
Goulart, João (president, Brazil)
136
grace, Ellacuría's views 52–3
Grande, Rutilio, assassination
(1977) 25, 29, 49
Gregory XV (Pope), canonizes
Ignatius of Loyola and Francis
Xavier 206n. 168
Guaraní people 84–5
Guatemala, repression of
indigenous peoples (1980s)
128, 129
Guayrá (Paraguay) 84
Guest Worker proposals 95
Gutiérrez, Gustavo 3, 59
creation of the liberation
metaphor 2
friendship with Segundo 60
on God's presence 112
involvement with the poor of
Lima 28
liberation theology, as viewed by
Segundo 66
metaphor of liberation 64
response to Vatican criticisms of
liberation theology 73
spirituality of liberation 144
theological orthodoxy
challenged by the CDF (1983)
70–1
on the theology of the Santo
Domingo conference 7
understanding of theology 174
Gutiérrez, Jaime Abdul, Colonel
196n. 74
Guzmán, Nancy (Chilean
journalist) 213n. 225

Hampson, Daphne 153, 154–5
Hartman, Nicolai 54

Index

Romero 147
as the viewpoint from which to
see theology 175–6, 178
prayer
Casaldáliga's views 144
in the Ignatian *Exercises* 209n.
198
importance for Jesuit life 81
Premio Vasco Universal (1999),
awarded to Sobrino 192n. 43
PRI (Revolutionary Institutional
Party), 'Acteal Massacre' 128
Primoli, Gianbattista 86
Príncipe de Asturias Prize,
awarded to the UCA (1990) 31
Pro Paz Committee 6, 82
'problem of generations' 1–3
prophecy, 'historical effectiveness'
198n. 86
Protestant Evangelicals,
population in El Salvador
26–7
Puchuncaví (Chilean detention
centre) 102
Puebla de Los Angeles (Mexico),
Latin American bishops'
conference (1979) 5, 35, 124
'Puerto Montt' 101
Puttnam, David 206n. 176

race, and liberation theologies
175–6
racism 124
Radio Exterior de España 48
Rahner, Hugo 46
Rahner, Karl 46, 197n. 81
defends Gutiérrez's theology
71
Foundation of Christian Faith,
views of the canon criticized by
Segundo 69
on relation between God and
humanity 76
theological pluralism 74

theology of the Church defended
by Ellacuría 52
Raiser, Konrad, on the violation
of human rights 110
Ramón Moreno, Juan,
assassination 43
Ramos, Celina (daughter of Julia
Elba Ramos), assassination 43
Ramos, Julia Elba, assassination
43
Ratzinger, Joseph *see* Benedict
XVI (Pope)
Rayan, Samuel, on the poor 185
Reagan, Ronald (president, USA)
96
reality
Ellacuría's views 57
Zubiri's views 56
reason, in theologies 178
reconciliation, process 106–7
rectors, university rectors 197n.
83
reducciónes 84, 85–6, 207n. 178
refugees, Jesuit involvement with
95
regency 46
Regimini militantis Ecclesiae
206n. 168
religion, and reconciliation 107
religions, as ethical framework
for human rights 110
religiosity, popular religiosity
194n. 57
religious traditions, Chiapas
(Mexico) 116
revelation, Segundo's views 67–8
Revista de Occidente (journal)
197n 80
*Revista Latinoamericana de
Teología* 49
Revolutionary Institutional Party
(PRI), 'Acteal Massacre' 128
Ribeirão Cascalheira (shrine)
146

government (Nicaragua), Jesuit
involvement in 95
Sanguinetti, Julio María
(president, Uruguay) 63
Santa Mónica Street 2338
(headquarters, Pro Paz
Committee) 82
Santiago Prison, Capuchinos
Annex, prisoners' welcome to
Salas and Cariola in
recognition of their work 82
Santo Domingo (Dominican
Republic), Latin American
bishops' conference (1992)
6–8, 188n. 13, 189n. 15
concerns with indigenous rights
13–14
São Félix do Araguaia diocese
(Brazil) 138–9
Schillebeeckx, Edward 76
School of the Americas (SOA)
98, 210n. 214
schools, Jesuit schools 81–2
Schweiger, Peter (Claretian
Superior General) 138
Second Vatican Council 5, 114,
138
impact on Latin American
theology 8
influence on Segundo's
ecclesiology 66
Ruiz García attends 117
Secretariado Internacional
Cristiano de Solidaridad con
América Latina (SICSAL) 117
security State, doctrine 98
Segundo, Juan Luis 58, 59, 168,
201n. 122
approach to theology 75
Christology, reflects concerns of
both John Paul II and Benedict
XVI 75
ecclesiology 65
education 59–60

educational work under the
Uruguayan military
dictatorship 62–3
Liberation of Theology, on
methodology in theological
developments 69–70
methodology 64–5
reflections on suffering 75
theology 19, 73–4, 75–6, 180–1
Theology and the Church, as
response to Vatican criticisms
of liberation theology 73–4
understanding of theology 174
views on liberation theology
66–70, 79
Seminary San José de la Montaña,
Ellacuría teaches at 46
Sepp, Antonius 86
SERPAJ (Uruguayan Peace and
Justice Service) 63
Servicio Internacional para la Paz
(SIPAZ) 122–3
sexuality
Althaus-Reid's views 150,
157–60
Church's attitude to 161–2
and theology 150
SICSAL (Secretariado
Internacional Cristiano de
Solidaridad con América
Latina) 117
'signs of the times', Segundo's
views 67, 68, 69
Simón Bolívar Prize, awarded to
Ruiz García (2000) 118
SIPAZ (Servicio Internacional
para la Paz) 122–3
Smith, Adam 10
SOA (School of the Americas)
98, 210n. 214
Sobre la esencia (Zubiri) 55,
199n. 101
Sobrino, Jon 2, 27–8, 52, 106
advocates the option for the

Index